South Congregational Church

A Half Century of the South Congregational Church

New Britain, Conn. - 1842-1892

South Congregational Church

A Half Century of the South Congregational Church
New Britain, Conn. - 1842-1892

ISBN/EAN: 9783337235383

Printed in Europe, USA, Canada, Australia, Japan

Cover: Foto ©Lupo / pixelio.de

More available books at **www.hansebooks.com**

A Half Century

OF THE

South Congregational Church

NEW BRITAIN, CONN.

1842 - 1892

NEW BRITAIN, CONN.
Published by the Church
1893

Press of The Case, Lockwood & Brainard Co., Hartford, Conn.

"WHEREFORE seeing we also are compassed about with so great a cloud of witnesses, let us lay aside every weight, and the sin which doth so easily beset us, and let us run with patience the race that is set before us, looking unto Jesus the author and finisher of our faith."

CONTENTS.

	PAGE
HISTORY OF THE CHURCH,	9
GOVERNMENT OF THE CHURCH, .	49
FORMULAS OF THE CHURCH,	57
CATALOGUE OF OFFICERS AND MEMBERS,	61
REPORT OF SEMI-CENTENNIAL SERVICES, .	117

HISTORY OF THE CHURCH.

The Parish, or Ecclesiastical Society, of the South Church in New Britain, occupies a portion of the original territory of the town of Farmington; and the Church, as an organized body of believers, derives its existence from the Puritans through the First Church of Hartford, the Farmington Church, the Kensington Church, and the First Church of New Britain. The First Church of Hartford was organized at Newtown, (Cambridge,) Mass., about 1632, and Rev. Thomas Hooker was ordained its pastor soon after his arrival from England, on October 11, 1633. This Church was composed principally of Puritans, who came from England between 1628 and 1632. In June, 1636, the Church, with its pastor, made the journey through the wilderness from Newtown to Hartford, where it was permanently established. Four years later a number of persons from this Church, with others from Wethersfield, commenced a settlement at Tunxis, afterwards named Farmington. In 1645 the town of Farmington was incorporated by the General Court, and included the territory now occupied by New Britain.

In 1652 the Church in Farmington was organized, with Rev. Roger Newton, Stephen Hart, Thomas Judd, John Bronson, John Cole, Thomas Thompson, and Robert Porter, constituting the seven pillars. Rev. Roger Newton was pastor, and Stephen Hart and Thomas Judd were chosen deacons.

The growth of the town and Church were remarkable for that age. In 1655, three years after the Church was organized, and ten years after the town was incorporated, there were but forty-six ratable persons in the town, indicating a population not far from two hundred. In 1756, about a hundred years later, Farmington had a population of 3,707, and in 1774, of

6,069, while Hartford at that time had but 5,031 inhabitants. The growth of Farmington had resulted in the settlement of the eastern and western parts of New Britain, and Great Swamp and the Blue Hills in Kensington, and in 1705 a part of the southeastern portion of Farmington was incorporated into a new Ecclesiastical Society, termed the "Great Swamp Society." A minister, the Rev. William Burnham, was obtained and a plain meeting-house was built at Christian Lane, near the Mattabeset river in Kensington. On December 12, 1712, a Church was organized in connection with the Great Swamp Society. The seven pillars of this Church were Rev. William Burnham, pastor, Stephen Lee, Thomas Hart, Anthony Judd, Samuel Seymour, Thomas North, and Caleb Cowles. Anthony Judd was appointed deacon. The name of the Church was changed to Kensington by the General Assembly in 1722. A portion of the members of the Kensington Church resided within the present limits of New Britain, and the Great Swamp, or Kensington Society, extended some distance north of the center of New Britain. The Kensington Church also had a rapid growth. From ten members at the beginning of 1713, it had grown to two hundred and twenty-four before the division in 1758.

In 1754, the north part of Kensington, with a small portion of Farmington and Wethersfield, was incorporated into a separate Ecclesiastical Society, and named New Britain. The First Church in New Britain was organized April 19, 1758, and included Rev. John Smalley, pastor, from the Church at Cornwall, Conn., fifty members from the Church in Kensington, and seventeen from the Church in Newington. Mr. Smalley was ordained the day the Church was organized. He was sole pastor for nearly fifty-two years, and continued in office until his death, June 1, 1820, sixty-two years. He died at the age of eighty-six years.

There were four other pastors of this Church before its division. Rev. NEWTON SKINNER was ordained as colleague pastor of Dr. SMALLEY, Feb. 14, 1810, and was sole pastor from 1820 until his death, March 31, 1825.

Rev. HENRY JONES was ordained and installed pastor Oct.

12, 1825. The failure of his health occasioned his dismission, Dec. 19, 1827. He died in Bridgeport, Nov. 9, 1878, aged 77 years.

Rev. JONATHAN COGSWELL was installed pastor April 29, 1829, and was dismissed April 29, 1834, having been appointed Professor of Ecclesiastical History in the Theological Institute at East Windsor, Conn. He died in New Brunswick, N. J., Aug. 1, 1864, aged 81 years.

Rev. DWIGHT M. SEWARD, the fifth pastor, was ordained Feb. 3, 1836. He was dismissed June 15, 1842, and was afterwards pastor of a church in Middlefield from 1842 to 1845; in West Hartford from 1845 to 1850; in Yonkers, N. Y., from 1852 to 1870; in New Providence, N. J., 1880, and in Portland, Me., from 1881 to 1884. During the interim of his settled pastorates he supplied the pulpit at West Hoboken, N. J., Schroon Lake and Moriah, N. Y., and other places, and has resided at South Norwalk since 1884.

When the New Britain Ecclesiastical Society was incorporated, there were from forty to fifty houses within its limits. These were chiefly in Stanley Quarter, East Street, and Hart Quarter, and the only public building was a small schoolhouse on East Street. For a few years after the society was organized, the Sunday services and other public meetings were held in this schoolhouse, or in dwelling-houses or barns on East Street. The first meeting-house was located by the county court, and was placed near a ledge of rocks, in a grove a half-mile northeast of the city square. It was a plain building, without steeple or bell, but became the place where preaching services and nearly all public meetings were held from 1756 until 1822, when a second and more convenient house of worship was erected at the corner of Main and East Main Streets. This latter house was the place of meeting at the time of the division of the Church.

The expediency of organizing another Congregational church had been considered for some time, when a communication having this object in view was presented to a meeting of the Church, June 14, 1842. The causes which led to this step were partly local, the feeling that a church was needed in the southern part of the village, and partly differences of opinion as to methods of work, with possibly different views in regard to theological questions, then occupying the attention of the churches of New England.

At a meeting of the First Church, June 28, 1842, it was

"*Voted*, That this church unite in calling a meeting of the Hartford South Consociation to assemble in this village, on Tuesday, the 5th day of July next, at nine o'clock A.M., in reference to forming and organizing a new Congregational church in this parish provided they deem it expedient."

The Consociation met in compliance with this call, the following members being present:

Rev. Calvin Chapin, D.D., and Jehiel Robbins, Rocky Hill.
Rev. Joab Brace and Jedediah Deming, Newington.
Rev. Royal Robbins and Milo Hotchkiss, Kensington.
Rev. John R. Crane and John B. Woodford, Middletown.
Rev. Harvey Talcott and Russell Penfield, Portland.
Rev. James H. Francis and Selah Galpin, Westfield.
Rev. James Smith, North Glastonbury.
Rev. Zebulon Crocker and Richard Warner, Upper Middletown.
Rev. Chauncey D. Cowles and Roderick Stanley, Plainville.
Rev. Aaron Snow and Leonard E. Hale, Eastbury.
William Woodruff, Southington.
Rev. Joseph Whittlesey and Rev. Dwight M. Seward, without charge.

After hearing the parties concerned, and deliberating upon the matter, the Consociation passed the following resolutions:

"*Resolved:*
"1. That the Consociation judge it expedient to comply with the request implied in the reference which the letters missive and the vote of the church express.
"2. That this Consociation will proceed to form the new church in accordance with the call which has convoked this standing mutual council.
"3. That the new church thus formed be designated and known by the name and style of 'The South Congregational Church in New Britain.'"

The new church thus founded by the advice and action of sister churches, as represented in the Hartford South Consociation, consisted of one hundred and twenty members, some of whom were direct descendants of those who constituted the pillars of the Church in Farmington, organized nearly two hundred years before.

Four days after the action of the Consociation, or July 9, 1842, the first business meeting of the Church was held, when Romeo Francis was appointed clerk, and Horatio Waldo superintendent of the Sunday-school. Six days later, July 15th, another Church meeting was held, and Elijah Francis was appointed first deacon, and Chauncey Cornwell second deacon. Both had been deacons of the First Church before the division. During the summer and early autumn of 1842, the pulpit was supplied chiefly by professors from the Theological Seminaries at New Haven and East Windsor; but in October, Rev. SAMUEL ROCKWELL was invited to preach. His services were so acceptable that on November 18th, or less than five months after the Church was organized, a call was extended to him, which was accepted in a letter dated December 5, 1842, and on January 4, 1843, he was installed pastor of the Church. Rev. Horace Bushnell, D.D., of Hartford, preached the sermon, Rev. Joab Brace, D.D., of Newington, made the ordaining prayer. The charge to the pastor was given by Rev. Noah Porter, D.D., of Farmington, and the right hand of fellowship by Rev. E. C. Jones of Southington.

The Church deemed itself fortunate in securing, at this critical period in its history, a pastor whose experience and good judgment guided it wisely in its earlier years, and whose kindly sympathy united it in strong bonds of fellowship. Mr. Rockwell, in a communication made to the Church the year before his death, says, " When I came I found a united Church, a praying Church, a Church waiting for the ministrations of the gospel . . . . On my first survey of the field, I felt that my work was more than half accomplished because that public sentiment among all the business and influential men of the place was so strongly in favor of good order, temperance, Sabbath-schools, and vital religion."

In the Church the spirit of self-sacrifice was inculcated. With no pretense or outward show, and with little noise, the great problems of Church life and laying wisely the foundations of Christian character, ministering to the poor and the sick, and sending the gospel to the heathen, were solved. Prayer meetings were regularly sustained and well attended. The Church meeting was held every Friday afternoon and a conference meeting every Friday evening. The monthly concert of prayer for foreign missions was established soon after the organization of the Church, and for many years was held the first Sunday evening in each month. The pastor was accustomed to prepare interesting papers upon the different missions, and these were illustrated by maps and charts, and the Sandwich Island mission, then a foreign mission field, the Nestorians, the Mahratta mission, Ceylon, China, and the Indian missions were terms almost as familiar as household words to the members of the Church. The Church and congregation were thus kept well informed in regard to most of the missions, and the attendance which kept the rooms of the vestry crowded was evidence of the interest taken in the monthly concert of prayer.

At the same time the interest in the Pagan world was so stimulated, the work at home was not neglected. The pastor was able to make visits to all the families of his people, and at the annual meeting in 1846 a person was appointed to circulate books and tracts among the members of the Church and congregation with a suitable compensation for his services. A few years later all the Evangelical Churches in the place engaged in evangelistic work in the organization of the New Britain Tract Society, and this Church was largely represented in that society during the more than thirty years of its active effort.

During Mr. Rockwell's pastorate there were added to the Church on confession of faith, one hundred and thirty-seven, and by letter, one hundred and thirty-three; total, two hundred and seventy. The net gain was one hundred and nineteen, or nearly one hundred per cent. Several of the members who had been active in the organization of the Church had passed away; but others had taken their places, and the Church had become firmly united as one band to carry forward Church work.

After his ministry with this Church of fifteen and a half years, Mr. Rockwell was dismissed at his own request, June 20, 1858; but he continued to reside in the parish until his death. He was born at Winchester, Conn., April 18, 1803. On his father's side, he was a direct descendant, the seventh generation, of Deacon William Rockwell, member and deacon of the Congregational Church originally organized at Plymouth, England, and on his mother's side he was the eighth generation in descent of Governor William Bradford of the Plymouth colony. He graduated at Yale college in 1825, studied theology at Andover and Yale Theological seminaries, and was licensed to preach in 1828. He was pastor of the Church in Plainfield, Conn., from 1832 to 1841, and in 1842 came to New Britain. He was a faithful pastor, endeared to his people by his kindly sympathy with them, and his constant interest in whatever concerned their welfare. While a settled pastor, he devoted his time and strength to the Church and parish, but after his dismission from the Church he was repeatedly chosen to offices of honor and trust. He was a member of the Connecticut Assembly, being in the House in 1862 and 1869, and in the Senate in 1865. He was the first treasurer of the Savings Bank of New Britain, holding the office from 1862 to 1879, and was judge of probate from 1864 to 1872. He was married to Julia Ann Plummer of Glastonbury, June 6, 1833. She died in 1838, and he married, May 5, 1840, Elizabeth Eaton of Plainfield. She died April 18, 1842, and he married July 29, 1844, Mrs. Charlotte Stanley, the daughter of Seth J. North, one of the founders of the Church. Mr. Rockwell died December 25, 1881.

With Mr. Rockwell's pastorate closed the first century of Church work in New Britain. The history of this period would be incomplete without some allusion to the men who contributed most to molding the thoughts and forming the character of the Church during this time. The first pastor of the First

Church in Hartford, Rev. Thomas Hooker, left a lasting impress on both Church and State in the whole colony, and this was probably nowhere felt more deeply than in the mother Church at Farmington. His son, Rev. Samuel Hooker, the second pastor of the Farmington Church, had the families of the Great Swamp Society, and what was afterwards Kensington and New Britain, in his parish during the latter part of his ministry. So long as he was pastor, the people at Great Swamp would go to the meeting-house in Farmington on foot or on horseback, six or eight miles, without complaint, to worship and be instructed by this eminent minister and faithful pastor. Other Farmington pastors and laymen, especially Rev. Timothy Pitkin and Rev. Noah Porter, D.D., and Colonel Fisher Gay, and Governor Treadwell, aided and befriended New Britain in its earlier days of weakness, and contributed to the social and religious character of the place.

One of the most active men in securing the organization of the Great Swamp Society was Stephen Lee, son of John Lee. one of the Hooker company that came to Hartford in 1636. When the Great Swamp Church was organized in 1712, in the list of the seven pillars the name of Stephen Lee was placed next that of the pastor, and when the meeting-house was seated, he was assigned to the post of honor, the pew next the pulpit. He was a conscientious supporter of the Great Swamp or Kensington Church, until he believed it necessary to have preaching in what was afterwards the New Britain Society. Then he headed the petition for that privilege, and for nearly fifteen years petitioned, counseled, and labored, until his prayer was answered and the request granted. On his death his mantle fell upon his grandson, Colonel Isaac Lee, then thirty-six years of age, who at once became a leader both in civil and religious affairs in the new parish. He had for several years joined his grandfather and others in petitioning for the new Society, and when it was incorporated in 1754, he gave it its name, "New Britain." On its organization he was appointed its clerk, and held the office nearly forty years. He was one of the original members of the First Church, a member of the standing committee from its organization, and deacon of the Church for the last thirty years of his life. He was a man of great energy of character, superior intelligence, and for thirty years the principal magistrate of New Britain, administering justice with wisdom and impartiality, and exhibiting a truly Christian life.

Rev. John Smalley, one of the most eminent of New England divines, as pastor of the First Church for more than sixty years of its earlier history, by his thought and teaching and commanding influence so molded the opinion and guided the practice of the community, that the impress of his mind remained long after he had passed away.

Other men, as the Norths, the Stanleys, the Smiths, the Harts, and others, all descendants of the Farmington Church, were active in laying the foundations both of the First Church and of the South Church.

In the autumn of 1858, Rev. CONSTANS L. GOODELL, who had been preaching a few weeks at the First Church, Hartford, was invited to New Britain. His first sermon here was given on November 7, and his services were so acceptable to the people on this day and the two following Sundays, that a call was extended to him, and he was ordained and installed over this Church, February 2, 1859. The sermon was preached by Rev. I. E. Dwinell, D.D., Salem, Mass. Rev. Noah Porter, D.D., of Farmington, made the ordaining and installing prayer. Charge to the pastor, by Rev. E. C. Jones, Southington ; right hand of fellowship, by Rev. L. Perrin, D.D., First Church, New Britain ; and the address to the people by Rev. S. Rockwell, the former pastor.

Mr. Goodell's pastorate began in the years of excitement preceding the civil war. The interest and attention of the community was, at the time, largely absorbed in the events connected with the nation's struggle, and this Church participated deeply in that interest. Its first pastor presided at the first war meeting held in the State. The captain of the first military company which went to the army from New Britain was a member of this Church. Other members were in the ranks. Many of the young men enlisted in the army. Some were killed or wounded in battle, and others were for many years absent from their homes. When the war broke out, other men and women were engaged in fitting out their brothers, fathers, or sons, for the part they were to take as immediate actors in the struggle, or in preparing supplies for camp and hospital, and ordinary Church work was interrupted.

When Mr. Goodell was installed, there were two hundred and twenty-seven members of the Church. At the close of his first year of service, there were but two hundred and twenty, and after his first five years as a pastor here, the year 1864 opened with the same number of Church members. In three of these years there had been net losses, and in the last year, the darkest year of the American conflict, the greatest loss of any one of these years; and the report at the end of the year indicated a Church membership less by fifteen than the number reported nine years before. After the war closed, society gradually resumed its normal condition, and an advance in Church work was inaugurated. The foundations of a new and larger Church edifice were laid; active and efficient efforts were put forth to bring the gospel to the neglected; larger additions were made to the Church, and the net increase in membership continued from year to year for nine years without interruption.

During this period over five hundred persons united with the Church, and the net gain over losses by death, dismission, and discipline was three hundred and twenty-two, or one hundred and forty-six per cent. The whole number uniting with the Church during Mr. Goodell's pastorate was five hundred and sixty-one, of whom two hundred and eighty-nine were received on confession of faith, and two hundred and seventy-two by letter. One hundred and sixty-three were dismissed to other churches, sixty-five were removed by death, and twenty-one by discipline. In less than two years after the settlement of Mr. Goodell, a convenient parsonage was completed and occupied, and later in his ministry the large stone church edifice was erected.

On the tenth of November, 1872, to the surprise of many and to the great regret of more, Mr. Goodell announced that "eminent physicians had decided that a change of climate was necessary on account of failing health in his household," and therefore with great reluctance he tendered his resignation as pastor of this Church. A mutual council was called, and after a successful ministry of nearly fourteen years he was dismissed, at his own request, Nov. 18, 1872. His pastorate here had been eminently successful in building up the Church and increasing its power. His pulpit utterances, enriched by his fertile genius and winning eloquence, his unostentatious manner, his methodical pastoral visits, his self-sacrificing spirit and devotion to the welfare of others, and especially his sympathy with the poor and unfortunate, with his loving consecration to the Master's service, had won for him a large place in the hearts of his people, who witnessed his departure with unfeigned sorrow. In the latter part of November, 1872, he began his work in St. Louis, where, as pastor of Pilgrim Church, his labors were continued with eminent success for more than thirteen years. In this time while several new churches went off from the Pilgrim Church, the membership of that Church was increased from one hundred and eighteen to nearly nine hundred, and its beneficent work was correspondingly increased. Mr. Goodell was born in Calais, Vt., March 16, 1830. He graduated at the University of Vermont in 1855, and at Andover Theological Seminary in 1858. He was married to Emily Fairbanks, daughter of Governor Erastus Fairbanks of St. Johnsbury, Vt., May 5, 1859. He visited Europe five times, and twice extended his visits to the Holy Land. He died suddenly, Feb. 1, 1886, in the midst of active work.

Rev. HENRY L. GRIFFIN was ordained and installed pastor of this Church Oct. 1, 1873. The sermon was preached by Rev. Noah Porter, D.D., of New Haven ; the ordaining and installing prayer was offered by Rev. N. J. Burton, D.D., of Hartford ; the charge to the pastor was given by Rev. N. H. Griffin, D.D., of Williamstown, Mass.; the right hand of fellowship by Rev. John H. Denison of the First Church, New Britain ; and the address to the people by Rev. Samuel Harris, D.D., of New Haven. During Mr. Griffin's pastorate of four years and two months, two hundred and thirty-eight members were added to the Church, one hundred and ninety on confession of faith, and forty-eight by letter. Sixty received letters to other churches, thirty-two were removed by death, and three by discipline; the gain in membership for the four years being one hundred and forty-three, or a little more than twenty-six per cent. On Sept. 23, 1877, Mr. Griffin read a communication to the Church, in which he said: "For the purpose of seeking rest by a prolonged season of travel abroad and study in a foreign university, in accordance with a plan formed last year, I herewith tender my resignation as your pastor, and ask you to unite with me in calling a council to advise in regard to the dissolution of the pastoral relation." The Church did not at once comply with his request, but at a meeting held Oct. 10, 1873, almost unanimously adopted the following preamble and resolutions:

"WHEREAS, our beloved pastor has, to our very great regret, and as we believe, contrary to our best interests as a Church, felt it his duty to offer his resignation, therefore

"*Resolved*, That by his earnest, acceptable, and successful labors among us the past four years, by his manifest love for and self-sacrificing devotion to his chosen work, his constant and unremitting zeal for the spiritual welfare and edification of his people — his warm and ready sympathy and co-operation in every benevolent and charitable enterprise — his kind encouragement and willing aid to the poor, the unfortunate, and the afflicted, thereby following in the steps and imitating the example of his divine Master, not less than by the beauty and growing power of his public discourses, he has so endeared himself to us, that we cannot willingly consent to the severance of ties so pleasant and tender, nor give up our claim to his maturer and, as we trust, still more profitable labors in the future among us.

"*Resolved*, That in view of the above, and pledging him our hearty sympathy, encouragement, and support, we hereby request him to reconsider, and, if possible, withdraw his resignation, believing such a course to be for the permanent good and prosperity of this church and people."

After due consideration, Mr. Griffin returned answer that he did not think it his duty to withdraw his resignation, and he was consequently dismissed by council, Dec. 20, 1877. After a few years of travel and study in Europe, he was installed over the Hammond Street Church, Bangor, Maine, in 1881, of which he is still pastor.

The present pastor, Rev. JAMES W. COOPER, was installed pastor of this Church, March 20, 1878, by aid of council, of which Rev. W. W. Woodworth of Berlin was Moderator, and Rev. Wm. R. Eastman of Suffield, Scribe. The sermon was preached by Rev. N. J. Burton, D.D., of Hartford; the installing prayer was offered by Rev. A. S. Cheesebrough of Durham; Rev. A. F. Beard, D.D., of Syracuse, N. Y., gave the charge to the pastor; Rev. A. W. Hazen of Middletown, the right hand of fellowship; and Rev. W. L. Gage, D.D., of Hartford, the address to the Church.

On Jan. 1, 1878, there were six hundred and seventy members of the Church. There have been added since, on confession, four hundred and fifty-two; by letter, two hundred and thirty-four, and three restored to membership; and the whole number of members, Dec. 31, 1892, was nine hundred. The Sunday-school has also largely increased in numbers, and various forms of church work have been introduced.

DEACONS.

Ten days after the organization of the Church, or July 15, 1842, two deacons were appointed and this number was continued until 1861, when, by the appointment of two deacons in addition to those serving, the number was increased to four. The whole number was further increased to six in 1874, and subsequently to eight. Seven is the present number.

LIST OF DEACONS.

Term of Service.

Elijah Francis,	July 15, 1842, to November 1, 1846.
Chauncey Cornwell,	July 15, 1842, to September 17, 1863.
Orson H. Seymour,	January 22, 1847, to December 3, 1864.
David N. Camp,	October 3, 1861.
Charles Peck,	October 3, 1861.
William H. Smith,	April 14, 1865, to August 20, 1873.

Term of Service.

John Wiard,	April 14, 1865.
George P. Rockwell,	January 13, 1874, to January 6, 1891.
Truman B. House,	January 13, 1874, to January 31, 1875.
John N. Bartlett,	April 14, 1876.
Isaac N. Carleton,	April 14, 1876, to January 4, 1884.
John B. Talcott,	January 4, 1884.
John H. Peck,	December 27, 1889.
Daniel O. Rogers,	December 27, 1889.

The terms of service of deacons Elijah Francis, Chauncey Cornwell, William H. Smith, and Truman B. House were terminated by death, of deacons Orson H. Seymour, George P. Rockwell, and Isaac N. Carleton by removal from town and resignation accepted.

STANDING COMMITTEE.

At a meeting of the Church held February 17, 1843, a committee consisting of the deacons and five other brethren was "appointed for the ensuing year, to act with the pastor in cases of discipline and the examination of candidates for admission to the Church." This was the first recognition or basis of the standing, or Church committee. For many years the number consisted of five, besides the deacons, and all were elected each year at the annual meeting. In 1868 the number of brethren besides the deacons was increased to six, who were divided into classes, so that two, or one-third of the number, were elected each year, and the term of service was extended to three years.

CHURCH OR STANDING COMMITTEE WITH TERM OF SERVICE.

Alvin North, 1843 to '46, '47 to '50, '52 to '62, '64 to '65.
Elnathan Peck, 1843 to '47.
William H. Smith, 1843 to '48, '55 to '61, '62 to '66.
Horace Butler, 1843 to '44, '46 to '51, '52 to '70.
Romeo Francis, 1843 to '46.
Francis Hart, 1844 to '46.
Joshua Carpenter, 1846 to '48.
Chester Hart, 1846 to '47.
Horatio Waldo, 1847 to '50.
Horace Clapp, 1847 to '48.

Henry Stanley, 1848 to '52, '72 to '81.
Samuel Hart, 1848 to '52.
Ethan A. Andrews, 1850 to '54.
Josiah Dewey, 1850 to '52.
Frederic W. Hart, 1850 to '52.
Henry North, 1852 to '54.
Lucius Woodruff, 1852 to '55, '57 to '59, '67 to '72.
Philo Pratt, 1854 to '55.
Abram Peck, 1854 to '55.
Grove W. Loomis, 1855 to '56.
Charles Peck, 1855 to '56, '59 to '61.
David N. Camp, 1856 to '60.
Oliver Stanley, 1856 to '57.
Charles T. Talcott, 1860 to '63.
John B. Talcott, 1861 to '67, '78 to '80, '83.
J. Henry Hart, 1862 to '69.
William S. Booth, 1864 to '67, '77 to '80.
Harvey G. Brown, 1865 to '69, '85 to '87.
Thomas A. Conklin, 1866 to '67, '79.
Frederic H. North, 1867 to '77.
George P. Rockwell, 1867 to '74.
Henry C. Bowers, 1869 to '72, '80 to '82.
Josiah Shepard, 1869 to '73.
Charles L. Mead, 1870 to '72.
Asa P. Meylert, 1872 to '75.
Horace H. Brown, 1873 to '79.
J. Warren Tuck, 1873 to '75, '81 to '83.
Isaac S. Lee, 1875 to '77.
John H. Peck, 1876 to '79, '83 to '85.
Edwin B. Lyon, 1876 to '77.
H. Dayton Humphrey, 1877 to '79, '86 to '88, '91 to
Thomas S. Hall, 1879 to '81, '89 to '91.
William E. Latham, 1880 to '81.
Frederick H. Churchill, 1880 to '81.
Philip Corbin, 1881 to '82.
John B. Smith, 1881 to '82.
Daniel O. Rogers, 1881.
Charles E. Hart, 1882 to '84.
John W. Stoughton, 1883 to '85.
Thomas W. Wilbor, 1884 to '86, '92 to
Phineas M. Bronson, 1884 to '86.
John H. Peck, 1884 to '85.
Francis H. Smith, 1885 to '87.

Charles E. Steele, 1886 to '88.
Martin S. Wiard, 1887 to '89.
Edward N. Stanley, 1887 to '89.
Clarence F. Carroll, 1888 to '90.
Burr A. Johnson, 1888 to '90.
John P. Bartlett, 1889 to '91.
Charles E. Wetmore, 1890 to '92.
Albert L. Wiard, 1890 to '92.
Robins Fleming, 1891 to
Henry J. Wheeler, 1892 to

CLERKS.

At a meeting of the Church held July 9, 1842, Mr. Romeo Francis was chosen clerk of the Church. In a few years the clerk came to act also as treasurer, which usage was continued to 1885. Since that time the offices of clerk and treasurer have been held by different persons.

The following is the list of clerks:

Names.	Time of Service.	Term of Office.
Romeo Francis,	1842—1846,	4 years.
Gad Stanley,	1847—1849,	2 years.
Frederic H. North,	1849—1856,	7 years.
Gad Stanley,	1856—1858,	2 years.
William H. Hart,	1858—1884,	26 years.
Daniel O. Rogers,	1885—1890,	5 years.
Edward N. Stanley,	1890—	

TREASURER FROM 1858.

William H. Hart.

SUNDAY-SCHOOL.

The Sunday-school, as an institution of the Church, has held an important place, contributing not only to the increase of the Church in membership, but to the training of the young for efficient service. The first officers of the Sunday-school were appointed at the first business meeting of the Church, and were as follows: Superintendent, HORATIO WALDO; Assistant Superintendents, CHAUNCEY CORNWELL and MRS. R. G. WILLIAMS; Secretary, FRANCIS HART; Librarians, R. G. WILLIAMS and

CHARLES LEWIS. Rules and regulations for the school were adopted at this meeting, which provided that the appointment of officers and the general care of the school should be in the hands of the Church. The sessions of the Sunday-school were held in the vestry of the church, but when the building was removed in 1866, to make room for the new edifice, the school was transferred to the audience room.

When the new chapel was completed in the spring of 1867, the school, which had been suspended for a short time, was opened in the new rooms, the primary department occupying the room on the west side of the chapel. These rooms it was supposed would afford ample accommodations for the Sunday-school, and it was thought that there would be no necessity of having classes in the audience room of the church. But with additional accommodations the school increased in number of members more rapidly than ever before, the net increase in numbers in a single year, 1869, being 114. For the first decade, 1842–52, the gain in number of members enrolled was 45; for the second decade, 1852–62, 38, and for the third, 1862–72, it was 436, or more than two hundred per cent. After the dedication of the new edifice and all the rooms were opened, the chapel, primary room and parlor, were soon crowded by the classes of the Sunday-school, and still additions were making to the school constantly. What was to be done? The audience room was new, and had not been constructed with reference to the convenience of Sunday-school instruction, and there was a considerable number of the members of the Church and Society who thought it not wise to have it occupied by classes.

After consultation and prayer for wisdom, without dissension or objection, or any vote by Church or Society, the doors were opened, first for a single class in one corner of the audience room, and then for more, until the entire room was occupied from pulpit to organ with classes engaged in the study of God's word. For some years this necessary arrangement, approved by all who sought the advancement of Christ's kingdom, was adequate, but the school continued to increase. The number of members enrolled at the close of the fourth decade of the history of the Church was three hundred and twenty-six greater than in 1872, and more than four and a half times as great as the number enrolled at the close of the second decade, or 1852. The chapel, church parlor, primary-class room, audience room, and pastor's room, were occupied by the school, and still more room was needed. Various plans for relief were proposed, as the extension of the chapel, or some addition to the church, when the late Cornelius B. Erwin, by his will, provided in part for the erection of a new building. The requisite amount was raised, satisfactory plans were obtained, and the new parish chapel was completed in 1890, and was occupied by a portion of the Sunday-school. With the accommodations afforded by this addition, the school was provided with room for all its departments and for far more efficiency in its work.

In March, 1881, the superintendent became a salaried officer of the Church, devoting his whole time to the interests of the school and to parish work. In 1891, the Church voted to establish a Home department of the Sunday-school. During the first year, although only a part of the parish was thoroughly canvassed, one hundred and eighty persons were enrolled, some of whom soon became members of classes in the school; and this department gave promise of becoming an important auxiliary.

The membership of the school at periods of ten years has been as follows:

1842.	1852.	1862.	1872.	1882.	1892.
130	175	203	649	975	1131

and 250 in the Home Department.

The Sunday-school at first had no library, but a few books were soon collected, principally for children, and a small library established. This seems to have been not entirely acceptable, for at a meeting of the Church, April 5, 1844, it was voted " that the officers of the school be a committee to select from the library such books as they deem unfit for use and to purchase such new books as they think necessary." At the annual meeting of the Church, January 9, 1846, Rev. Samuel Rockwell, Prof. E. A. Andrews, Horatio Waldo, and O. B. Bassett were appointed "a committee to examine the Sunday-school library, to see what books are needed, and whether some books of a higher order may not be useful;" they were also to recommend such books as they shall think conducive to the interest and welfare of the school. This committee seems to have taken a broader view than simply to provide books for the Sunday-school, for in a few months a collection of nearly four hundred books was secured and catalogued to constitute the "New Britain South Church Congregational Library." The books seem to have been selected for a parish library and intended for older persons than the classes then found in the Sunday-school. Among these books were secular, or political, histories of America, Europe, India, China, etc., books for farmers and for trades and professions, the English dramatists and poets, translations of the Latin and Greek classics, and some religious works. The perusal of these volumes, whether by old or young, must have helped to strengthen character and to train up thoughtful men and women. This library was in use several years, the books being exchanged on week days, or on the evenings of the conference meeting.

When the first meeting-house was to be moved and the basement rooms where the library was kept were demolished, the books were placed in the rooms of the New Britain Institute. It was found that many of the books were missing, and as the Sunday-school library was enlarged, and the town library increased the number of its volumes, there was little demand for the parish library, and it has never been recalled from the Institute.

The Sunday-school library had received additions of new books from time to time, but some had become worn out or lost, and in 1862, after the library had been carefully renovated, some of the books rebound and new books added, the little twelve-page catalogue published of all the books in the library had titles of only 330 books. Other books were added, and in 1868, another catalogue, three and a half inches by two in size, with twenty-two pages, and names of 463 books, was issued. In 1870, through the generosity of Dr. Lucius Woodruff, the teachers' library was established. This was a reference library, and consisted principally of commentaries and works on the Bible. The next year a catalogue of the books for the youth's department, with twenty-two pages and 600 titles, was printed. During the next four years new books were added, so that the catalogue published in 1875 had in all 890 volumes. In this catalogue the books for the senior department, or older members of the school, had a distinctive mark, and the 160 volumes in the teachers' library were catalogued separately. In 1878, after the senior department had been removed to the church, two catalogues were issued, one for teachers and the senior department, of thirty-two pages, including the teachers' or reference library, and 766 volumes; and one of twenty pages and 480 volumes for the junior department, in all 1,246 volumes. Supplements were printed two years later with 121 new books. In 1881, additions were made to the teachers' library, and for the first time, a separate and complete catalogue issued, with more than twice the number of books that were in this library at first. In 1882, there were 180 books purchased for the primary department and a four-page catalogue printed.

In 1884 large additions were made to both departments of the general Sunday-school library, the books were classified, analytical accounts of the more important were prepared, and two catalogues, one for each department, with an aggregate of seventy pages, were published, with titles of more than 1,400 volumes. Between 1884 and 1890, six supplements, in all thirty-five large pages, with 510 new books were issued. In 1891–92, the teachers', or reference library, was re-classified and the books numbered anew, additions of new and standard works were made to several classes, a larger catalogue was published which embraced over 500 volumes, a new case was procured, and the library carefully arranged for convenience of use. Arrangements were also made for a department of books on missions. New books were added to the circulating library in 1892 and a new catalogue issued for the senior and junior departments.

The library has thus been a growth, keeping pace with the growth of the school and the demands of the times. Great care has been exercised in the selection of books, but additions have been made frequently and generously until more than two thousand volumes, most of them of high character, have been collected for the use of the Sunday-school, making one of the most extensive and comprehensive Sunday-school libraries in the country.

SUPERINTENDENTS.

Names.	Time of Service.	Term of Office.
Horatio Waldo,	1842—1844,	2 years.
Osias B. Bassett,	1844—1848,	4 years.
Orson H. Seymour,	1848—1854,	6 years.
David N. Camp,	1854—1855,	1 year.
John B. Talcott,	1855—1856,	1 year.
Hubert F. North,	1856—1858,	2 years.
Lucius Woodruff,	1858—1861,	3 years.
George D. Rand,	1861—1862,	1 year.
Lucius Woodruff,	1862—1864,	2 years.
Henry C. Bowers,	1864—1868,	4 years.
John Wiard,	1868—1872,	4 years.
Isaac N. Carleton,	1872—1873,	1 year.
John Wiard,	1873—	

CONTRIBUTIONS TO BENEVOLENT OBJECTS.

This Church, early in its history, adopted the practice of systematic benevolence, its gifts the first year after its organization amounting to nearly four hundred and thirty dollars. The money raised was at first placed in the pastor's hands for distribution, and then committed to the pastor and deacons. Contributions for Foreign Missions were taken up at every monthly concert, and other occasional contributions for specific objects were made in connection with Church services, but the principal collections were received by individuals appointed by the Church to call on each of its members.

After a few years, the contributions for Home and Foreign Missions were made — the first in May, and the latter in October, through the personal solicitation of collectors appointed annually, and the contributions for other objects were made in Church on specific days appointed by the pastor and Church committee.

In May, 1860, the Church adopted the following minute:

"Since in this age the providence of God has opened a wide field for Christian benevolence, blessed the Church with temporal prosperity, and crowned its charities for the spiritual elevation and redemption of man with favor, we deem it a duty to practice according to our ability prayerful and systematic benevolence."

Certain months of the year were set apart, or recommended for each of the principal societies, but the collections were still made in part by calls of committees from house to house. At a Church meeting held April 2, 1875, the plan of systematic giving by weekly contributions, as a part of worship, on each Lord's day morning, was adopted; and the amount collected, not specifically appropriated to some definite object by the donors, was distributed to the various missionary and benevolent societies and charitable objects by giving a certain percentage to each. The percentages were slightly changed, but this plan was followed until 1883, when special months were devoted to special objects, and envelopes dated for each Sunday in the year were furnished to all who desired to use them for the weekly offering. While the benevolent contributions have not been as large as in some wealthier churches, they have been made freely for objects at home and abroad. A commodious, substantial church edifice and a convenient chapel and Sunday-school rooms and social rooms have been secured and paid for in full. Local objects have been freely aided. The Church has had a special interest in the cause of Christian education, the cause of missions, and of aid to the depressed classes in our own country, and while other objects of Christian effort and opportunity have not been overlooked, for no cause have its contributions been more regular and systematic than for Foreign Missions. The following table has the principal contributions for fifty years:

Contributions of the South Cong'l Church to Benevolent Objects, from its Organization to 1892.

Year.	Foreign Missions.	Home Missions.	Freedmen. Colonization Society.	Christian Education.	Church Building.	Bible and Tract Cause.	Sunday-School Cause.	Miscellaneous.	Total.
1843	$170.50	$105.37	$40.00	$35.28		$38.50	$19.74	$20.00	$429.39
1844	191.10	101.50				127.64	33.43	31.17	484.84
1845	201.01	125.00		26.75		221.06		64.75	641.57
1846	210.51	100.60	31.00	22.00		116.85	28.83	52.84	562.63
1847	341.00	300.00	23.00	25.35		145.25		166.40	1,001.00
1848	380.00	145.00	40.00			151.60	34.00	36.42	787.02
1849	360.00	211.50				160.25		99.60	832.88
1850	400.00	241.00		21.53		157.00		32.80	880.80
1851	412.00	263.00		50.00		152.34		66.72	894.06
1852	362.55	278.00	70.50			107.25		28.28	846.58
1853	516.25	530.00		29.04		172.00	19.67	169.88	1,436.80
1854	597.70	450.00	164.50			568.45		122.84	1,903.49
1855	440.00	295.12				32.90		55.74	823.76
1856	364.57	323.00	36.00	17.00		37.15	60.04	522.35	1,360.11
1857	286.65	183.18	106.00			69.82	36.00	77.05	758.72
1858	300.23							43.97	344.20
1859	450.35	66.60	96.00	360.00		71.35	106.19	144.16	1,234.65
1860	570.79	91.62		350.00	28.00	57.89	27.03	215.51	1,380.84
1861	476.19	346.53		11.40	25.00	139.86	16.29	275.11	1,290.38
1862	700.78	481.16	25.00	25.00		210.57	85.77	225.94	1,756.22
1863	701.47	605.69	57.50	446.00	25.00	170.52	12.55	519.87	2,538.62
1864	918.00	837.91	46.40	500.00		82.05	105.41	1,142.14	3,631.91
1865	1,086.51	1,185.26	66.00	93.33	120.00	166.39	177.43	834.70	3,729.62
1866	1,205.72	1,267.95	152.70	1,500.00	117.53	174.00	155.57	636.39	5,209.86
1867	1,412.84	1,339.01	312.65	230.00	72.60	368.29	158.31	1,483.09	5,356.79
1868	1,515.89	1,447.60	50.00	1,805.00	76.23	171.40		770.27	5,836.39

CONTRIBUTIONS—CONTINUED.

Year.	Foreign Missions.	Home Missions.	Freedmen. Indians, etc., A. M. A.	Christian Education.	Church Building.	Bible and Tract Cause.	Sunday-school Cause.	Miscellaneous.	Total.
1869	$1,631.78	$1,541.10	$297.00	$2,105.00	$150.00	$232.69	$250.00	$1,041.57	$7,249.14
1870	1,736.26	1,707.05	148.35	1,685.00	117.00	222.09	300.00	1,679.80	7,595.55
1871	2,017.76	1,655.04	745.35	4,786.65	....	198.43	....	1,693.85	11,097.08
1872	2,368.90	2,574.16	582.00	6,236.35	....	334.55	131.00	1,474.47	13,701.43
1873	772.80	1,757.97	99.38	1,154.70	....	91.81	....	1,216.67	5,093.33
1874	957.30	1,325.00	130.21	....	....	188.48	....	1,108.05	3,709.04
1875	1,162.91	1,387.06	90.65	315.65	88.65	180.71	....	721.43	3,947.06
1876	1,223.58	1,412.79	144.58	137.59	125.58	225.70	20.00	629.86	3,919.68
1877	955.13	1,264.82	94.35	89.35	89.36	187.22	100.00	652.66	3,432.89
1878	1,285.00	1,435.52	242.19	71.22	71.22	184.05	105.00	1,196.73	4,590.93
1879	876.77	896.80	272.15	3,243.00	66.00	129.80	375.00	2,950.70	8,810.22
1880	1,292.13	1,694.82	840.46	581.39	176.40	135.73	100.00	4,715.36	9,536.29
1881	1,498.44	1,878.73	1,582.05	1,478.15	1,133.77	439.03	100.00	1,682.44	9,792.61
1882	1,311.80	1,158.85	863.03	1,028.22	691.65	414.02	192.64	1,697.79	7,358.04
1883	2,021.22	2,044.93	1,299.09	2,413.45	1,067.52	240.00	200.00	315.00	9,601.21
1884	1,349.39	1,702.00	389.67	592.63	869.64	60.00	128.46	1,991.34	7,283.13
1885	1,305.03	1,466.83	621.55	566.24	226.72	75.00	176.49	2,334.09	6,771.95
1886	1,095.72	1,815.55	802.96	352.12	396.62	86.00	147.00	4,104.00	8,799.27
1887	1,156.86	1,678.25	631.84	453.15	94.66	70.00	123.53	3,929.72	8,138.01
1888	1,277.20	1,701.74	727.25	181.26	827.47	75.00	108.28	4,113.63	9,011.83
1889	943.95	1,735.36	646.18	352.56	1,039.61	61.75	185.59	1,765.52	6,730.52
1890	1,464.78	1,482.64	821.51	376.12	1,603.84	48.34	114.03	2,110.56	8,022.02
1891	1,724.90	1,649.41	666.72	117.72	2,231.00	45.00	120.70	1,137.24	7,692.69
1892	1,587.93	1,162.32	999.13	318.78	2,238.24	40.00	194.00	2,514.60	9,054.00
	$47,390.15	$49,453.34	$15,254.24	$34,123.94	$13,719.31	$7,827.98	$4,250.00	$54,615.29	$226,933.25

ASSOCIATIONS AND SOCIETIES.

For several years after the organization of the Church, its general work, aside from that of the Sunday-school, was prosecuted chiefly by the Church acting as one body, in planning and executing the various projects for advancing Christ's kingdom. A Church meeting was held every Friday afternoon, at which schemes for active Church work were freely discussed, and the final action was the result of the concurrent judgment of all or of the majority of the Church present. As these meetings were well attended by nearly all the members, and especially by those having the greatest influence, the whole Church participated in the onward progress of its distinctive work. As opportunities for Christian effort and counsel multiplied, and the Church itself embraced a greater variety of age and condition of members, much of its work has been done by societies and associations formed within the Church and working together in harmony to accomplish its mission. A few of these societies were nearly contemporaneous with the Church in organization, but the greater part have been formed within the last twenty years.

LADIES' BENEVOLENT SOCIETY.—Before the Church was organized, some of the ladies who were among its original members met at private houses to sew and plan to raise money for furnishing the new Church edifice then building. For the better prosecution of their work, they formed themselves into a society, with the name of the "Ladies' Benevolent Society." The first meeting as a society was held October 29, 1841; this is therefore the oldest association in the Church, anticipating by more than eight months the beginnings of church life as a separate Church. In less than a week after the society was organized it had fifty members. Its work at first had direct and special reference to preparing cushions for the pulpit and the furnishing of the meeting-house, dedicated in June, 1842. But from that time through the more than fifty-one years of its existence, it has been an instrumentality for good, working on varied lines, as the Providence of God has presented opportunities.

By its well-directed, systematic efforts, its persevering diligence and watchful attention to the needs of others, it has not only in a large degree ministered to the needy, and relieved distress in the home parish, but it has become an efficient aid in redeeming our whole country to Christ by its coöperation with State and National societies, in its contributions to their treasuries, and in ministrations to their missionaries and families. This Society has a board of directresses who have charge of boxes sent to home missionaries, a committee on missionary intelligence, an entertainment committee, a flower committee, and a committee of welcome. It contributes one hundred dollars annually toward the yearly expenses of the parish chapel, and its contributions in cash and boxes to Home missionaries amount to several hundred dollars annually. For several years this Society has been auxiliary to the Woman's Home Missionary Union of Connecticut.

MATERNAL ASSOCIATION.—The first Maternal Association in New Britain was held at the house of Samuel Hart, M.D., March 30, 1836, when a few ladies of the Church, upon the invitation of Mrs. Hart, met to consider the matter of forming an association. At the next meeting held April 17th of the same year, a constitution was adopted and a complete organization effected. The constitution provided for two officers, a directress and a secretary. Mrs. L. H. Seward, the wife of the pastor, was appointed directress, and Mrs. N. Stanley, secretary. Meetings were held by the members monthly, quarterly, and annually. At the annual and quarterly meetings the pastor, or some other gentleman, frequently made an address. After the division of the Church, the members of this Society continued to meet together as before for several years, until a division of the Association was deemed wise.

The first meeting of the Maternal Association of the South Church was held at the house of Rev. Samuel Rockwell, July 2, 1846. Mrs. Rockwell was chosen directress at this meeting, and held the office until her death, June 2, 1887. The meetings were held at her house for more than thirty-five years, when, on account of her illness, they were transferred to the Church parlor, November, 1881, and Mrs. J. W. Tuck then had charge of them. Since Mrs. Tuck's death in 1889, the meetings have been under the care of Mrs. J. N. Bartlett.

JUVENILE MITE SOCIETY.—In the winter of 1860-61, Mrs. C. L. Goodell invited girls too young to attend the Ladies' Benevolent Society, to meet at her house, where she interested them in missions. The meetings became regular, and the girls to the number of twenty-five were organized into a Society, November 2, 1861, under the name of the Juvenile Mite Society. The number of members was soon increased to thirty or more, who were accustomed to meet at the house of the pastor to listen to missionary intelligence, and to sew or engage in other work for the cause of missions. They also contributed money for the same cause. This Society continued its work for eight or ten years, or until its members were old enough to unite with other societies.

YOUNG LADIES' SEWING SOCIETY.—During a time of business depression in 1871-72, when there were many families in need, the older girls and young ladies of the Church, upon the invitation of Mrs. Goodell, met at the parsonage regularly, to sew and provide garments for the needy in the Sunday-school. When this had been accomplished, the work was broadened to include provision not only for the deserving poor of the Church and congregation, but to some extent for others, who in a time of lack of work, either by themselves, or families, would suffer if relief were not provided. No formal constitution was adopted at the time, but by request Miss Annie L. Smith served as secretary, and Miss Ellen R. Camp as treasurer of this circle.

The visits to the needy were made by the young ladies individually and unofficially, to avoid as far as possible arousing the prejudices of such as would shrink from receiving aid from a society. The work progressed so satisfactorily that other young ladies joined the circle, and an organization was formed which took the name of the Young Ladies' Sewing Society. To the local work in New Britain was added sending boxes or barrels of clothing to families of Home Missionaries, and furnishing aid to the school at Hampton and other places at the South. This Society was successfully continued for twelve or fourteen years, when it became merged with the Ladies' Benevolent Society, and most of its members became connected with that Society.

LADIES' FOREIGN MISSIONARY SOCIETY.—The Ladies' Foreign Missionary Society was organized April 11, 1874, with Mrs. Samuel Rockwell, president; Mrs. J. W. Tuck, recording secretary and treasurer, and Mrs. Charles Peck, corresponding secretary. January 6, 1877, Mrs. Rockwell resigned, and Mrs. William H. Smith was elected president. Mrs. Tuck died May 2, 1889, and Miss Alice C. Tuck has since been secretary and treasurer. In January, 1890, Miss Mary D. Eastman was appointed vice-president and acting president. This Society has been efficient in collecting and disseminating missionary intelligence, and especially have its members and others been kept fully acquainted with the missions and missionary work of the American Board of Commissioners for Foreign Missions. Its meetings held once a month have been well sustained, and its contributions, amounting to several hundred dollars annually, have been an important aid to missionary work. This organization for many years was an auxiliary of the New Haven Branch of the Woman's Board of Missions, but in the spring of 1892 its relations were transferred to the Hartford Branch.

THE CHEERFUL GIVERS, consisting of a group of girls interested in charitable and benevolent work, was formed in 1875. Their efforts were directed mainly to raising money for charitable objects, and in 1875 they contributed two hundred and five dollars to the cause of missions. In 1877 their contributions to Foreign Missions was one hundred and ten dollars, and twenty-five dollars to the Sunday-school Union.

THE CHRISTIAN BROTHERHOOD was organized in the winter of 1875-76, with a view to enlist the men in the Church in definite personal work. It was in some respects a forerunner of the Young People's Society of Christian Endeavor, and the Men's Union for Christian Work, in laying specific obligations upon its members. It was active and did good service through the great revival of 1876, thus proving the timeliness of its organization and its adaptation for this work. After the special season of interest was over, its active work was allowed to diminish, and at last the Society was discontinued.

THE LITTLE HELPERS' MISSION CIRCLE, organized February 17, 1877, by Mrs. Charles Peck, was at first composed of forty-three girls from five to twelve years of age, who met on alternate Saturdays at the house of their leader, for counsel and social intercourse. The number has varied from year to year, as new members have joined and the older ones have left to join other societies. This circle has been a training-school for girls interested in missionary work and afterwards joining other societies. The information imparted has given to the members a knowledge of the missionaries and their families, and they have brought their gifts willingly to send to Turkey, India, Micronesia, and elsewhere to aid the cause of missions. The total amount contributed the first ten years was $924.78. The meetings have for late years been held at the chapel, several young ladies in turn having charge of the Circle.

THE YOUNG MEN'S MISSIONARY SOCIETY was first known as The Banian Seeds Mission Band. It began February, 1878, with five boys, meeting under the charge of Miss Harriet M. Eastman, but the number soon increased. The Band was accustomed to meet weekly, the boys bringing their gifts, and their leader giving them information upon missions, or reading to them from some helpful work. In 1889, the name was changed to the Young Men's Missionary Society, and the meetings for the last few years were held in the parish chapel on Sunday afternoons. These were continued with interest until 1891, when other appointments led to their suspension. Fifty different persons were connected with the Society, and the contributions amounted to over four hundred dollars.

THE BOARD OF LADIES FOR HOME WORK, instituted in 1881, though not distinctively a society, has been an instrumentality for good. It consists of twelve ladies, four of whom are appointed each year for three years, who, by periodical visits in their several districts, alleviate distress and accomplish for the parish much of what the Tract Society did for the whole town.

THE GERMAN MOTHERS' MEETING was established under the charge of Mrs. Horace H. Brown as directress, and Mrs. William S. Booth as secretary, in 1882. There were at first but five members, but others joined, until twenty-two German mothers have belonged to the Association, which has been to them what the Maternal Association has been to other mothers in the Church, a helpful means of elevating and strengthening family life.

YOUNG WOMAN'S CHRISTIAN LEAGUE.—In the autumn of 1882, the Board of Ladies for Home Work appointed a committee of three of their number, with Mrs. J. W. Tuck chairman, to consider what could be done for some of the girls who were busily occupied in shops or elsewhere through the day, and had little opportunity for social and intellectual improvement. On invitation, several members of classes of girls in the senior department of the Sunday-school met the committee and a society was formed, termed the Class Union. The regulations were very simple. Meetings were held weekly, or fortnightly, for social purposes, mutual improvement, and charitable work. In 1889, after Mrs. Tuck's death, the plan and work of the Society were enlarged and the name changed to the Young Woman's Christian League of New Britain, with Miss Elizabeth R. Eastman president. When the parish chapel was completed, classes were organized in singing, dress-making, embroidery, stenography, and cooking. The rooms of the Society in the chapel were opened two evenings in a week, a teacher of cooking was employed, and aid was given in other work. Some other classes have been added, and some have been dropped for a time. The committee having the matter in charge endeavor to introduce exercises and employments which will interest and instruct, and help to the formation of character, and the making of pleasant homes. The members pay a regular fee, and contribute to the Ecclesiastical Society towards the expenses of the parish chapel, and also engage in charitable work for the needy and for missions. A prayer meeting is held once a month. There have been over a hundred members connected with this Society.

THE STANDARD BEARERS' MISSION CIRCLE was organized in November, 1882, under the charge of Miss Elizabeth R. Eastman. It is composed of boys from fourteen years of age upwards, who meet Sunday afternoons in the parish chapel. They receive intelligence from Foreign Missions, and the members sometimes hold correspondence with missionaries and sons of missionaries, and receive letters which are read at the meetings. The contributions of this Society are made to the American Board.

YOUNG LADIES' MISSIONARY SOCIETY.—When the Little Helpers' Mission Circle had been continued nearly seven years, some of the older members had become young ladies in age and capacity, beyond the class for which that Circle was designed, and their leader, Mrs. Charles Peck, in 1883, organized them into a separate society, called the Young Ladies' Mission Band. This Society raised for missions over one hundred and fifteen dollars the first year of its work. Under the name of the Young Ladies' Mission Band, Young Ladies' Mission Circle, and Young Ladies' Missionary Society, its work has been continued and reported to the Church. Its special object has been to promote an interest in Foreign Missions, and with the exception of one year, since 1884, it has had Mrs. James W. Cooper for its president.

THE YOUNG PEOPLES' SOCIETY OF CHRISTIAN ENDEAVOR was organized under that name in April, 1887. Many of the young people had before this been organized into a society with pledges, and, under the direction and advice of the pastor, had entered upon work for others and upon systematic training in Christian character. Their constitution and methods were so similar to those of the Christian Endeavor societies that they adopted the name, and have cordially engaged in the work of that organization. The number of members at the time of organization was ninety-one; in a year the membership increased to one hundred and fifty-one. This Society at first held its meetings on Tuesday evenings, taking the place of the Young

People's meetings established in 1864. In September, 1891, the time of meeting was changed to Sunday evening. In February, 1890, the Society assumed the support of a missionary in Africa, and raised five hundred dollars a year for that purpose. This Society has the following working committees: lookout, prayer-meeting, missionary, junior endeavor, music, and social; and special committees are appointed when demanded. It still contributes towards the support of a missionary in Africa.

THE KING'S MESSENGERS MISSION CIRCLE was organized by Miss Elizabeth R. Eastman, February 4, 1888, to take a younger class of boys than those she was accustomed to meet in the Standard Bearer's Circle. The boys at first were from seven to ten years of age, and the Circle consisted of ten. The number has increased until there are from twenty to twenty-five members from nine to fourteen years of age. The boys contribute to Foreign Missions and prepare scrap-books, cards, and other articles, which are sent direct to Mission fields, and letters are received in return, which are read at the meetings. Other missionary intelligence is given, and questions asked and answered. The meetings are held once in two weeks on Saturday mornings at the parish chapel.

THE MEN'S UNION FOR CHRISTIAN WORK was organized in the autumn of 1889, with six committees for various kinds of Christian work. In 1890 the number of committees was increased to seven by adding a temperance committee. The meetings of the Union are usually held once a month, after the regular service on Sunday evenings.

THE JUNIOR ENDEAVOR SOCIETY was formed in February, 1892. It consists of children from eight to fifteen years of age, under the immediate charge of the pastor, who is assisted by four or five young ladies from the Young People's Society of Christian Endeavor. Meetings are held every Friday afternoon, at which the pastor is generally present when in the city. In his absence, one of the young ladies has charge of the meeting. This Society has for its object the training of children for service in the Church. By means of pledges and various exercises, their attention is directed to religious thought and obligation. During the last four years there have been various other groups, or circles, of children, as the Andrew and Philip Circle, Children of the Cross, and Young Pilgrim Band, that have met the pastor at the parsonage or at the chapel, and receive instruction for a time, and have then been merged in other societies or circles.

GROWTH OF THE CHURCH.

The history of the Church for these fifty years has been marked by few periods of powerful revival or great decline. The special seasons of unusual religious interest and of largest accessions were in 1843, 1847, 1866, 1869, 1872, 1876, and 1886. The growth for the most part has been steady, healthful, and continuous, indicating the abiding presence of the power of the Holy Spirit in the regular and constant work of the Church. During a few of these years the Church has suffered a loss in aggregate membership, but the greatest losses have been in the years when there were the largest number of dismissions to churches in other places.

During the half century of the history of the Church, there have been many changes. Only nine of the one hundred and twenty original members are now connected with the Church. Two only of the four pastors are living, one still ministering to the Church, and the other a pastor in another state. Not one of the deacons for the first third of this period is living. The first twenty members of the standing committee, who served so faithfully the first dozen years, have all passed to their reward.

The Church has been signally blessed in having never been without a settled pastor for a year at any one time since its organization, and never for a continuous period of six months without either an installed pastor, or one who had accepted a call to settle. The whole number of members added to the Church since its organization is seventeen hundred and sixty-five; the number removed by letters of dismission, or by death and discipline, nine hundred and eighty-five, and the net gain in membership, seven hundred and eighty. The number of members December 22, 1892, is nine hundred.

The following table gives the additions and dismissions, with gain or loss for each year:

Years.	Additions.			Removals.			Total.		Total Membership.
	Confession.	Letter.	Restored.	Dismission.	Death.	Discipline.	Gain.	Loss.	
July 5. 1842									120
1842		2			1		1		121
1843	20	10		4	2		24		145
1844		7		3			4		149
1845		9			4		5		154
1846		10		6	2		2		156
1847	40	8		1	4		43		199
1848	5	9		6	3		5		204
1849		3		4	4			5	199
1850	1	8		3	1		5		204
1851	7	10		7	8	2	9		213
1852	5	17		9	4		9		222
1853	4	6		11	6			7	215
1854	15	10		7	3		15		230
1855		2		10	4	3		15	215
1856	4	7		9	8			6	209
1857	24	5		7	2		20		229
1858	12	1		10	5			2	227
1859	2	4		10	3			7	220
1860	1	20		7	1	10	3		223
1861	3	1		9		1		6	217
1862	4	15		2	5		12		229
1863	4	2		9	6			9	220
1864	9	14		11	4	3	5		225
1865	16	15		11	3		17		242
1866	46	37		12	4		67		309
1867	14	13		10	6		11		320
1868	9	43		7	6		39		359
1869	75	31	1	12	3		92		451
1870	13	29		21	6		15		466
1871	17	26		16	11	5	11		477
1872	73	22		23	7		65		542
1873	4	4		10	7			9	533
1874	20	10	1	14	8	1	8		541
1875	5	12		8	9	2		2	539
1876	157	21		15	7		156		695
1877	7	5		24	8			20	675
1878	8	9		19	10			12	663
1879	9	27		11	12	17		4	659
1880	14	12	1	16	5		6		665
1881	43	9		13	12		27		692
1882	16	9		20	12	6		13	679
1883	15	3		16	14	1		13	666
1884	37	35		19	9	7	37		703
1885	37	21		18	15	3	22		725
1886	108	15		24	4		95		820
1887	6	12		14	8			4	816
1888	23	10	2	23	16	5		9	807
1889	25	15		16	12		12		819
1890	24	8		16	13		3		822
1891	21	15		6	9	9	12		834
1892	66	40		15	9	11	66		900
	1,068	697	5	574	325	86	923	143	

CHURCH AND SOCIETY FUNDS.

Dr. Lucius Woodruff, who was a member of this Church from 1850 until his decease in 1872, left the following legacies to the Church and Sunday-school:

Ten thousand dollars ($10,000) to be invested as a permanent fund, the income of which shall be expended, under the direction of the acting pastor and Church committee, in such manner as they shall deem best calculated to promote the interest of the Church, particularly advising them that, in the expenditure of the income of this fund, they be careful always to remember the poor and indigent of the Church; and

Five thousand dollars ($5,000) to be invested as a permanent fund, the income of which shall be expended for the benefit of the library of the Sunday-school, both for teachers and scholars, under the direction of the acting pastor and the acting superintendent of the Sunday-school.

These funds are securely invested, and the income appropriated as provided by the donor.

Cornelius B. Erwin, a member of this Church from 1857 until his death, March 22, 1885, had been a liberal contributor to its funds during his life, and had deeded to the Society as a gift the site upon which the parish chapel was afterwards erected. By his will, he gave twelve thousand five hundred dollars ($12,500) towards the cost of the chapel; and also left to the Society his premises on Washington street, with all the buildings and appurtenances, for the uses of a parsonage, and twenty-five thousand dollars ($25,000) as a fund, the use and income of which should be used to keep the premises in good order and repair, and to pay taxes thereon.

He left to the pastor and standing committee of the Church, eighty thousand dollars ($80,000) to purchase a suitable lot of land in the town of New Britain, and to erect thereon a building or buildings, as a home for worthy and indigent women of the town of New Britain, and for the maintenance of the same.

These liberal bequests have been carefully managed, and made to contribute not only to the enlargement of church work and to the welfare of the members of this Church, but have been the means of relieving distress and ministering to the comfort of those of other folds, or not connected with any church.

In addition to these bequests Dr. Woodruff gave $10,000, and Mr. Erwin $163,333 to the New Britain Institute. Mr. Erwin also bequeathed to missions, Christian colleges, the cause of Christian education, churches of other denominations, and to various benevolent objects, different sums, in all aggregating with the foregoing, $866,419, besides the residuary estate not yet divided. Other smaller bequests have been made by other members of the Church.

WOMAN'S HOME.

The Erwin Home for women, though entirely undenominational, is really an institution of this Church, under the care and management of the pastor and Church committee.

In compliance with the provisions of the will of Cornelius B. Erwin, the pastor and Church committee, on the receipt of the legacy for this purpose, purchased a lot bounded by Bassett, Ellis, Edson, and Warlock streets, and caused to be erected thereon a building for the purposes mentioned in the will. This building is fitted up with convenient apartments, in which worthy women who have little or no property, find comfortable homes, and a relief from much of the trials and anxiety which their circumstances sometimes entail. While the administration of this bequest involves grave responsibilities and a large amount of care, it gives to the Church an additional opportunity to follow the example of its Divine master in ministering to the poor. More than twenty persons are now enjoying the blessings of this bequest.

ECCLESIASTICAL SOCIETY.

The South Congregational Society of New Britain was organized May 9, 1842, when a constitution was regularly adopted and signed by fifty members. At the first meeting the officers were appointed as follows: Henry Stanley, clerk; Henry North, treasurer; Elnathan Peck, William H. Smith, and William F. Raymond, society committee. A committee was also appointed for supplying the pulpit, and another to make arrangements for the dedication of the House of Worship, then nearly completed. More than half the members of the Society have been members of the Church, and the most cordial and harmonious relations have always existed between the Church and Society. The Society provides for the general financial needs of the Church, and has charge of the Church buildings and parsonage. The greater part of the current expenses is met by the annual rental of pews. Henry Stanley was clerk of the Society from its organization until 1875, and, during the thirty-three years of his service, carefully kept and preserved its records, and by his excellent taste in church architecture contributed to the beauty of the Lord's house.

Oliver Stanley was for forty years, or until his death, chairman of the Society's committee, and sixteen years treasurer, and by his careful methods, exact accounts, painstaking, self-denying vigilance for the Society's interests, to a large degree promoted the welfare both of Church and Society. The officers of the Society for 1892 were as follows:

Society's Committee, Philip Corbin, A. P. Collins, E. B. Lyon, E. N. Stanley; *Clerk*, H. Dayton Humphrey; *Treasurer*, Edward N. Stanley; *Collector and Sexton*, L. A. Gladding.

HOUSES OF WORSHIP.

The first House of Worship was commenced in the autumn of 1841, more than six months before the Church was organized, and completed in the spring of 1842. Three brothers, Seth J. North, then the leading manufacturer in the place, Alvin North, and Henry North, all business men interested in the prosperity of New Britain, and in its moral and religious character, believing the time had come for the organization of another church, met and consulted together, and subscribed half the amount necessary for the erection of a house of worship before asking others for contributions for this object. Their appeal then met with willing responses, the necessary funds were raised, and the building was erected. It was a plain, substantial structure of wood with basement rooms, four pillars in front, a clock and bell, standing on the corner of Main and Arch streets, near the site of the present church. It contained, including the galleries on three sides, which were put in some time after the church was constructed, about five hundred sittings. It was built by Mr. Elnathan Peck, at a cost of about $8,000. It was dedicated June 29, 1842. Rev. Joab Brace, D.D., Newington, preached the sermon from Ps. 84.

This building was occupied for twenty-five years. In the spring of 1864 it was removed a few yards to the east, to make room for the present house; the congregation, however, still worshiped in it till the present one was nearly completed. The last religious services were held in the old house on the eve of November 3, 1867. Rev. Samuel Rockwell preached the discourse from Matt. xii: 6. Subject: "The Unwritten History of the Sanctuary." The old house was then dismantled, and converted the following season into a public hall, and was afterwards destroyed by fire.

The present stone edifice was commenced in April, 1865. The corner stone was laid with appropriate ceremonies on the 23d of August following. Address by Rev. Samuel Rockwell. Prayer and laying the stone by Rev. C. L. Goodell.

The chapel was finished and dedicated March 29, 1867, and used after that for all the evening meetings of the Church. The main house of worship was completed the succeeding winter, and dedicated January 16, 1868. Sermon by the pastor, Rev. C. L. Goodell, from Rev. xxii: 9. Subject, "Christian Worship; its nature, claims, and uses, together with some of the dangers to be avoided." Consecrating prayer by Rev. Jonathan Brace, D.D., Hartford.

The building committee were C. B. Erwin, F. H. North, Henry Stanley, Oliver Stanley, Horace H. Brown, Philip F. Corbin, and Lucius Woodruff. The architect was George F. Meacham of Boston.

The church cost $140,000, and will seat about eight hundred people.

The new, or parish chapel, was erected to meet the demand for more room for Church and Sunday-school work. In material and style of architecture it is the same as the main church building, and was designed by the same architect. It was commenced in June, 1889, and completed in 1890, and dedicated June 30th, with addresses by Rev. Graham Taylor, D.D., of Hartford, and Rev. Drs. Cooper, Wright, Stidham, and Pullman of this city. This chapel affords commodious rooms for the senior and primary departments of the Sunday-school, an ample library room, convenient and pleasant social rooms, and facilities for promoting the various forms of Christian work undertaken by the Church. Its cost was $25,000, and about $2,000 more was expended in furnishing the rooms. It was dedicated entirely free from debt. The building committee were Oliver Stanley, D. O. Rogers and T. W. Wilbor.

CHURCH EDIFICE ERECTED IN 1842.

GOVERNMENT OF THE CHURCH.

"Ye are fellow citizens with the saints, and of the household of God, being built upon the foundation of the apostles and prophets, Christ Jesus himself being the chief corner stone."—*Eph. 2: 19-20.*

The local Church holds its charter of life from Christ, its head, and is competent, under Christ, to choose and induct its officers, admit and dismiss its members, exercise Christian discipline, administer the sacraments, conduct public worship, organize and maintain forms of Christian service, and do all other acts necessary to the attainment of the ends for which a church is established.

While thus independent of external control, every local church is bound by the law of Christian love to seek to maintain relations of mutual fellowship, communion, and coöperation with other churches walking in the truth of Christ, and to realize that unity set before us in the prayer of our blessed Lord, that we all may be one, and the world may believe in Him whom the Father has sent.

This Church is, therefore, Congregational, in that, while it recognizes the fellowship of the churches, and seeks the unity of the kingdom of God, it assumes under Christ the sole responsibility of its own actions, resting in the wisdom and grace which shall be given by the Holy Spirit to the whole brotherhood of its believing members. While it controls its own affairs according to its understanding of the Word of God, it will extend to sister churches and expect from them, that communion, counsel, sympathy, and aid, which the law of Christ demands.

To promote good order and efficiency in its life and work, it adopts the following

RULES OF ORDER.

"That thou mayest know how men ought to behave themselves in the house of God, which is the church of the living God, the pillar and ground of the truth. — 1 Tim. 3: 15.

I. RELIGIOUS SERVICES.

1. The public worship of God will be maintained on the Lord's Day, morning and evening, with a service for Bible study immediately after the morning worship.

2. The Sacrament of the Lord's Supper will be administered on the first Sundays in January, March, May, July, September, and November, except that the appointment for July shall be on the Sunday preceding the fourth of that month. A preparatory service will be held on the Friday evening preceding each Communion Sunday. The Church invites to the Lord's Table those who love our Lord Jesus Christ in sincerity and are living by faith in Him.

3. The Sacrament of Baptism will also be administered, when desired, on Communion Sundays and on the second Sunday in June, known as Children's Day. Children of the Church will be baptized, according to the form prescribed for the baptism of children, on presentation by their parents. Adults will be baptized on the confession of their Christian faith, according to the form for the reception of members into the Church.

4. The weekly prayer and conference meeting of the Church is held every Friday evening.

5. Other services, according to appointment, as circumstances may require.

II. BUSINESS MEETINGS.

1. There shall be an annual meeting of the Church on Friday preceding the first Sabbath in January. At this meeting, reports shall be submitted by the standing committee, the clerk, the treasurer, and the various societies connected with the church; a clerk, treasurer, two members of the standing

committee, and four members of the board of ladies for home work shall be chosen; a schedule shall be adopted for the benevolent contributions of the ensuing year, and such other business transacted as may be deemed necessary.

2. Ordinary business, such as the receiving and dismissing of members, may be transacted at any regular Church service.

3. Special business meetings may be called by the pastor or standing committee, notice being given at a regular Church service. On petition of fifteen voting members such a meeting shall be called.

4. All members of the Church in good standing, who have reached the age of twenty-one years, are entitled to vote in Church meetings.

III. OFFICERS.

1. The officers of this Church shall be a pastor, deacons, clerk, treasurer, a standing committee, and board of ladies for home work.

2. The pastor shall be an ordained minister of the gospel, elected by ballot, and installed in his office by council, and his dismission shall be effected in like manner. In addition to his ministerial duties, he shall preside at the business meetings of the Church.

3. The deacons shall be elected by ballot, and shall hold their office during life, or until their resignation, unless removed by vote of the Church. Their duties shall be to provide for and minister at the Lord's table; to give special care to the poor of the Church, and to assist the pastor in his various labors for the spiritual welfare of the Church.

4. The clerk and treasurer shall be elected by ballot. The clerk shall keep a true record of all the transactions of the Church, together with a complete roll of its members. The treasurer shall keep an account of all moneys received and disbursed.

5. The standing committee shall consist of the pastor, deacons, and six brethren, two of whom shall be chosen each year

to serve for three years, though they shall not be eligible to re-election until one year after their term of office shall expire. The clerk and treasurer, *ex officio*, shall also be members of this committee.

It shall be the duty of the standing committee to recommend candidates for admission to the Church; to investigate and bring before the Church cases of discipline; to recommend to the Church objects for benevolent contributions, and generally to have a care of the prudential affairs of the Church. Seven shall constitute a quorum for the conduct of business.

6. The board of ladies for home work shall consist of twelve ladies appointed by the Church on the nomination of the standing committee, four each year for a term of three years.

It shall be the duty of this board, under the direction of the pastor, to engage in systematic parish visitation, welcome strangers, and encourage forms of Christian work.

IV. ADMISSION OF MEMBERS.

1. Members are received into this Church either on the confession of their faith in the Lord Jesus Christ, or by letters of commendation from other churches.

2. Candidates for admission to the Church, on their confession of faith, will meet the standing committee, and on its recommendation they shall be propounded to the Church at least one week previous to their admission. Having been accepted by vote of the Church, they shall become members by confessing their Christian faith according to the form for the reception of members.

3. Members of other churches bringing letters of recommendation, after being approved by the standing committee, shall be reported to the Church, and if accepted by the Church at any succeeding meeting, they shall be enrolled as members of this Church.

4. Members of churches whose rules forbid them to give letters of recommendation to this Church, may be received as above, on a certificate of their regular standing after giving assent to our Covenant.

5. Members of other churches intending to commune with the Church for more than one year, are requested to bring their letters and enter into fellowship with us.

V. DISMISSION OF MEMBERS.

1. Members of this Church in regular standing may receive letters of dismission and recommendation to other churches by vote of the Church, but their relations to this Church will not cease until actually received by another church.

2. If any member of this Church shall leave its fellowship and unite with another church without asking a letter of dismission, his name may be dropped from the roll of membership by vote of the Church.

3. Members of this Church who remove their residence from this place and become permanently located within a convenient distance of an evangelical church, are expected to transfer their relation to some other church within one year, and such members shall be reminded of this rule by the pastor or clerk of the Church.

4. It shall be the duty of the standing committee to make an annual examination of the roll of membership and enter upon a separate list of "Absent Members," the names of such persons as have been absent from the place for more than one year, and are permanently resident in some other locality.

5. Absent members who have been duly notified of rule 3, in this section, if, after two years from the time of their removal, they neglect to give satisfactory reasons for not taking their letter or to ask for a dismission, may, by vote of the Church, upon recommendation of the standing committee, be dropped from the roll of membership.

VI. DISCIPLINE OF MEMBERS.

1. The object of all discipline shall be to reclaim the erring. Only when this shall fail shall the Church withdraw its fellowship from any member, for the maintenance of its own purity in the sight of God and the world.

2. In case of private or personal offense, the procedure must be according to the rule presented by our Lord in Mat-

thew xviii: 15-17. If the aggrieved member shall be unable to remove the difficulty, he shall bring the matter to the notice of the standing committee, who, in the name of the Church, shall endeavor to effect a reconciliation. If this cannot be done, the aggrieved member may prefer a formal complaint before the Church against the offending member. If the Church entertains the complaint, it shall appoint a time for hearing of the same and proceed with an investigation.

3. In case of public offenses, such as flagrant immorality, open rejection of our confession of faith or violation of covenant engagements, it shall be the duty of the standing committee to bring the case before the Church without waiting for personal complaint, reasonable endeavor having first been made to reclaim the transgressor.

4. When complaints are brought before the Church the member charged with fault shall, unless absent in parts unknown, be seasonably furnished by the clerk with a copy of the charges against him in all their specifications, and be entitled to a full hearing. If on such hearing the Church is satisfied of his guilt, it may suspend him for a definite period or withdraw its fellowship from him.

5. Instead of trying a member before the body of the Church, the Church may refer the charges to a committee, who shall have whatever power and authority the Church possesses to hear and try the case. When the case shall have been heard and tried by this committee, it shall report the facts with its opinion on them to the Church. The final decision of the case shall rest with the Church, due regard being always paid to the opinion reported by the committee.

VII. BENEVOLENCES.

1. The offering of gifts for missionary and charitable purposes shall be made a part of the worship of this Church at each Sunday morning service.

2. In the schedule of benevolences adopted at the annual Church meeting, special objects shall be assigned to such Sundays as the Church may determine, and the collections received

on other Sundays shall be appropriated by the standing committee. But gifts designated for any worthy benevolence will be always received and forwarded by the Church treasurer.

VIII. SUNDAY-SCHOOL.

1. This Church shall seek to gather into its Sunday-school for systematic Bible study, its own members and their children, and all others, both old and young, who are providentially dependent upon it for instruction in the things of Christ. The Church shall have the general oversight of the school and shall appoint its officers.

2. The annual meeting for the Sunday-school shall be held on the last Friday in September; at which time the officers shall be chosen, and a report of the condition of the school, including the state of the treasury and library, shall be presented by the superintendent and placed on file by the clerk.

3. The officers shall be a superintendent of the school, a superintendent of each department, secretary, treasurer, librarians, an executive committee, a library committee, and such other officers and committees as the Church may determine. The superintendents shall be chosen by ballot.

4. The superintendent shall be responsible for the management of the school, secure for its classes wise and sympathetic instruction and provide for its growth. When practicable, he shall assist the pastor in general parish work by visitation and such other service as he may be able to render. The department superintendents shall conduct the general exercises and have the immediate oversight of their respective departments. Other officers shall perform the duties usually rendered in their several offices.

5. The executive committee shall consist of the pastor, superintendent, department superintendents, and four other members, two of whom shall be ladies. This committee shall recommend the course of study; suggest objects for benevolent contributions, and disburse at their discretion such contributions as are not otherwise designated; advise with the superintendent in relation to teachers and classes, and generally seek to

promote the efficiency of the school. The superintendent shall be its chairman.

6. The library committee shall, with the approval of the pastor and superintendent, select and care for the books of the Sunday-school library.

7. A temperance committee may be also appointed, who shall, with the pastor and superintendent, provide for instruction in the principles of temperance, and encourage total abstinence from all intoxicants among the members of the school.

IX. ORGANIZATION OF CHURCH WORK.

1. The Church encourages the organization within its fold of various forms of Christian work, for the quickening of the spiritual, moral, intellectual, and social life of the Church and congregation; for the development of an intelligent interest in Christian missions, both home and foreign, and for their support; and for evangelistic effort in behalf of the unsaved about us.

2. These organizations shall be formed and maintained with the consent and advice of the pastor and subject to the oversight of the standing committee, and shall make yearly reports to the Church at its annual meeting.

X. AMENDMENTS.

Amendments to these rules, or changes in the formulas of the Church, may be made by a two-thirds vote of all the members present at an annual meeting, or at any other meeting regularly called for that purpose.

FORMULAS OF THE CHURCH.

To set forth in order, a declaration of those things which are most surely believed among us.—*Luke 1: 1.*
So the service of the house of the Lord was set in order.—*2 Chron. 29: 35.*

CONFESSION OF FAITH.

Hold fast the form of sound words.—*2 Tim. 1: 13.*

We, as a church, believe in one only living and true God, infinite and eternal, the Father, Son, and Holy Ghost.

We believe in the Scriptures of the Old and New Testaments, as the inspired record of God's revelation of Himself in the redemption of the world, and as our only perfect rule of faith and practice.

We believe in God, the Father Almighty, Maker of heaven and earth, Who governs the worlds in wisdom, justice, and love.

We believe in the Lord Jesus Christ ; Who in the beginning was with God and Who was God : Who took upon Him our humanity and by His sufferings and death made atonement for the sins of the world, that all who repent and believe in Him may be pardoned and justified : Who rose from the dead and ascended into heaven and liveth forevermore.

We believe in the Holy Spirit, by Whom alone the fallen race of man can be renewed in heart, delivered from sin, and perfected in holiness, to be kept by the power of God through faith unto salvation.

We believe in the moral responsibility of man : that although saved by grace yet the law of God is binding upon all, and the fruits of regeneration will be manifest in a humble, holy, and righteous life.

We believe in the visible Church, the ordinances of which are Baptism and the Lord's Supper.

We believe in the ultimate triumph of the kingdom of our Lord and Saviour Jesus Christ on earth, and in His glorious appearing; in the resurrection of the dead; and in the final judgment, the issues of which are eternal punishment and eternal life.

This form of words is not imposed as a test for membership in the Church, but is a general declaration of the faith of the Church and is to be used for the instruction of its members and of their children. It is to be read by the pastor at the Communion Service or on other appropriate occasions of worship, in his discretion.

FORM FOR RECEPTION INTO THE CHURCH.

Come, and let us join ourselves to the Lord in a perpetual covenant that shall not be forgotten. — *Jer.* 50 : 5.

The minister will say:

With the heart man believeth unto righteousness; and with the mouth confession is made unto salvation. Those who are now to make confession of Christ and enter into covenant with His Church, as their names are called, will present themselves before the Lord's Table.

The minister will read the names of such as have been accepted by the Church, and when they have come forward he shall proceed.

DEARLY BELOVED: called of God to be His children through Jesus Christ, we give hearty thanks to God, who by His Spirit has opened your eyes to see and your hearts to receive Jesus as Lord; and who has inclined you to offer yourselves at this time to made confession of Him.

Lift up your hearts with us, while we pray that God may count you worthy of His calling and that His Name may be glorified in you. *Let us pray.*

Prayer will here be offered by the minister.

THE CONFESSION OF CHRIST.

You do now confess yourselves the disciples of the Lord Jesus Christ; declaring the Father, Son, and Holy Ghost to be your God, and the Holy Scriptures the rule of your faith and practice. You give yourselves up to God, to be governed by His laws, to be guided by His Spirit, and to be saved by His grace, promising to receive the pure doctrines of the gospel, and to be henceforth the followers of Christ.

<small>The candidate will respond, "*I do.*"</small>

THE COVENANT OF BAPTISM.

You, who are children of the covenant by the consecration of Christian parents, do you gratefully own that covenant and accept for yourselves the seal of Baptism, to which you were brought in the arms of faith and love in your infancy?

<small>Those who were baptized in infancy will respond, "*I do.*"</small>

You who now enter into the everlasting covenant of grace, do you humbly yield yourselves to God in Baptism, as the seal of your covenant with God in Christ and the sign of the renewal wrought in you by the Holy Spirit?

<small>Those who have not been baptized will respond, "*I do*," and the minister calling each one by the Christian name shall baptize them, saying:</small>

A. B.: *I baptize thee into the Name of the Father, and of the Son, and of the Holy Ghost, Amen.*

THE FELLOWSHIP OF THE CHURCH.

BELOVED IN THE LORD: do you cordially seek the fellowship of this Church of Christ, engaging to walk with us in Christian charity and helpfulness, to unite with us in the worship of God and the ordinances of the Gospel, and to labor with us for the salvation of our fellowmen?

<small>The candidate will answer, "*I do.*" The members of the Church will then rise and remain standing to the end.</small>

We, then, do receive you to be members with us of the visible Church, and in token thereof we rise about you and by this right hand of fellowship welcome you with joy to this communion of Christian love. We give thanks to God for you: we promise to treat you with Christian affection, to watch over and help you, and to offer our prayers that the great Head of the Church may build you up and give you an inheritance among all them which are sanctified.

And now unto Him who is able to keep us from falling and to present us before the presence of His glory with exceeding joy, to the only wise God our Saviour, be glory and majesty, dominion and power, both now and ever. Amen.

FORM FOR BAPTISM OF CHILDREN.

For the promise is unto you and to your children. — Acts 2 : 39.

DEARLY BELOVED : rejoicing in your privilege as Christian parents to seek for your children that covenant of grace and renewal of the Holy Spirit of which the rite of Baptism is the divinely appointed sign and seal ; do you now present both yourselves and them a willing offering to the Lord, in humble reliance upon His promised blessing, and do you engage to faithfully train your child for Him by precept, prayer, and Christian example?

The parents will answer, "*I do,*" and the minister, naming each child with a Christian name, shall baptize them, saying :

A. B.: I baptize thee into the Name of the Father, and of the Son, and of the Holy Ghost. Amen.

After baptism, prayer may be offered by the minister, and the choir may sing some appropriate selection.

CATALOGUE OF OFFICERS AND MEMBERS.

"*Ye are the body of Christ.*" — 1 Cor., 12 : 24.

Officers.

Pastor.
JAMES W. COOPER.

Deacons.

DAVID N. CAMP,
CHARLES PECK,
JOHN WIARD,

JOHN N. BARTLETT,
JOHN B. TALCOTT,
JOHN H. PECK,

DANIEL O. ROGERS.

Clerk.
EDWARD N. STANLEY.

Treasurer.
WILLIAM H. HART.

Standing Committee.

Pastor, Deacons, Clerk, and Treasurer, *ex officio.*

H. DAYTON HUMPHREY,
ROBINS FLEMING,
HENRY J. WHEELER,

THOMAS W. WILBOR,
THOMAS S. HALL,
SPENCER H. WOOD.

Board of Ladies for Home Work.

Mrs. J. H. PECK,
Mrs. J. N. BARTLETT,
Miss ELIZABETH R. EASTMAN,
Mrs. ISAAC PORTER,
Mrs. H. H. BROWN,
Mrs. H. C. BOWERS,

Mrs. E. P. SWASEY,
Mrs. E. H. PRESTON,
Mrs. W. S. BOOTH,
Mrs. C. W. WELLES,
Mrs. PHILIP CORBIN,
Miss KATHARINE A. STANLEY.

Sunday-School Superintendent and Pastor's Assistant.
JOHN WIARD.

MEMBERS.

"One shall say, I am the Lord's; and another shall subscribe with his hand unto the Lord, and surname himself by the name of Israel." — Isaiah, xliv; 5.

One hundred and twenty persons, whose names stand first in this Catalogue, were members of the First Church in New Britain; they became members of this Church at its organization, July 5, 1842. They stand here in the order in which they are found in the original petition.

EXPLANATIONS.

The year of admission is placed over the name.

L — placed before a name, signifies that the person was received by letter from another church; all others were received on the confession of their faith.

The date at the right of the name denotes the year that the relation to the church was dissolved.

L — placed before the date, signifies that the person has been dismissed by letter to another church.

D — placed before the date, signifies that the person was removed by discipline, which includes those from whom watch has been withdrawn on account of long absence.

* — signifies that the person is deceased.

The name enclosed in a parenthesis, following the Christian name of a female, was her maiden name.

The names of husband and wife standing together in the catalogue are connected with a brace.

```
 1  Elijah Francis,            * 1846
 2  Chauncey Cornwell,         * 1863
 3  Seth J. North,             * 1851
 4  Alvin North,               * 1865
 5  Samuel Hart,               * 1863
 6  Norman Woodruff,           L 1866
 7  Henry North,               * 1853
 8  Ozias Hart,                * 1845
 9  Dennis Sweet,              D 1855
10  Andrew P. Potter,          L 1848
11  Josiah Dewey,              * 1851
12  Elijah Hart,               * 1856
13  John Judd,                 * 1875
14  Abijah Flagg,              * 1842
15  Alonzo Stanley,            * 1851
16  Aaron C. Andrews,          * 1847
17  George Hart,               * 1891
18  William Bassett,           D 1851
19  William H. Smith,          * 1873
20  Chester Hart,              D 1860
21  George L. Tibbals,         L 1850
22  Edmund Steele,             * 1879
23  Theodore A. Belknap,       L 1854
```

24 Charles A. Warner, ... * 1868
25 S. Waldo Hart, ... L 1847
26 Salmon Hart, ... * 1857
27 Horace Butler, ... * 1870
28 Joshua Carpenter, ... L 1848
29 Robert G. Williams, ... L 1843
30 James Judd, ... D 1855
31 Eliza A. (Gains) Marshall, w. of William, L 1843
32 Ezekiel Andrews, ... L 1880
33 Elnathan Peck, ... L 1863
34 Henry Stanley, ... * 1884
35 Catharine A. (Stanley) Stanley, . . * 1881
36 Curtis Waples, ... * 1882
37 Esther (Meigs) Lee, wid. of Thomas, . * 1865
38 Abigail (Hart) Seymour, wid. of Moses, . * 1858
39 Mary A. (Seymour) Palmer, wid. William, L 1843
40 Dorothy (Percival) Francis, wid. of Edwin, * 1886
41 Edmund Warner, ... * 1853
42 Elizabeth (Woodruff) Warner, . . * 1845
43 Francis Hart, ... * 1845
44 William B. Stanley, ... * 1883
45 Charles M. Lewis, ... * 1886
46 Polly (Belden) Clark, w. of Abner, . * 1855
47 Romeo Francis, ... * 1849
48 Catharine (Andrews) Francis, . . L 1852
49 Nancy M. (Judd) Eddy, w. of Lorenzo.
50 Matilda (Wright) Slater, w. of Elam, . * 1848
51 Dolly (Stanley) Gridley, w. of Solomon D., * 1868
52 Nathan R. Cook, ... D 1860
53 Lucy B. (Judd) Cook, . . . * 1851
54 Jane (Clark) Francis, wid. of Elijah, . * 1849
55 Orpha (North) Hart, w. of Samuel, . * 1847
56 Lauretta (Smith) North, wid. of Henry, . * 1885
57 Amelia S. (Gould) Williams, w. of Robert G., * 1843
58 Orpha (Hart) Butler, wid. of Horace.
59 Charlotte (North) Rockwell, wid. of Rev. Samuel, . * 1887
60 Sarah E. (North) Brace, w. of Samuel, . L 1848
61 Georgiana M. (North) Hart, w. of Rev. Levi W., L 1855
62 Louisa B. (North) Ward, w. of Alex. M., L 1869
63 Lucinda (Hart) Smith, wid. of William H.
64 Lydia S. (Coslett) Dewey, wid. of Josiah, * 1864
65 Clarissa (Burnham) North, wid. of Alvin, * 1871
66 Elizabeth (Stanley) North, wid. of Seth J., * 1862
67 Sarah (Clark) North, wid. of Oren S., * 1890
68 Ann (Watson) Burritt, wid. of Elijah H., L 1849
69 Mary G. (Coslett) Cornwell, wid. of Chauncey, * 1879
70 Sarah G. Cornwell, ... * 1889
71 Maria (Stanley) Seymour, w. of Orson H., L 1865
72 Julia A. (North) Hall, w. of Thomas S., . L 1867
73 Mary (Dewey) Peck, wid. of Elnathan, . L 1863
74 Esther Dewey, ... * 1852
75 Caroline U. (Hart) Sweet, wid of Dennis.
76 Mary C. (North) Emerson, w. of Joseph, L 1853
77 Sarah (Burgers) North, wid. of William B., * 1882
78 Abigail (Booth) Woodruff, w. of Norman, L 1866

79 Louisa (Hart) Flagg, w. of Rev. Jared B., . . L 1848
80 Lois (Evans) Bassett, w. of William, . . L 1848
81 Mary S. Bassett, ... L 1848
82 Lucretia (Moore) Smith, wid. of William, . * 1866
83 Sarah M. (Smith) Hinsdale, wid. of Gilman.
84 Harriet (Smith) Brown, wid. of Horace H.
85 Elizabeth A. Smith, ... * 1869
86 Betsey (Hart) Judd, wid. of John, . . * 1878
87 Betsey (Hull) Carpenter, wid. of Joshua, * 1846
88 Alma Woodruff, ... * 1853
89 Honor Flagg, wid. of Abijah, . . * 1851
90 Melvina (Chamberlain) Stanley, w. of F. T., . * 1843
91 Chloe (Andrews) Stanley, wid. of Gad, . * 1851
92 Abigail (Lee) Stanley, wid. of Cyrus, . * 1867
93 Maria (North) Erwin, w. of Cornelius B., . * 1884
94 Electa (Barret) Andrews, wid. of Aaron C., . * 1882
95 Harriet A. Stanley, ... L 1868
96 Elizabeth F. (Booth) Hart, w. of George, . * 1862
97 Hannah (Eddy) Root, wife of Joseph, . * 1852
98 Selina (Hart) Churchill, w. of Solomon, . * 1845
99 Elvey (Wells) Hart, wid. of Chester, . * 1885
100 Lucy (Newell) Steele, w. of Edmund, . * 1878
101 Marilla (Collins) Callender, w. of Ira, . * 1849
102 Matilda (Clark) Warner, wid. of Charles A., . * 1880
103 Almira (Woodruff) Warren, wid. of Alanson, * 1879
104 Rosetta (North) Hart, wid. of Salmon, . * 1863
105 Maria (Wright) Steele, w. of Ira, . . * 1862
106 Mehitable (Dewey) Hart, w. of Edmund, . * 1853
107 Louisa (Warren) Hart, wid. of Elijah, . * 1870
108 Eliza (Howd) Judd, w. of Richard, . . L 1844
109 Gunilda (Bass) Judd, wid. of James, . * 1883
110 Sarah E. (Parker) Andrews, w. of Ezekiel, . L 1880
111 Sarah (Kelsey) Whiting, w. of Henry W., . * 1876
112 Sarah (White) Hart, wid. of Stephen, . * 1859
113 Mary (Mather) Gridley, w. of Eben, . * 1856
114 Lucy (Hollister) Winchell, wid. of Miles C., . * 1868
115 Mary (Penfield) Curtiss, wid. of Shubel, . * 1871
116 Julia A. (Curtiss) Hall, wid. of Jarvis, . L 1851
117 Lucy Wright, ... * 1874
118 Sylvia Hart, ... * 1864
119 Olive (Belden) Wright, wid. of Oni, . * 1864
120 Catharine A. Francis, ... * 1849

1842.

121 L Gad Stanley, ... * 1858
122 L Thomas F. Griswold, . . . * 1883

1843.

123 Henry W. Whiting.
124 Arabella (Dewey) Stanley, w. of James.
125 H. Clarissa (North) Shepard, w. of Josiah, . L 1856
126 Elam Slater, ... D 1871
127 Isaac H. Potter, ... L 1846
128 J. W. Humphrey, ... D 1851
129 Lester P. Buell, ... L 1846

130 Oliver Stanley, * 1890
131 Lydia (Bronson) Kelsey, w. of Samuel, * 1853
132 Mary A. (Curtis) Eddy. w. of Walter, D 1860
133 Henrietta (Hart) Francis, wid. of Darwin, L 1851
134 Julia A. (Cornwell) Booth, w. of William S., * 1855
135 Orson H. Seymour, L 1865
136 Elizabeth C. (Lusk) Whaples, wid. of Curtis.
137 Catharine (Pearl) Landers, w. of George M., * 1884
138 Eliza N. (Seymour) Bass. w. of Charles, L 1859
139 L Mary (Richards) Eno, wid. of Salmon, * 1883
140 L Jane (Eno) Lewis, w. of Horatio. L 1846
141 Stephen T. Ford, L 1846
142 Jane B. (Wilmot) Strickland, w. of George W., * 1848
143 Elizabeth (Smith) Post, w. of Peter B., L 1846
144 Franklin Woodruff, L 1844
145 L Amzi Stanley, L 1843
146 L Betsey (Cornwell) Porter, wid. of Richard S., L 1856
147 L Ethan A. Andrews, } * 1858
148 L Lucy (Cowles) Andrews, } L 1859
149 L George W. Strickland, L 1856
150 L Virgil C. Taylor, L 1844
151 L Horace Clapp, } # 1851
152 L Sarah (Woodruff) Clapp, } * 1847

1844.

153 L William F. Raymond, L 1862
154 L Mary Andrews, L 1859
155 L Cynthia Hart, w. of Stephen, L 1851
156 L Elizabeth (Henshaw) Meigs, wid. of John, * 1847
157 L Horatio Waldo, * 1863
158 L Ozias B. Bassett, } * 1878
159 L Emeline (Eno) Bassett. }

1845.

160 L Abigail Clark, L 1856
161 L Russell Upson, } L 1861
162 L Adeline (Tuttle) Upson, } L 1861
163 L Samuel Upson, L 1846
164 L Lydia D. Parker, L 1851
165 L Dorothy (Hart) Wright, wid. of Joseph, * 1878
166 L Sarah C. Hart.
167 L Harriet (Upson) Hendrick, wid. of Abel, * 1890
168 L Jane M. (Hendrick) North, wid. of Hubert F., * 1888

1846.

169 L William Gaylord, D 1860
170 L Selah Steele, } L 1857
171 L Phebe (Baldwin) Steele, } * 1856
172 L Lucy P. (Gager) Lewis, wid. of George, * 1852
173 L Frederic W. Hart, * 1883
174 L Harriet N. (Lampson) Finch, w. of Amon L., * 1853
175 L George Hooker, } * 1876
176 L Sally (Woodruff) Hooker, } * 1877
177 L Jane A. (Hooker) Norton, w. of Isaac, L 1860
178 L Elizabeth C. (Kirkham) Brown, w. of Martin, * 1885

1847.

179 L	Roswell Smith, }	*1874
180 L	Mariva (King) Smith, }	*1876
181 L	Sidney Smith,	L 1852
182	J. Henry Hart,	*1869
183	Edward Doen,	D 1871
184	Charles S. Andrews,	L 1852
185	Ellen A. Andrews,	L 1859
186	Eliza A. (Hart) Humphrey, w. of H. F.,	L 1852
187	Julia A. Smith,	*1855
188	Viana (Perry) Hart, wid. of Edward,	*1863
189	Cordelia M. (Smith) Hart, w. of S. Waldo,	*1857
190 L	Hubert F. North,	*1863
191 L	Burnham S. Slater,	*1848
192 L	Mary (Francis) Humphrey, w. of J. W.,	L 1853
193	William S. Booth,	*1888
194	Lucius S. Booth,	D 1860
195	Henry C. Bowers. }	
196	Augusta M. (North) Bowers. }	
197	James B. Merwin,	L 1851
198	Frank Corbin.	
199	Charles Peck,	L 1849
200	Samuel W. Carpenter,	D 1860
201	James P. Brainard,	L 1853
202	Elizabeth L. (Whaples) Post, w. of George R.,	L 1862
203	Augusta C. (Hart) Humphrey, w. of Henry,	L 1852
204	Sarah B. (Stowe) Woodruff, w. of John E.,	L 1866
205	Sarah H. (Judd) Sweetland, w. of Aaron W.,	L 1861
206	Cordelia H. (Peck) Stanley, w. of Oliver,	*1881
207	Abigail B. (Peck) Lee, w. of Isaac N.,	L 1856
208	Caroline E. (Hart) Pratt, w. of S. B.,	L 1852
209	Elizabeth A. (Cornwell) Peck, w. of Henry F.,	L 1863
210	Ellen S. (Cornwell) Camp, w. of L. L.,	L 1856
211	Julia W. (Burritt) Dunham, w. of Warren,	L 1849
212	Lucy W. (Seymour) Smith, w. of Ira B.	
213	Emeline Judd,	L 1851
214	Helen J. (Bassett) Doen, wid. of Edward.	
215	Caroline North,	*1852
216	Elizabeth (Butler) Westover, wid. of Edwin,	D 1875
217	Mary E. (North) North, w. of F. H.,	*1877
218	Adelaide J. (Francis) Fish, w. of W. J M.,	L 1855
219	Louisa B. (Waldo) Jackson, w. of John,	L 1861
220	Elizabeth C. (Andrews) Ortiz, w. of Pedro P.,	L 1859
221	Clara (Hudson) Cassady, w. of Joseph,	D 1860
222	Ann E. (Burritt) Hawks, wid. of Joseph,	L 1849
223	Elizabeth S. (Whiting) Smith, wid. of Levi O.,	*1892
224	Jane E. Smith,	L 1853
225 L	Philip Corbin.	
226 L	Harriet (Robinson) Case, w. of Hiram,	L 1854

1848.

227 L	Frederic H. North,	L 1877
228 L	Chauncey Hale, }	*1866
229 L	Clara (Miller) Hale, }	*1856
230 L	Mary E. Hale,	L 1852

231 L Julia A. (Hale) Clark, w. of Almond, . . . L 1853
232 L Richard Gillett, } *1855
233 L Elizabeth (Frink) Gillett, } . . . L 1860
234 L Catharine (Burt) Frink, wid. of Luke, . . *1856
235 L L. Ann (Andrews) McKinley, w. of William, . L 1850
236　Israel F. Hale, } . . . . . L 1855
237　Grata (Rugg) Hale, } *1850
238　Thomas S. Hall, ... L 1867
239　Thomas Royden, ... *1854
240　Annette Powell, ... L 1850

1849.

241 L Mary (Tuttle) Bailey, w. of John G., . . L 1855
242 L Huldah Deming, ... *1851
243 L Cornelia E. (Cooke) Flagg, wid. of Henry W.

1850.

244 L Abram Peck, ... L 1856
245 L Sarah F. (Gridley) Bingham, w. of William.
246 L Lucius Woodruff, } *1872
247 L Harriet L. (Buell) Woodruff, } . . . *1872
248 L Henry M. Clark, } *1858
249 L Harriet (Shelton) Clark, } . . . *1888
250 L Charles T. Talcott, } *1889
251 L Jerusha (Gager) Talcott, } . . . *1891
252　Margaret M. Lewis, ... L 1855

1851.

253　Henry Wright, } . . . L 1858
254　Sarah (Larkin) Wright, } . . L 1858
255　Henry B. Judd, ... D 1861
256　Hercelia A. Wright, ... *1854
257　Hannah J. Hart, ... *1853
258　Mary A. (Woodruff) Durgie, . . L 1866
259　Jane (Bingham) Lee, wid. of Philip.
260 L Joseph H. Stephens, ... L 1853
261 L Marietta (Holcomb) Wetmore, w. of E. B., . L 1852
262 L Sarah A. (Noble) North, w. of Orrin A., . L 1851
263 L Rev. Timothy D. P. Stone, } . . . L 1853
264 L Phebe Stone, } . . . L 1853
265 L Augustus P. Collins. } . . . *1890
266 L Harriet P. (Beckley) Collins, } . . *1890
267 L Harriet M. (Beckley) Lewis, w. of James F., L 1885
268 L Mary Mudford, ... L 1853
269　Chloe (Chamberlain) Dutton, wid. of Jesse, *1868
270 L Lydia Buell, ... *1854
271 L Charles Peck.
272 L Ann (Watson) Burritt, wid. of Elijah H., . L 1854
273 L Ann E. (Burritt) Hawks, wid. of Joseph, . L 1857
274 L Julia W. (Burritt) Dunham, w. of Warren, L 1852
275 L S. Waldo Hart, ... L 1859
276 L Levi W. Wells.
277 L Alvah Cumings, ... L 1855
278 L Phebe (Congdon) McLean, wid. of Silas O., L 1855

1852.

279 L Maria (Johnson) Callender, w. of Ira,		*1873
280 L Sophia (Hart) Dunham, wid. of Ralph,		*1870
281 L William Hunter, ⎫		D 1860
282 L Sarah Hunter, ⎭		L 1869
283 Ellen A. (Clark) Everest, w. of Cornelius,		L 1854
284 L Elisha H. Butler, ⎫		L 1854
285 L Catharine B. (Wright) Butler, ⎭		L 1854
286 L Ira E. Leonard,		L 1854
287 L Frederick Platt,		L 1853
288 L Eliza B. (Seymour) Giddings, w. of Alden,		L 1858
289 L Mary A. (Beckley) Corbin, w. of Frank.		
290 L Julia Parker,		*1858
291 L Sophronia (Lord) Hale, w. of Israel F.,		L 1855
292 L Marietta (Crow) Upson, w. of Thomas,		L 1871
293 L William Giddings, ⎫		L 1858
294 L Cornelia A (Seymour) Giddings, ⎭		L 1858
295 L John Gridley,		L 1853
296 Charles Lydall. ⎫		
297 Margaret (Risdon) Lydall. ⎭		
298 James Donaldson, ⎫		D 1860
299 L Anne Donaldson, ⎭		D 1860
300 L. Sophia (Hale) Peck, w. of Abram, Jr.,		*1856

1853.

301 J. Bernard Judd.		
302 Jane E. (Griswold) Hart, w. of J. Henry,		*1864
303 Ann Doyle,		L 1860
304 Mary J. (Peck) Stanley, w. of Walter H.		
305 L John B. Talcott. ⎫		
306 L Jane C. (Goodwin) Talcott, ⎭		*1878
307 L Philo Pratt, ⎫		L 1857
308 L Sarah L. (Southworth) Pratt, ⎭		L 1857
309 L Wallace A. Humphrey,		D 1855
310 L Lydia Newell,		L 1858

1854.

311 L Roger H. Mills, ⎫		L 1855
312 L Harriet A. (North) Mills, ⎭		L 1855
313 L Ellen F. Bartlett,		L 1859
314 L Mary F. (Davis) Peck, wife of Charles.		
315 L George Scott,		*1888
316 L William W. Clemens, ⎫		L 1857
317 L Mary Clemens, ⎭		L 1857
318 L David N. Camp. ⎫		
319 L Adeline (Howd) Camp, ⎭		*1883
320 Jane A. (Bartholomew) Porter, w. of Mortimer S.,		*1867
321 L Mary Mudford,		L 1867
322 Fanny L. (Moore) Stanley, wid. of Gad,		*1889
323 Elizabeth (Mygatt) Northrop, w. of E. G.,		L 1860
324 Grove W. Loomis,		*1856
325 Addison Maguire, ⎫		L 1856
326 Cornelia C. Maguire, ⎭		L 1856
327 Mary J. (Moore) Corbin, w. of Andrew,		L 1865

328	Emily (Upson) Bunce, w. of L. Edgar,	L 1861
329	Eveline (Upson) Lyman, w. of Rev. C. N.,	L 1861
330	Jane A. (Hart) Lewis, w. of John G.,	L 1861
331	Harriet A. (Seymour) Bird, w. of William M.,	L 1859
332	Mary E. (Flagg) Bailey, w. of Lester R.,	L 1866
333	Eliza H. (Keeney) Judd, w. of J. Bernard.	
334	Frederic W. Judd,	L 1870
335	Mortimer A. Warren,	L 1865

1855.

336 L	Erastus W. Pierce,	L 1858
337 L	Flora M. (Clark) Pierce,	L 1858

1856.

338 L	John Stanley,	* 1871
339 L	Martha J. (Forbes) Stanley,	* 1859
340 L	Abigail (Andrews) Hewlet, w. of Comfort,	* 1877
341 L	Harriet (Whaples) Faichney, w. of David,	L 1864
342 L	Alexander M. Ward,	L 1869
343 L	James Booth,	* 1859
344 L	Amanda F. (Clarke) Brown, w. of Harvey G.	
345	Mary N. (Lee) Massey, w. of Wells,	L 1860
346	Ellen F. (Lee) Massey, w. of George L.,	L 1857
347	Jane M. (Dickinson) Cook, w. of John R.,	L 1864
348	H. Anna (Hendrick) Stillman, w. of J.,	L 1877

1857.

349	Ellen M. Hart,	L 1858
350	Martha G. (Lewis) Cody, w. of D. D.,	L 1869
351	Emily A. (Benjamin) North, w. of Frederic M.,	L 1866
352	Amelia R. (Benjamin) Bunce, w. of J. A.,	L 1870
353	Mary E. (Bassett) Mumford, w. of Joseph P.,	L 1865
354	Milton H. Bassett.	
355	Jane E. Case.	
356	George S. Dewey,	L 1860
357	Harvey G. Brown.	
358	Theron Upson,	L 1858
359	Martin Brown,	* 1890
360	William H. Hart.	
361	Martha (Peck) Hart.	
362	George P. Rockwell,	L 1890
363 L	Eliza S. (Ames) Rockwell,	* 1871
364	Emily L. Stanley.	
365	Elizabeth E. Rockwell,	* 1866
366	Theodore A. Stanley,	* 1862
367	Ellen N. (Judd) Gridley, w. of George C.,	* 1892
368	William Corbin,	* 1860
369	George S. Corbin,	D 1864
370	Cornelius B. Erwin,	* 1885
371	Adeline E. Henderson,	L 1863
372	Almira S. (Clark) Brittain, w. of Geo. S.,	L 1873
373	Louisa M. (Eddy) Howard, w. of H. W.,	L 1863
374 L	Eliza (Hart) Pearl, wid. of Ralph,	* 1876
375 L	Samuel Brace,	L 1864
376 L	Sarah E. (North) Brace,	L 1864
377 L	Mary J. (Hart) Doolittle, w. of Julius,	L 1866

1858.

378 L	Laura A. Ward,		* 1865
379	Edwin L. Hendrick,		L 1861
380	Alfred W. Stephenson,	⎫	L 1859
381	Rhoda (Steele) Stephenson,	⎭	L 1859
382	Edward S. Hart,		L 1864
383	Isaac W. Hart.		
384	Emma L. (Hart) Graham, w. of John C.,		L 1870
385	Thomas A. Conklin,	⎫	* 1879
386	Martha (Fitch) Conklin.	⎭	
387	Catharine W. (Flagg) Park, w. of Boyd S.,		L 1875
388	Henrietta B. (Flagg) Latham, w. of William E.		
389	Adeline (Hart) Wells, w. of Levi W.		
390	Francina T. (Whiting) Corbin, w. of Philip.		

1859.

391 L	Sarah A. (Lewis) Risley, w. of C. W.,	L 1860
392 L	Clarissa (Orvis) Andrews, wid. of Thompson,	L 1881
393 L	Cornelia (Hall) Beckley, wid. of Lyman,	L 1865
394 L	Mary E. Hale,	L 1870
395	Jennie M. (Bassett) Hart, w. of Frederick W.	
396	Ellen R. Camp.	

1860.

397 L	David L. Isham,		L 1871
398 L	Sarah A. Isham,		L 1871
399 L	William Wheeler,	⎫	L 1865
400 L	Sarah J. (Allen) Wheeler,	⎭	L 1865
401 L	George D. Rand,	⎫	L 1865
402 L	Martha J. (Crossman) Rand,	⎭	L 1865
403 L	Emily (Fairbanks) Goodell, w. of Rev. C. L.,		L 1872
404 L	Amy A. (Langdon) Woodworth, w. of W. W.,		* 1889
405 L	Henry B. Buckham,		L 1871
406	Mary T. Cuyler,		L 1864
407 L	Theron Upson,		L 1861
408 L	Jane E. Smith,		* 1867
409 L	Solomon D. Gridley,		L 1872
410 L	George C. Gridley.		
411 L	Wealthy A. (Gridley) Woodruff, w. of F. H.,		L 1871
412 L	Grove W. Henderson,	⎫	L 1863
413 L	Elizabeth Henderson,	⎭	L 1863
414 L	Mary J. (Bissell) Bronson, w. of Merritt,		L 1878
415 L	Betsey (Cornwell) Porter, wid. of Richard S.,		* 1888
416 L	Fidelia M. (North) Booth, w. of William S.,		* 1874
417 L	Sarah J. (Avery) Hart, w. of Philo W.		

1861.

418	Fanny Oldershaw,		* 1862
419	Edward McCormick,	⎫	L 1863
420	Grace A. (Watson) McCormick,	⎭	L 1863
421 L	Sarah T. (Robbins) Woodruff, w. of Nelson P.		

1862.

422	Cordelia B. North,	* 1881
423	Sarah (Allen) Whiten, w. of Charles.	
424	Annie L. (Smith) Churchill, w. of F. H.,	L 1876

425 Helen M. Andrews,	* 1866
426 L David Faichney,	L 1864
427 L Leverett H. Luce, }	L 1864
428 L Elvira (Clark) Luce, }	L 1864
429 L Norman E. Purple, }	L 1878
430 L Mary (Clark) Purple, }	L 1878
431 L Alfred W. Stephenson, }	D 1864
432 L Rhoda (Steele) Stephenson, }	D 1864
433 L Rev. Constans L. Goodell,	L 1872
434 L Albert Clark, }	L 1874
435 L Mary A. (Luce) Clark, }	L 1874
436 L Ralph C. Dunham, }	
437 L Charlotte (Rumrill) Dunham, }	
438 L Sarah L. Evans,	L 1868
439 L Elizabeth (King) Butts, wid. of O. H.,	L 1864
440 L Catharine Butts,	L 1864

1863.

441 William Hubbard,	* 1867
442 Jane E. (Bingham) Breckenridge, w. of W. J.,	L 1870
443 Mary L. Stanley.	
444 Elizabeth (Ellsworth) Hart, w. of George,	* 1882
445 L Henrietta A. (Johnson) Plumley, w. of Henry,	L 1870
446 L Josephine (Perry) Hart, w. of Rev. H. E.,	L 1866

1864.

447 Celia A. (Stuart) Rowe, w. of Henry,	L 1868
448 Catharine L. Warren,	L 1886
449 Alice A. (Baker) Moore, wid. of Henry W.	
450 Harriet (Granger) Seymour, w. of Frederic S.,	* 1873
451 Hannah (Foulds) Dawson, w. of James,	* 1879
452 Harriet E. (Andrews) Fowler, w. of Anson F.,	L 1865
453 Adelaide P. (Campbell) Ives, w. of Nelson H.,	L 1881
454 Harriet O. (Clark) Shepard, w. of Norman.	
455 L Susan M. (Martyn) Booth, w. of Edward M.,	L 1867
456 L Ann (Oldershaw) Tyler, w. of Geo. L.,	* 1879
457 L Mary (Oldershaw) Blakeslee, w. of B. A.,	* 1867
458 L John Wiard. }	
459 L Jenette R. (Buell) Wiard. }	
460 L Lester P. Buell, }	L 1873
461 L Louisa M. (Tuttle) Buell, }	L 1873
462 L Jane (Chalmers) Muir, w. of Hugh.	
463 L Jessie Richardson,	L 1866
464 L T. Woodford Kilbourn, }	L 1882
465 L Lucy (Staples) Kilbourn, }	L 1882
466 L Sarah (Doolittle) Conklin, w. of Hiram K.,	* 1883
467 L Samuel Moore,	L 1885
468 Frederick D. Winton,	D 1871
469 L Martin S. Wiard.	

1865.

470 Elizabeth R. Woodworth.	
471 L Rev. Charles Nichols, }	* 1879
472 L Louisa (West) Nichols, }	* 1890
473 L Laura A. (Nichols) Denison, w. of Rev. A. C.,	L 1867
474 L Lucy F. (Nichols) Smith, w. of John B.,	L 1866

475 L Elizabeth (Jones) Ashley, w. of Evans,		L 1885
476 Emma C. (Hayes) Hale, wid. of Henry K.		
477 Mary E. (Allen) Rossetter, w. of L. G.		
478 Jane E. (Byington) Winston, w. of DeWitt,		L 1868
479 L Simeon Woodruff,		* 1871
480 L Caroline (Hibbard) Prentice, wid. of Francis D.,		* 1877
481 L Ruth A. (Page) Roberts, wid. of Eleazer.		* 1879
482 L John Henderson,		D 1871
483 Charles H. Lum, }		L 1867
484 L Jane (Buckingham) Lum, }		L 1867
485 L Caroline R. Long,		L 1871
486 Rhoda (Cogswell) Penfield, w. of Hiram,		* 1887
487 Rev. Charles E. Steele,		L 1876
488 George H. Bingham,		* 1884
489 S. Sophia (Brown) Bronson, w. of Nathan S.,		L 1880
490 Sarah M. (Bingham) Bronson, w. of Phineas M.		
491 L Gilman Hinsdale,		* 1885
492 L Robert M. Reynolds,		L 1866
493 Frances T. (Whitney) Camp, wid. of Benajah,		* 1870
494 Emma A. (Wells) Clark, w. of A. H.		
495 Jane (Bingham) Austin, w. of John H.		
496 Emily Bingham.		
497 Harriet E. Brown,		* 1873
498 Alice E. (Bingham) Mead, w. of Arthur,		L 1866
499 L Edwin L. Hendrick,		D 1875
500 L Jane (Beebe) Hendrick,		L 1888

1866.

501 Albert L. Wiard.		
502 Edward S. Clark,		L 1876
503 Betsey A. (Taylor) Gifford, w. of Lester F.		
504 L Sarah D. Acker, w. of Rev. Henry J.,		L 1869
505 L Lovica (Seymour) Moore, w. of Perry,		* 1872
506 L Jane (Allen) Muir, w. of Robertson B.,		* 1875
507 L Mary J. (Thompson) Booth,		L 1868
508 L Elisabeth (Wiard) Smith, wid. of Hector.		
509 L Francis H. Smith. }		
510 L Ruth A. (Usher) Smith. }		
511 L Samuel N. Chapin. }		
512 L Emily M. (Forbes) Chapin. }		
513 L Alanson H. Merriman, }		L 1868
514 L Ellen A. (Griggs) Merriman, }		L 1868
515 Susan P. (Loomis) Bingham, w. of Henry,		* 1888
516 Diodamia (Carter) Belden, w. of Hiram,		* 1887
517 Julia C. (Smith) Townsend, w. of Heber,		L 1869
518 Helen Mead,		L 1870
519 L Cynthia S. (West) Ely, wid. of Heman,		* 1871
520 L Joshua N. Oviatt, }		L 1880
521 L Martha A. (McNary) Oviatt, }		L 1880
522 L Mary S. Bassett.		
523 L Warren J. Breckenridge,		L 1870
524 L Eliza M. (Foote) Fuller, w. of A. J.		
525 L Florence A. (Fuller), Bowen, w. of Geo. D.,		* 1875
526 L John H. Peck. }		
527 L Harriet B. (Dibble) Peck, }		* 1871

528 L Henry C. Strickland,	}	L 1886
529 L Mary E. (Douglass) Strickland,	}	L 1886
530 William A. Spaulding.	}	
531 Anna A. (Hart) Spaulding.	}	
532 Lucy L. Johnson, . . .		* 1868
533 Ella E. Graves, ...		D 1879
534 Harriet B. (Collins) Edgar, w. of J. Blanchard,		L 1874
535 Lillian L. Lewis, ...		L 1885
536 Harriet E. (Camp) Chipman, w. George T.,		* 1881
537 Mary F. (Hale) Wessell, w. of Frederick.		
538 Martin A. Boardman.	}	
539 Mary S. (Allen) Boardman.	}	
540 Julia E. Bugbee, ...		D 1892
541 Harriet C. (Loomis) Humphrey, w. of H. D.		
542 Julia E. (Bassett) Lee, w. of Isaac S., .		L 1886
543 Annie N. Bowers.		
544 Maria L. Brown, .		L 1868
545 Meigs H. Whaples.		
546 Isabella E. Whaples.		
547 Jane S. (Mac Millan) Muir, wid. of James,		* 1882
548 Thomas Muir, ...		D 1884
549 Charles E. Foster, . . .		L 1867
550 John P. Stanley, . . .		D 1874
551 Mary Simpkins. . . .		D 1879
552 Dwight N. Steele. . . .		* 1875
553 Frederick N. Steele.		
554 Walter P. Steele.		
555 Helen C. (Tuttle) Richmond, w. of John,		L 1870
556 Caroline M. Steele, . . .		* 1873
557 Harriet A. Steele.		
558 Henry B. Goodrich,	}	* 1880
559 Laura A. (Hart) Goodrich.	}	
560 John C. Bingham.		
561 Alfred H. Clark.		
562 Charles S. Landers.		
563 Julia E. Blinn.		
564 Elizabeth A. (Hills) Hubbard, wid. of William, .		L 1867
565 Mary P. Allen.		
566 Sarah R. (Rossiter) Thomas, w. of J. H., .		L 1869
567 Emeline (Brewer) Arnold, w. of Wilbur F.		
568 Charles O. Collins.		
569 L Josiah Shepard,	} . . .	L 1870
570 L H. Clarissa (North) Shepard,	} .	* 1870
571 L Margaret S. (Todd) Dunham, w. of Raymond, .		L 1867
572 L Helen Slate, ...		L 1880
573 L Alfred Juckett,	} . . .	* 1869
574 L Harriet A. (Slate) Juckett,	} . . .	L 1879
575 L Susan M. Noble, ...		* 1888
576 L Philander Rand,	} . . .	L 1870
577 L Mary F. (Dutton) Rand,	} . .	L 1870
578 L Mary Rand, ...		L 1870
579 L Carrie F. Rand, ...		L 1870
580 L George D. Rand,	} .	L 1871
581 L Martha J. (Crossman) Rand,	} .	L 1871
582 L James Hollister,	} . . .	L 1869
583 L Jane A. Hollister,	} . .	L 1869

1867.

584 L Ann (Watson) Burritt, wid. of Elijah H., . . *1871
585 L Adelaide J. (Francis) Fish, w. of W. J. M.
586 L Charlotte A. (Comstock) Tomlinson, w. of Charles, . L 1871
587 L Mary A. (Connor) Kennedy, w. of John, . . . D 1879
588 L James D. Smith, ... L 1869
589 L Nathan S. Clement, ⎱ . . . L 1885
590 L Mary J. (Loucks) Clement, ⎰ . . . . L 1885
591   Robertson B. Muir.
592   James S. Muir, ... *1892
593   Margaret (Muir) Wilson, wid. of Thomas.
594   Jessie (Muir) Wilson, w. of Henry, . . *1881
595   Catharine (Host) Minderlein, w. of Charles.
596   Anna (Host) Scipel, w. of Henry B.
597   Mary A. Host.
598 L Caroline T. (Cary) Talcott, w. of C. Myron, . L 1872
599   Rev. William A. Lamb, ⎱ . . . L 1884
600 L Elizabeth T. (Kidder) Lamb, ⎰ . . . *1867
601   Julia A. Slate, ... L 1886
602   Virginia E. Thorpe, ... D 1879
603 L Margaret (Anderson) Bassett, w. of Frederic A.
604 L Electa (Shipman) Buell, wid. of Tillson, . . *1891
605 L Harriet E. (Freeman) Hawkins, w. of Hiram J., . *1890
606 L William Cowan, ... D 1871
607   Ada E. Buell, ... *1887
608   William W. Scott.
609   Leonard Wilhelmy. ⎱
610   Catharine B. (Berg) Whitney. ⎰

1868.

611 L Daniel M. Rogers. ⎱
612 L Phileua H. (Knapp) Rogers, ⎰ . . . *1890
613 L James B. Hawkins, ⎱ . . . L 1872
614 L Ellen L. (Bennett) Hawkins, ⎰ . . . L 1872
615 L Maria A. (Evarts) Warren, w. of William J., *1871
616   Lucy J. (Dewey) Hart, w. of Nelson, . . L 1877
617   Lydia A. (Richards) Ellis, w. of Martin.
618   Daniel Steele. . . . . . L 1870
619   Newell F. Deming, ... L 1885
620 L Homer B. Sprague, ... L 1870
621 L John W. A. Beers, ⎱ . . . *1882
622 L Mary A. (Bradley) Beers. ⎰
623 L Charles Vishno, ⎱ . . . L 1877
624 L Delina (Osborn) Vishno, ⎰ . . . . L 1877
625 L John J. Slate, ... *1883
626 L Louisa (Hitchcock) Humiston, w. of Luther.
627 L John L. Dowd, ... L 1881
628 L Julius Fenn, ... *1881
629 L Ida J. Fenn.
630 L Louisa F. (Peck) Wiard, w. of M. S.
631 L Elnathan B. Frisbie, ⎱ . . L 1870
632 L Mary E. (Gibbs) Frisbie, ⎰ . . L 1870
633 L Mary E. Frisbie, ... L 1870
634 L Edwin B. Lyon, ⎱
635 L Charlotte (Ward) Lyon, ⎰ *1874

636 L Jane Butler.	
637 L John Payne, }	L 1880
638 L Jane (Taylor) Payne, }	L 1880
639 L Hiram J. Hawkins.	
640 L Arthur E. McLean,	L 1878
641 L Mary L. (Pierce) Clark, w. of Theron E.,	* 1872
642 L Henry C. Stephens, }	L 1876
643 L Elenor B. (Kimball) Stephens, }	* 1886
644 L Charles A. Northend, }	L 1878
645 L Martha M. (Giddings) Northend, }	* 1873
646 L Charles H. Johnson, }	L 1883
647 L Caroline (Cleveland) Johnson, }	L 1883
648 L Martha E. (Stanley) Cornwell, w. of Charles H.,	L 1881
649 L Sophia Hall,	* 1882
650 Edwin H. Lyman, }	L 1882
651 Mary J. (Goodrich) Lyman, }	L 1882
652 Abigail (Benham) Hart, wid. of John G.,	L 1872
653 Helen M. (Hart) Cary, w. of William H.,	L 1872
654 L Rev. Samuel Rockwell,	* 1880
655 L Delia (Wood) Steele, w. of Daniel,	L 1870
656 L Truman B. House, }	* 1875
657 L Mary E. (Hall) House. }	
658 L William O. Campbell, }	L 1872
659 L Clara P. (Little) Campbell, }	L 1872
660 L Solomon E. Bailey, }	L 1872
661 L Anna (Edwards) Bailey, }	L 1872
662 Emma A. Bailey,	L 1872

1869.

663 L Charles L. Mead, }	L 1884
664 L Isabella (Martin) Mead, }	L 1884
665 L Christine (Woodburn) Andrew, wid. of John,	* 1888
666 L Mary (Capron) Freeman, wid. of L. W.	
667 Franklin Evarts, }	L 1871
668 L Mary (Bidwell) Evarts, }	L 1871
669 Edward L. Prior.	
670 Pascal D. Murray,	* 1872
671 L Phineas M. Bronson.	
672 L Mary E. (Dix) Hart, wid. of Thomas A.	
673 L Sarah J. (Loomis) Loomis, w. of C. D.	
674 L Henry R. Kelley, }	* 1870
675 L Sarah J. (Bloss) Kelley. }	
676 L Elizabeth Bishop,	L 1872
677 L Sarah B. (Stowe) Woodruff, w. of John E.,	L 1871
678 L John N. Bartlett. }	
679 L Ellen (Strong) Bartlett. }	
680 L Ellen S. Bartlett,	L 1888
681 L Salome (Buel) Case, wid. of Hiram,	* 1888
682 Edward H. Case.	
683 L Olivia (Cowles) Hart, w. of B. Kellogg,	* 1883
684 L Edward L. Deming, }	L 1874
685 L Elizabeth (McIndoe) Deming, }	L 1874
686 L Sabra A. (Skinner) Lyon, wid. of Asa,	* 1888
687 Darius Gates, }	L 1873
688 L Anna E. (Lyon) Gates, }	L 1875

689	Oren S. North,	* 1874
690	Horace H. Brown,	* 1879
691	Levi O. Smith,	* 1883
692	Frederick T. Stanley,	* 1883
693	Frances B. (Hawkins) Clay, w. of George C.,	L 1872
694	Mary Whiting.	
695	Daniel O. Rogers.	
696	Flora (Woodruff) Loomis, w. of Simeon,	* 1891
697	Dwight P. Mills. }	
698	Sarah A. (Skillin) Mills. }	
699	Charlotte Boone.	
700	Jane (Boone) Lloyd, w. of Charles H., .	D 1882
701	Lucinda (Boone) Diehl, w. of Joseph.	
702	James D. Slate,	D 1892
703	Ada L. Clark,	* 1874
704	Emma J. (Camp) Rogers, w. of D. O.	
705	Mary S. Porter.	
706	Marcellus Lawrence,	L 1874
707	Mary (Thompson) Smith, w. of James D., .	L 1869
708	George W. Andrew.	
709	Marion A. Andrew.	
710	James H. Brown, .	* 1885
711	Eda M. Callender.	
712	Ella A. (Bulkley) Wiard, w. of A. L.	
713	Albert H. House.	
714	Samuel P. Piper, .	L 1875
715	William E. Latham.	
716	Thomas D. Towle,	D 1885
717	Anna (Sterling) Towle, .	D 1879
718	William Hunter (Restored), .	L 1869
719 L	Ellen E. (Hamlin) Forbes, wid. of Samuel G.	
720 L	Henrietta E. (Clark) Cadwell, w. of Samuel.	
721 L	Henry E. Clark.	
722 L	John Barclay, }	L 1870
723 L	Mary Ann (Haltaufderhidey) Barclay, }	L 1870
724 L	J. Warren Tuck, }	* 1891
725 L	Phronia (Norris) Tuck, }	* 1889
726	Perry Moore, .	* 1885
727	Jay S. Stone. }	
728	Anna E. (Warner) Stone, }	* 1876
729	Eli H. Porter, }	* 1877
730	Ella M. (Field) Porter, }	
731	William C. Williams, }	L 1885
732	Geraldine V. S. (Jennings) Williams, }	L 1885
733	Elizabeth M. (Bishop) Griswold, wid. of Thomas F.	
734	Herbert W. Warren,	D 1892
735	William H. Lee,	L 1873
736	William H. Bowers.	
737	Elisabeth U. Smith.	
738	Julia M. (Roberts) Carleton, w. of John W.	
739	Anna I. (Smith) Chamberlain, w. of V. B., .	L 1873
740	Maria (Schermerhorn) Ross, w. of William,	L 1887
741	David B. Judd. }	
742	Ellen J. (Frost) Judd, }	* 1885
743	Isabella J. (Coleman) Nash, w. of H. O.	

744	Adeline L. (Barbour) James, w. of Charles J.,	L 1886
745	Elizabeth C. (Lander) Shepard, w. of Joseph.	
746	Henry C. Bulkley,	* 1883
747	Susan (Butler) Bulkley.	
748	Aurelian M. Brown,	L 1878
749	Charles F. North,	L 1877
750	Grace E. North,	L 1877
751	Mary (Schine) Cheever, w. of ———,	D 1882
752	Anna J. Hart,	* 1879
753	Mary L. (Peck) Thomson, w. of Elihu.	
754	Frederick A. Clark,	L 1878
755	Mary M. Callender.	
756	Carrie F. (Farnham) Clark, w. of Theodore F.	
757	Hannah M. (Wainwright) Ralph, w. of J. E.	
758 L	Clarence T. McLean,	L 1874
759 L	Elbert H. Preston.	
760 L	Emma I. (Andrew) Preston.	
761	Orville Jones.	
762	Caroline (Cutter) Jones.	
763	Charles E Hart.	
764	Jennie (Wainwright) Hart.	
765	Harriet A. Blinn.	
766	Rev. William M. Brown,	L 1888
767	Fannie L. Brown.	
768	Martha C. (Kilbourn) Hooker, w. of Edward B.,	1880
769	Albert G. Kilbourn,	L 1882

1870.

770	Mary L. (Hart) Woodruff, w. of Charles E.	
771	Asa P. Meylert,	L 1875
772 L	Harriet E. (Hodgdon) Meylert,	L 1875
773 L	Joseph K. Kilbourn,	D 1892
774 L	Jane (Skillin) Kilbourn,	D 1892
775 L	Isaac S. Lee,	L 1886
776 L	Mary (Mabew) Davis, wid. of Rev. E. Davis, D.D.,	* 1882
777 L	Isaac N. Carleton,	L 1884
778 L	Laura (Tenney) Carleton,	L 1884
779 L	Edwin A. Kimball,	L 1875
780 L	Edward A. Boardman,	L 1877
781 L	Grace H. (Judd) Landers, w. of Charles S.	
782 L	Prudence M. (Butler) Bassett, w. of Milton H.	
783 L	Orin Slate,	* 1872
784 L	Catharine W. (Miller) Slate,	L 1872
785 L	Genevieve M. Slate,	L 1872
786 L	Wilford C. Andrew,	L 1876
787 L	Ann E. (Johnson) Andrew,	L 1876
788 L	Lucius Clark,	* 1871
789 L	Catharine (Powell) Clark,	* 1874
790	Marcia E. (Curtis) Chamberlain, w. of Frederic C.	
791	Julia A. (Pratt) Ensworth, w. of J. C.	
792	Charles H. Porter,	D 1879
793 L	Eva M. Butler) Porter,	L 1876
794 L	Eunice (Wooding) Buell, wid. of E. L.,	L 1883
795 L	William H. Giddings.	
796 L	Frederick W. Giddings.	

797 L	John Gill,	L 1871
798	C. Frederick Zimmerman.	
799	Annie (Conklin) Stephens, w. of Henry C.,	L 1876
800 L	Abbe L. (Lyon) Draper, w. of A. S.,	L 1872
801	Stella E. (Hill) Clark, w. of Edward S.,	L 1876
802	Mary J. (Basney) Harris, w. of Leonard S.,	L 1876
803 L	Charles Taylor, }	L 1871
804	Frances A. (Irish) Taylor, }	L 1871
805	Richard M. Burr,	L 1877
806	Isabella (Aiken) Clark, wid. of Charles,	L 1877
807	Anna (Williams) Dolan, w. of Henry P.,	D 1882
808 L	Lewis S. Allen, }	L 1876
809 L	Susan C. (Bernard) Allen, }	L 1876
810 L	Wesley F. Boland, }	L 1872
811 L	Angeline (Warner) Boland, }	L 1872

1871.

812	Lethiel E. Nichols, }	D 1879
813	Caroline M. (Castle) Nichols. }	
814	William Stino, }	L 1877
815	Adora (Moore) Stino, }	L 1877
816	Mary H. (House) Gladden, w. of Fred. W.	
817	Alice C. Tuck.	
818 L	Elizabeth H. Kilbourn,	* 1878
819 L	Emma M. (Goldthwaite) Pease, w. of L. H.,	L 1876
820 L	Ella S. (Smith) Osborne, w. of Rev. C. P.,	L 1873
821	Chauncey W. Welles. }	
822	Anna A. (Stevens) Welles. }	
823	Barbara (Stewart) Muir, w. of Thomas,	D 1884
824	Jane E. Law.	
825 L	Harriet (Newell) Judd, wid. of James,	* 1878
826 L	Agnes (Hawthorn) Johnston, wid. of Robert,	L 1871
827 L	Spencer H. Wood, }	L 1875
828 L	Melissa (Bliss) Wood, }	L 1875
829 L	Lemira H. (Whipple) Cole, w. of L. W.,	L 1872
830 L	Cornelia R. (Neff) Williams, w. of H. C.	
831 L	John R. Andrew,	L 1877
832	Katherine A. Stanley.	
833	Catherine (Boback) Huebuer, w. of Adolph.	
834	Catherine (Taylor) Harlow, w. of Horace,	* 1871
835	John H. Austin,	* 1892
836 L	Frank H. Emerson,	L 1879
837 L	Ann (Sturman) Timbrell, w. of Isaac.	
838 L	Thomas S. Hall. }	
839 L	Julia A. (North) Hall. }	
840 L	Mary (McCardy) Sutherland, wid. of Robert,	* 1873
841 L	Edwin Bennett. }	
842 L	Ruth M. (Wheeler) Bennett. }	
843 L	Wallace T. Munger, }	L 1883
844 L	Emma D. (Murray) Munger, }	L 1881
845 L	Sarah L. Evans,	* 1888
846	William Killam, }	L 1888
847	Eunice M. (Pinney) Killam, }	L 1888
848	Harriet A. Strout,	L 1878
849 L	Mary A. (Foss) Hackett, w. of Jeremiah,	L 1888

850 L	Alice A. (Hackett) Just, w. of William H.,	L 1879
851 L	Nancy (Stone) Fielding, w. of W. I.	
852 L	Chauncey A. Bacon,	D 1891
853 L	Jennie C. (Deming) Bacon,	D 1891
854 L	Merab R. (Heaton) Blakeslee, wid. of C. W.,	* 1892

1872.

855	Horace E. Sherman,	D 1891
856	Emma (Pettibone) Andrews, w. of William R.	
857	Sarah J. (Shephard) Bartram,	L 1880
858	James G. Barnett,	* 1885
859 L	Emily Latimer,	L 1878
860 L	William W. Giddings.	
861 L	Cornelia A. (Seymour) Giddings.	
862 L	Elizabeth Pond.	
863	Elizabeth M. (Goodrich) Bingham, w. of George H.	
864	Mary E. (Elam) Scott, w. of William.	
865 L	George C. Root.	
866 L	Mary P. (Rowley) Root.	
867 L	Fannie M. Ordway.	
868	Luther Humiston.	
869	Jedediah C. Ensworth.	
870	James Hall.	
871	Annie (Tatem) Hall.	
872	Anna (Scott) Richardson, w. of Wm. H.,	L 1882
873	William Scott.	
874	Annie (Hurst) Downton, w. of Nathaniel.,	L 1880
875	Henrietta (Howd) Huisler, w. of F. W.	
876	Pauline (Shoutze) Johnson, w. of Henry J.	
877	Thomas E. Lukey,	* 1890
878	James H. Wise,	L 1873
879	Lucy (Masterman) Wise,	L 1873
880	Henry P. Dolan,	D 1882
881	Julia A. (Curtis) Hall, wid. of Jarvis.	
882	Franklin N. E. Bassett.	
883 L	Celia A. (Shearer) Bassett,	* 1874
884	Roxa A. Perry,	L 1877
885	Jarvis Miller,	* 1876
886	Jane (Grimley) Taylor, w. of Thomas.	
887	George A. Conklin,	L 1892
888	William E. Peck,	L 1882
889	Charles W. Hart,	* 1875
890	Edward N. Stanley.	
891	Charles F. Corbin,	L 1882
892	S. Willis Rockwell,	L 1888
893	Katharine M. Brown.	
894	Alice M. (Smith) Gridley, w. of Eben C.	
895	Susan C. (Flagg) Middlemas, w. of Wm.	
896	Ellen W. Hart,	* 1881
897	John C. Talcott,	* 1877
898	Ellen J. Talcott,	* 1877
899	Emily M. Slate,	L 1872
900	Hattie E. Judd,	* 1881
901	George L. Clark,	L 1874

902 John P. Bartlett.
903 Alice S. (Moore) Stanley, w. of Frederick N.
904 Susie G. Mills.
905 Mary A. (Barrett) Barnes, w. of Wm.
906 Theresa Beck, ... L 1872
907 Ella M. (Buell) Moore, w. of E. A.
908 Mary J. (Emerson) Ellis, w. of Chas D., *1889
909 Fanny S. (Conklin) Bastian, w. of J. H.
910 Cora A. Hart.
911 Ella G. (Pond) Morris, w. of William H. D 1888
912 Olive J. Lydall.
913 Ellen (Rackliff) Williams, w. of Russell, L 1873
914 George H. Dickerson, ⎫ . . D 1879
915 Mary B. (Brading) Dickerson, ⎭ . . D 1879
916 Adele B. Adler, ... D 1879
917 Charles B. Howd, ... L 1874
918 Albert W. Macomber, ... L 1879
919 Washington K. Hewlett, . . . D 1879
920 Herbert E. Johnson, ... D 1884
921 Katie E. (Judson) Palmer, w. of James, L 1886
922 Carrie L. Stanley.
923 L Jane M. (Yale) Shepard, w. of Josiah, . . L 1879
924 L Elizabeth A. (Hills) Hubbard, wid. of Wm., *1874
925 L Edward F. Hotchkiss, ... L 1877
926 L Mary E. Potter, ... L 1882
927 L Wilfred B. Rice, ... L 1877
928 L H. Dayton Humphrey.
929 L Franklin Woodruff, ⎫ . . L 1874
930 L Elizabeth (Andrews) Woodruff, ⎭ . . L 1874
931 L William McConnor, ... *1872
932 L Rachael (Perkins) Humiston, wid. of Russell, *1887.
933 Sarah M. (Cornish) Steele, w. of Thomas.
934 Sarah (Lee) Allen, wid. of Joseph P.
935 Harriet (Ambury) Eads, w. of Frank, . . D 1879
936 Adaline (Ford) Scott, w. of Wm. W., . . L 1890
937 Hannah K. Hart, ... *1892
938 Annie (Hedley) Martin, w. of Wm. H., . L 1882
939 Louise (Goodrich) Norton, w. of Henry, . *1882
940 Hattie E. (Butler) Dowd, w. of Edward W., L 1880
941 Helen S. (Butler) Hemenway, w. of Fred. M., L 1883
942 Louise S. Gladden, ... *1881
943 Mary E Bingham.
944 Mary Harriet Rogers.
945 Noah C. Rogers, . . . L 1883
946 L Jay H. Brown, . . . L 1882
947 L Maria S. Kelsey, . . . *1892
948 L Julia A. Kelsey.
949 L Mary J. (Moore) Corbin, w. of Andrew.

1873.

950 Thirza (Clark) Miller, w. of S. T., . . . L 1878
951 Amelia T. (Adams) Whiting, wid. of H. W., Jr.
952 Henry Boehm.
953 L Nellie L. (Savage) Boardman, w. of E. A., . L 1877
954 L J. Elizabeth (Fairchild) Porter, w. of Isaac.

955   Dwight M. Hull.
956 L Chauncey W. Blakeslee, ... *1875
957 L Catharine (Bartholomew) Howd, wid. of Augustus. *1888

1874.

958 L Nancy (Norton) Munger, wid. of Truman, *1879
959 L Ellen A. (Munger) Relay, w. of Robert J.
960   John Henderson (Restored), . . . L 1874
961   Charles A. Blair, ... L 1876
962 L Clara (Higby) Rockwell, w. of George P., . . L 1890
963 L Anna (Kreeger) Shaffer, w. of George, . L 1877
964 L Elizabeth A. (Stubbings) Collins, w. of Chas. O.
965 L Lucinda (Lane) Hart, w. of Isaac W., . . *1875
966   Charles Webster, ... L 1876
967   George E. Richmyer, ... L 1877
968   Caroline (Gamerdinger) Kaupert, . . L 1877
969   Catherine (Seibold) Geisser, wid. of Theodore.
970   Joseph Tatem.
971 L Hezekiah W. Hamlin, } . . L 1885
972 L Catherine (Cowles) Hamlin, } . . L 1885
973   Frank Schutz, } . . . D 1892
974   Dora (Ebert) Schutz, } . . *1878
975   Ida (Pohlman) Jones, w. of Frank, . . L 1886
976   Hattie H. (Samlow) Berre, w. of August.
977   Catherine C. (Host) Siering, w. of George.
978   Anna (Wight) Haman, w. of Martin.
979   Libette (Houtt) Scheidler, w. of Fred. G.
980   Mary Stino, ... L 1877
981 L Emeline (Hammond) Wheeler, wid. of Daniel, . L 1878
982 L Jennie E. Wheeler, ... L 1878
983   Mary G. (Clark) Burr, ... L 1878
984   George L. Allen, ... D 1879
985   George Unwin, ... D 1879
986   Eunice (Unwin) Bedford, w. of Wm. H. B.
987   Joseph Unwin, ... D 1891
988   Sophie R. (Gamerdinger) Barrett, w. of Willard.

1875.

989   Sarah H. (Brown) Porter, w. of Frank J.
990 L Alfred K. Seymour, ... L 1882
991 L Lydia Newell, ... *1879
992 L Cornelia A. (Hart) Humphrey, w. of Henry.
993 L Jennie (Kempton) Francis, wid. of J. P., . L 1886
994 L William N. Shepard, ... L 1879
995 L Frederick G. Gleason, ... L 1879
996   Lucie (Kenyon) Hull, w. of Dwight Martin, *1875
997   Louisa (Patz) Schutz, w. of John.
998 L George W. Banning. }
999 L Ellen (Wheelock) Banning. }
1000 L Eliza (Bartholomew) Woodruff, wid. of Urbane, *1885
1001   George W. Eddy.
1002   Henry J. Wheeler.
1003 L Mary (Reed) Eastman, wid. of Rev. Orman, *1878
1004 L Harriet M. Eastman.

82   A HALF CENTURY.

1005 L Mary D. Eastman.
1006 L Sarah F. (Waterman) Peck, w. of John H.
1007   Arisoma (Fitch) Seymour, wid. of Alfred P.,   * 1882

1876.

1008 L Mary (Arthur) Woods, w. of William A., .   L 1888
1009   Maria (Thompson) Avery, w. of Joseph, .   * 1888
1010 L Celestia D. (Browning) Comins, w. of J. S.,   L 1881
1011   Ella M. Boardman.
1012   Annie G. Bartlett.
1013 L Julia M. (Baldwin) Edmonson, w. of ———,   L 1883
1014   Mary A. (Booth) Peck, w. of Edward F., .   L 1887
1015   Henry Boehm, 2d,   .   .   .   D 1888
1016   Dietrich Bruemmer,   }   .   D 1888
1017   Wilhemina (Seavers) Bruemmer,   }   * 1883
1018   Henry A. Bruemmer, ...   D 1884
1019   William C. Bruemmer,   .   .   .   D 1885
1020   George F. Bird.   }
1021   Sarah (Charlesworth) Bird. }
1022   Edward H. Brush,.   .   .   .   L 1877
1023   Kate (Jerry) Boehm, w. of Henry.
1024   Henry Boehm, Jr., ...   L 1887
1025   Frederica W. (Poehlman) Beinhausen, wid. of Philip,   L 1882
1026   Mary E. (Spence) Booth, wid. of Wm. S.
1027   Emma L. (Conklin) Clark, w. of Edward H.,   .   L 1887
1028   Annie E. (Conklin) Fair, w. of Thomas A.,   .   L 1892
1029   Martha J. (Cole) Bissell, w. of Henry.   .   L 1891
1030   Estelle S. (Corbin) Wetmore, w. of Charles E.
1031   Grace M. Carleton,   .   .   .   L 1884
1032   Ann (Woolley) Charlesworth, w. of J.,   .   * 1882
1033   Samuel Cadwell.
1034   J. Willard Callender, .   .   D 1883
1035   Joseph H. Clark, .   .   L 1882
1036   Ira Callender.
1037   Abner W. Dickinson.   }
1038 L Fidelia S. (Hall) Dickinson.   }
1039   Almeria B. Dickinson,   .   .   .   L 1888
1040   Celia S. (Dickinson) Stevens, w. of John H.
1041   Nellie F. Dickinson,   .   .   .   * 1877
1042   Serrilla E. Dickinson.
1043 L Mary E. (Dickinson) Northend, w. of John,   .   L 1878
1044 L S. Anna (Dickinson) Knapp, w. of Isaac N.
1045   Edward B. Doen.
1046   Mary J. (Doen) Hart, w. of George P.
1047   H. Kate (Doen) Rice, w. of E. Wilbor.
1048   Sylvester C. Dunham.
1049   Edward W. Dowd,   .   .   .   L 1880
1050   Ralph C. Dunham.
1051   Rosa (Diehl) Bechstedt, w. of John F.,   .   L 1882
1052   Eliza (Withwan) Dyson, w. of George.
1053   Dora (Maeland) Etzold, w. of Fred. G., .   .   L 1883
1054   Jennie I. (Ellis) Carpenter, w. of Walter L.
1055   Ella L. (Freeman) Kimball, w. of George H.,   .   * 1888
1056   Caroline Foulds, ...   * 1889
1057   Josephine (Fenton) Bixby, w. of William.

1058	Cordelia (Blinn) Fenney, w. of Robert.	
1059	Mary (Homer) Farnham, w. of J. D.	
1060	Louisa (Flagg) Scribner, w. of Charles,	L 1883
1061	John L. Foss. }	
1062	Lizzie J. (Marston) Foss. }	
1063 L	Adeline F. Fish,	* 1892
1064 L	Caroline S. Fish,	* 1891
1065	William Farnham.	
1066 L	Mary (Stoughton) Giddings, w. of Fred. W.	
1067	Bertha (Gussman) Fenton, w. of H. S.	
1068	Lester F. Gifford.	
1069	Mary (Allen) Gamerdinger, wid. of Wm. F.	
1070	Charles H. Gamerdinger.	
1071	George W. Giddings.	
1072	Frederick M. Goodrich.	
1073	Geanna L. (Osborne) Giddings, w. of Wm. H.	
1074	Ada (Heins) Schmallfuss, w. of Frank.	
1075	Hattie Hendrick,	L 1880
1076 L	Jeremiah Hackett,	L 1888
1077	Benjamin K. Hart,	* 1884
1078	George P. Hart.	
1079	Reuben L. Hubbard. }	
1080	Lucy M. (Hooker) Hubbard. }	
1081	Johanna M. (Boehm) Hauser, w. of John,	D 1888
1082	Julia H. Hoffman.	
1083	Elizabeth M. Hoffman.	
1084	Louis Hoffman.	
1085	Frederick D. Hart.	
1086	Cora L. House.	
1087	Frederick Berthe Herman.	
1088	Albert Hallbauer.	
1089	Lina (Host) Thrall, w. of Ira W.	
1090	Frederick H. Humphrey,	L 1892
1091 L	Eleanor (Porter) Hart, wid. of Wm. C.	
1092	Frederick H. Heinisch, }	D 1884
1093	Anna (Ludewig) Henisch, }	D 1884
1094	Anna (Boone) Johnson, w. of Elmer.	
1095	Lina (Kelly) Corbin, w. of George W.	
1096	Henry P. King, }	D 1885
1097	Hattie (Bullard) King. }	
1098	Arthur A. Kaempf,	D 1882
1099	Lista W. (Lincoln) Dunham, w. of Martin R.,	L 1881
1100	Leontine J. S. (Leger) McCormick, w. of ———,	L 1883
1101	Emily A. (Taylor) Lyon, w. of E. B.,	* 1884
1102	Stephen Miller, }	* 1889
1103	Christina (Brukhos) Miller, }	D 1892
1104	Daniel McNiel. }	
1105	Jane (Pollock) McNiel. }	
1106	Jennie (McNeil) Sloan, w. of John Jr.	
1107	Jane (Pember) Moore, w. of Samuel A.	
1108	Reuben Mitchell. }	
1109	Jane (Cowlan) Mitchell. }	
1110	Lillie (Mitchell) Foulds, w. of John.	
1111	Jennie (Mitchell) Blake, w. of John A.	

1112 Samuel Muir. }
1113 Margaret (Pollock) Muir. }
1114 George Mather. }
1115 Mary (Cliff) Mather, } *1881
1116 L Willis W. Mildrum, } . L 1892
1117 L Anna S. (Webster) Mildrum, } . L 1892
1118 L Charles L. Moore.
1119 Mary (Palmer) Marsh, w. of William, *1889
1120 Louisa (Neinman) Pilz, w. of August.
1121 William Nichols.
1122 Emma (Nichols) Sargent, wid. of Samuel D.
1123 Kate (Nichols) Lydall, wid. of Henry.
1124 Orrin M. Otis, ... L 1884
1125 L Mary E. (Porter) Burnham, w. of Arthur, . L 1881
1126 Jennie (Porter) Mitchell, w. of Edwin R., . L 1881
1127 L Charlotte (Watson) Palmer, w. of John C., L 1878
1128 Edward F. Peck, ... L 1887
1129 Clara F. Preston, ... *1884
1130 Henry Pratt, } . . . L 1878
1131 Mary (Charlesworth) Pratt, } . . . L 1878
1132 George Polson. }
1133 Ann (Walker) Polson. }
1134 Spencer C. Page.
1135 Mary E. (Painter) Williams, w. of John, . L 1884
1136 Eliza (Steele) Piatt, w. of George, . . *1884
1137 Sarah (Schatz) Phillippi, w. of Charles P., D 1879
1138 Arthur D. Preston, ... L 1877
1139 Sarah P. Rogers.
1140 Julia P. (Rockwell) Roby, w. of Sidney J., L 1891
1141 Elizabeth (Nash) Reed, w. of Thos. E., . L 1890
1142 L Joseph Selden, } . . . L 1877
1143 L Emma (Fuller) Selden, } . . . L 1877
1144 Edward C. Samlow, ... *1881
1145 Gustav H. Samlow, ... L 1784
1146 Mary (Wagenblast) Steele, w. of Walter T., L 1878
1147 Lousia (Siering) Muller, w. of Louis J., . L 1884
1148 Frederick E. Smith, ... D 1882
1149 Anna (Siering) Berner, w. of Paul.
1150 Lina (Siering) Gilbert, w. of Wilbur F.
1151 L Frederic E. Sage, ... D 1884
1152 Emma J. P. (Spencer) Loomis, w. of C. D., Jr.
1153 Jefferson W. Steele. }
1154 Mary N (Steele) Steele. }
1155 Laura J. (Steele) Scoville, w. of Albert A.
1156 Lizzie J. Stone.
1157 Mary Schultz, . D 1879
1158 Edward F. Schutz.
1159 Henry Scherman. }
1160 Elizabeth (Bollerer) Scherman, } . . *1890
1161 George Smedley, ... *1889
1162 Anna S. (Schmidt) Thompson, w. of Willard A.
1163 Anna (Falk) Schmidt, w. of John A.
1164 Henry K. Smith, } . . . L 1890
1165 Leontina (Steele) Smith. }
1166 Margueretta (Jones) Seymour, w. of Alfred K., L 1882

1167 Albert P. Seymour,   L 1889
1168 Marie L. Tuck.
1169 George L. Tyler, .   D 1892
1170 John Ward, .   * 1876
1171 Estelle A. Whiting.
1172 W. Howard Whiting.
1173 Frederick Wessell.
1174 Arthur L. Woodruff.
1175 Minnie (Webster) Hansel, w. of William J.
1176 Hattie L. (Webster) Clark, w. of Emerson G.,   L 1882
1177 Henry Wilson,   * 1887
1178 Mary E. (Rowell) Wheeler, w. of H. J.
1179 Margaret (Hodgson) Woods, w. of Thomas.
1180 George Wilhelmy. }
1181 Mary (McGucken) Wilhelmy, }   D 1891
1182 Elizabeth Young.
1183 Jacob Young.

1877.

1184 L Spencer H. Wood. }
1185 L Melissa (Bliss) Wood. }
1186 L Florence E. Frisbie, .   L 1882
1187 John Marsh. }
1188 Johannah (Behrent) Marsh. }
1189 Carrie Eger.
1190 Hannah L. (Houth) Meisner, w. of Irtman.
1191 John Scheiblin, }   * 1891
1192 Louisa (Weber) Scheiblin. }
1193 Anna N. (Shepard) Rogers, w. of Noah C.,   L 1879
1194 L Emily (Blinn) Stevens, w. of Willard.
1195 L Elizabeth (Arthur) Muir, w. of David,   L 1880

1878.

1196 L Rev. James W. Cooper. }
1197 L Ellen (Hilliard) Cooper. }
1198 L Cornelia (Woodruff) Lewis, wid. of C. M.
1199 Sophia (Wiess) Lindgren, w. of Alfred.
1200 Ellen (Sharp) Pillard, w. of O. E.,   L 1882
1201 Caroline M. Lewis.
1202 Arabelle G. (Lewis) Paine, w. of Richmond P.
1203 George D. Waddell,   * 1878
1204 Mary (Waddell) Middlemas, w. of Robert.
1205 William B. Slater,   D 1891
1206 L Laura M. Stebbins,   * 1880
1207 L Samuel J. Chaffee, }   L 1887
1208 L Sarah M. Chaffee, }   L 1887
1209 L Harriet E. Chaffee.   * 1884
1210 L Jannette E. (Eno) Tuller, wid. of Rufus,   * 1889
1211 Louise A. (Scheiblin) Hand, w. of John, .   L 1886
1212 L Emma A. (Wells) Bodwell, wid. of Thos. L.

1879.

1213 L Frederick H. Churchill, }   * 1881
1214 L Annie L. (Smith) Churchill. }
1215 L Sarah J. (Allen) Wheeler, wid. of William,   L 1884

1216 L Mary E. (Armstrong) Parsons, wid. of Edward E., .   L 1880
1217 L Janet McNaughton, ...   L 1879
1218 L Elizabeth (Henry) White, w. of William.
1219 L Rebecca (Davis) Stone, w. of Jay S.
1220   John Sloan. ⎱
1221   Mary (Kennedy) Sloan. ⎰
1222   Amelia Winger.
1223   Charlotte S. Lyon, ...   * 1880
1224   Edward C. Riecker, ...   D 1891
1225 L Ellen R. (Woodford) Abbe, w. of Robert M., .   L 1889
1226 L Elizabeth R. Eastman.
1227 L Abigail (Merwin) Noble, wid. of David D.,   * 1891
1228 L Laura S. (Noble) Copley, w. of George D.
1229   Sarah (Gordon) Lambert, w. of William.
1230   Nettie S. (Bulkley) Matthewson, w. of Herbert L., .   L 1884
1231   Ida Griswold, ...   L 1879
1232   Kai Chong Chu, ...   D 1892
1233 L John B. Smith. ⎱
1234 L Lucy F. (Nichols) Smith. ⎰
1235 L Mary Julia Smith.
1236 L Fannie L. (Smith) Rogers, w. of Dwight L.
1237 L Lena (Adolf) Heisler, w. of Edward.
1238 L John W. Stoughton. ⎱
1239 L Sarah B. (Ellsworth) Stoughton. ⎰
1240 L Ellen F. (Williams) Sugden, w. of N. Wales, .   * 1892
1241 L Luther A. Parker. ⎱
1242 L Nancy E. (Woodruff) Parker. ⎰
1243 L David G. Gordon, ⎱ . . . .   L 1881
1244 L Helen (Hazen) Gordon, ⎰ . . . .   L 1881
1245 L Fannie L. (Grant) Hazen, wid. of James A.,   L 1881
1246 L Fannie H. (Hazen) Talcott, w. of John B.
1247 L Ella A. (Townsend) Brown, wid. of James H.
1248 L Susan E. (Hanchett) Humphrey, w. of F. H., .   L 1892

1880.

1249 L Seymour Strong, ⎱ .   L 1883
1250 L Ellen (Welton) Strong, ⎰ .   L 1883
1251 L Anna E. Strong, . . .   L 1883
1252   James M. Belden, . .   D 1888
1253   John Sloan, Jr.
1254   George Ernest Root.
1255 L Matilda (Hathaway) Doyle, w. of Dennis, .   L 1883
1256 L Mary (Loady) Norman, wid. of Joseph.
1257   Herbert Elam.
1258   Chu Kai You, ...   D 1892
1259   Laura C. (Tenney) Wright, w. of G. S.,   L 1885
1260 L Samuel H. Beard.
1261   Theodore A. Stanley.
1262   William T. Schneider.
1263   Ida A. (Bristol) Steele, w. of Walter P.
1264   Andrew B. Huntington, ...   L 1892
1265   Charles H. Johnson, ...   L 1884
1266   Frederick M. Hemenway, ...   L 1883
1267 L Caroline T. (Cary) Talcott, w. of C. Myron.

1268 L Allie J. (Church) Hemingway, w. of John P.
1269 L Margaret K. (Schicker) Hockmuth, w. of August.
1270 L William Middlemas.
1271   Alice M. (Neal) Otis, w. of Orrin M , .   .   L 1884
1272   Minnie L. (Tomlinson) Brown, w. of G. E.,   L 1885
1273 L William H. Just,   }   .   .   .   L 1886
1274 L Alice A. Hackett) Just, }   .   .   .   L 1886

1881.

1275 L Emma A. (Covell) Abbe, w. of Henry E.
1276   Anna (Barrett) Sherman, w. of Chauncey, .   L 1884
1277 L William H. Huntley,   }   .   .   * 1882
1278 L Laura P. (Ellsworth) Huntley, } .   .   L 1892
1279 L Thomas W. Wilbor.
1280 L Charles Hummell,   .   L 1886
1281 L John H. Bastian.
1282 L Annie B. (Miles) Beard, w. of Samuel H.
1283   John Boyle.   }
1284   Margaret (Young) Boyle.   }
1285   Nettie (Konold) Samlow, w. of Gustave H.,   L 1884
1286   Emily (Haaga) Bollerer, w. of Frederick.
1287   Ellen L. (Marsh) Boehm, w. of Henry,   L 1887
1288   Elizabeth (Grimley) Smith, w. of Francis A.
1289   Emma L. Hawkins.
1290   Bessie S. (Booth) Preston, w. of Wilfred E.
1291   Alice M. Doen.
1292   Mary E. (Bassett) Sage, w. of Geo. H.,   L 1889
1293   Anna L. (Smith) Waterman, w. of Frank N.
1294   Lucy M. (Boehm) Montague, w. of Wm. B.
1295   Clara L. Carleton, ...   L 1884
1296   Mary W. Lyon.
1297   Bertha Fannie Montague.
1298   Grace R. (Stanley) Moore, w. of A. J. P.
1299   Charles E. Wetmore.
1300   Fannie (Moore) Learned, w. of E. C.
1301   Lettie H. Learned.
1302   Mary C. Bowers.
1303   Carolyn Peck.
1304   Elizabeth (Rockwell) Russell, w. of Isaac D.   L 1891
1305   Martin Haman, ...   * 1883
1306   Nellie M. (Haman) Chapman, w. of Wm. E.
1307   Fannie C. (Gridley) Vile, w. of Henry J. N.
1308   Bertha M. Schmidt.
1309   Carl A. Molender, ...   L 1886
1310   Selma A. Johanson, ...   L 1881
1311   Josephine (Johanson) Molender, w. of C. A., * . L 1886
1312   Alida J. Johanson) Rosangran, w. of N. A.,   L 1886
1313 L Louisa M. (Barnes) Moses, wid. of Luther.
1314 L Agnes J. (Moses) Abbe, w. of Edwin W.
1315   Burr A. Johnson.   }
1316   Jennie E. (Rowell) Johnson. }
1317   Anna S. Hart.
1318   William A. House.
1319   Emma C. Scheiblin.
1320   Augusta H. Scheiblin.

1321 Christine N. (Johanson) Johnson, w. of Chas. F.
1322 Lillie C. Brown.
1323 Lillian W. Hart.
1324 Carrie B. (Copley) Rundlett, w. of L. J.
1325 Mary L. (Rounds) Welles, w. of George M.
1326 Amy (Bridgman) Cowles, w. of George B., Jr.,   L 1889

1882.

1327 Martha E. (Hart) Moore, w. of Ethelbert A.
1328 Emma (Hallbauer) Nash, w. of Jesse L.
1329 Johanna S. (Trick) Guenther, w. of Frederick.
1330 Bertha (Foel) Hummell, w. of Charles,   L 1886
1331 Harriet L. (Andrus) Mallory, w. of E. A.
1332 Bertha M. Church.
1333 Frank N. Waterman.
1334 William S. Stone.
1335 L George D. Copley.
1336 L Helen W. (Christy) Osgood, wid. of Dr. D. W.
1337 Elizabeth W. Welles.
1338 Estelle M. Hart.
1339 L Delora J. (French) Boyington, wid. of B. C.,   L 1882
1340 L Ellen F. (Marsden) Dyson, w. of Joseph.
1341 L Helen Maria (Beach) Seelye, w. of A. S.
1342 Pauline E. (Early) Scheidler, w. of Christian,   L 1884
1343 Rosa M. (Schonfeld) Snowman, w. of Herman.
1344 Elizabeth C. Georgi.
1345 L Leonard Kurtz,   L 1883
1346 L Charles Cornwell,   L 1886
1347 L Charles D. Barnes, }   L 1886
1348 Cora B. (Norton) Barnes, }   L 1886
1349 Jennie E. Chapin.
1350 Laura C. Smith.
1351 L Cornelia A. (Borst) House, w. of Albert H.

1883.

1352 Carrie A. Crabtree.
1353 Gertrude M. (Moore) Pierce, w. of John,   L 1892
1354 Walter L. Carpenter.
1355 L Jane (Skidmore) Wainwright, wid. of J. W.
1356 David W. Johnson.
1357 Joanna (Burkhardt) Petry, wid. of Gustave.
1358 Emily Jost.
1359 Elisha H. Cooper.
1360 Frederick A. Bassett.
1361 Elizabeth (Smith) Deming, w. of Newell F.,   L 1885
1362 Edwin Johnson. }
1363 Anna M. (Baxter) Johnson. }
1364 Minnie E. (Johnson) Dunham, w. of E. P.,   L 1884
1365 Joseph Landgren. }
1366 Charlotte (Olson) Landgren. }
1367 Nellie J. (Barrett) Case, w. of Geo. T.,   L 1892
1368 Electa C. (Andrews) Hartman, w. of Wm. T.
1369 Harriet N. (Hitchcock) Merwin, w. of Chas. P.

THE SOUTH CHURCH.

1884.

1370	Edwin C. Gillette,	l. 1885
1371	Mary (Hoffman) Sengle, w. of Baltus.	
1372 l	Edwin H. Lyman.	
1373 l	Effie (McLeod) Lyman.	
1374 l	Anna M. (Pickett) Rockwell, w. of S. Willis,	l. 1888
1375 l	Henry J. Gillette,	l. 1885
1376 l	Rachel L. (Whiton) Gillette,	l. 1885
1377 l	Sarah A. (Harrington) Dickey, wid. of Monroe,	l. 1887
1378 l	Anna (Yale) Allis, w. of Fortis H.	
1379 l	Ella J. (Childs) Searle, w. of Henry L.	
1380 l	Charles H. Thurston,	l. 1888
1381 l	Carrie A. (Frost) Thurston,	l. 1888
1382 l	Charles E. Steele.	
1383	Carrie K. (Stone) Hale, w. of Charles H.	
1384	Elizabeth (Jenkins) Davey, w. of John.	
1385	Lucia E. (Case) Case, w. of Cromwell O.	
1386	Peter Fodt.	
1387	Minnie (Nobz) Fodt.	
1388	William Blair.	
1389	Robert W. Boyle.	
1390	James T. Muir.	
1391	David Muir.	
1392	Hugh M. Muir,	* 1888
1393	Agnes C. Muir.	
1394	Helen E. Harris,	L 1889
1395	Eliza A. (Timbrell) Dyson, w. of Geo. H.	
1396	Sarah M. (Wheeler) Hall, w. of H. C.,	l. 1892
1397	Antoinette R. Smith.	
1398	Alice M. Booth.	
1399	Nathan M. Doen.	
1400	Albert B. Johnson.	
1401	Fred. A. Searle,	l. 1886
1402	Frank W. Thurston,	l. 1888
1403	Robert H. Stanley.	
1404	George S. Talcott.	
1405 l	John R. Ayer,	l. 1884
1406 l	Adaline M. (Taylor) Evans, wid. of Wm. H.,	* 1885
1407 l	Rev. William Miller.	
1408 l	Hannah E. (Button) Miller,	* 1890
1409 l	Lizzie (Dunham) Wolcott, w. of Wm. H.,	L 1890
1410 l	Ann Eliza Shipman.	
1411 l	Henry Nash.	
1412 l	Hermine (Sterzing) Gerber, w. of Herman.	
1413 l	Emma (Gerber) Wetzel, w. of Henry.	
1414 l	Amelia Gerber.	
1415 l	Arthur J. Reynolds.	
1416 l	Loraine E. (Sheldon) Reynolds.	
1417	Catharine M. (Ague) Martin, w. of Jacob.	
1418	Eva (Martin) Senf, w. of George.	
1419	Emma J. (Muir) Newell, w. of I. N.,	l. 1891
1420	Mary J. (Muir) Grocock, w. of Samuel.	
1421	Georgia A. (Zeickler) Downs, w. of Geo. A.,	l. 1890
1422	Lottie B. Bassett.	

1423 L George Crabtree.
1424 L Lena B. (Rowell) Crabtree.
1425   John W. Carleton.
1426   Sarah E. Kelley.
1427   Mary E. Goodrich.
1428   Joseph H. M. Clark, ... L 1890
1429   Elizabeth F. (Brown) Clark, . . . * 1885
1430 L Mary E. (Buckminster) Kibbe, w. of M. J.
1431 L Frank N. Welles.
1432 L Fannie C. (Brown) Welles, . * 1885
1433 L Harriet A. Ludington.
1434 L Rowena (Jackson) Higby, w. of William, . L 1890
1435 L James A. Muir, ... * 1885
1436   Ervin E. Osgood.
1437 L Mary A. (Stanley) Prior, w. of Edward L.
1438 L Clarence F. Carroll.
1439 L Julia (Webster) Carroll.
1440 L Grace (Stanley) Wilbor, w. of Thomas W.
1441 L Caroline C. (Johnson) Starr, w. of Edward, L 1887

1885.

1442   August Wolfe, . D 1891
1443   Wilfred E. Preston.
1444   Frederick Bridgman, . L 1889
1445   Henry M. Bridgman, . L 1889
1446   Andrew A. Scheidler.
1447   Alice C. Smith.
1448   Emile (Houtt) Miller, w. of Chas. F.
1449 L James H. Thompson, . . L 1889
1450 L Alida (Ingraham) Thompson, . . L 1889
1451 L George A. Fowler, . . . L 1890
1452 L Mary T. (Bosworth) Stanley, w. of E. N.
1453   Cromwell Padelford, . . L 1886
1454 L Anna E. (Tolman) Padelford, . . L 1886
1455   Albert W. Goodwin.
1456   Amelia D. (Zimmerman) Goodwin,
1457   Lizzie M. (Jost) Jiingst, w. of Louis C.
1458   Nettie S. Jost.
1459   Fannie Spring.
1460   Susanna C. (Seibler) Schmidt, w. of Adolph.
1461   Minnie (Boehm) Cowles, w. of Geo. B.
1462   Margaret (Bowers) Zimmerman, wid. of Frank.
1463 L John White.
1464 L Mary A. (Rathbun) White.
1465   Henry E. Abbe.
1466   Buell B. Bassette.
1467   Alfred H. Boehm, ... * 1885
1468   Margaret (Bodmer) Hall, w. of Samuel T.

1885.

1469   Emma (Diebold) Rowland, w. of L. W., 1888
1470   Caroline (Gussman) Barnard, w. of W. L.
1471   Erskine H. Kelley.
1472   Eugene W. Parker.

1473   Clayton A. Parker.
1474   Herbert H. Wheeler.
1475 L Henry N. Penfield.
1476 L Harriet (Bodwell) Penfield.
1477 L Hope S. (Martyn) Swasey, w. of E. P.
1478 L Charles H. Johnson.
1479 L Caroline (Cleveland) Johnson.
1480   Louis E. Hart.
1481   Thomas Scholes.
1482   Ann (Smyrk) Scholes.
1483   Ellen V. Brundin.
1484   Margaret (Siering) Benz, w. of Frank.
1485   Mary (Ritchie) Belden, wid. of Jas. W., . L 1889
1486   Annie M. (Belden) Kimball, w. of M. J., . D 1889
1487 L Lydia A. (Smith) Styles, w. of E. L.
1488 L Mary G (Smith) Smith, w. of Gilbert A.
1489   Frank Story, ... L 1887
1490   Lena Sheldon.
1491   Amelia A. (Howe) Steele, w. of V. H., L 1890
1492   Alice (Howe) Steele, w. of Willard.
1493   Edwin W. Abbe.
1494   Caroline Grimley.
1495 L L. Gay Sheldon.
1496 L Sarah M. (Reynolds) Sheldon.
1497 L Emma (Blue) Steele, w. of Charles E.
1498 L C. Wallace Healey.
1499 L Amelia A. (Greenleaf) Healey.

1886.

1500 L John Webster.
1501 L Lydia (Francis) Webster.
1502 L Frances E. (Webster) Camp, w. of Waldo C.
1503 L Ella C. Steele.
1504   Herbert C. Abbe.
1505   Daniel Andrew.
1506   George W. Banning, Jr., . . . L 1888
1507   Ellen (Warren) Barrett, w. of Francis.
1508   Edwin Barrett.
1509   Franklin E. Bassett.
1510   Lizzie R. Beh.
1511   Mary B. (Beh) Goodrich, w. of Henry.
1512   Bertha M. Bowers.
1513   Caroline M. Button.
1514   Waldo C. Camp.
1515   Wilfred H. Chapin.
1516   George Cryne.
1517   L. Howard Curtis.
1518   Marie A. Daniels.
1519   Watson Davis.
1520   Louise J. Doen, .   . * 1886
1521   Sarah H. Dyson.
1522   Henrietta (Eichel) Hall, w. of Wm. B.
1523   Charles J. Elam.
1524   Ella M. (Lord) Elam.

1525 John Grimley.
1526 Ann (Bacon) Grimley.
1527 Howard S. Hart.
1528 Alice L. (Humiston) Johnson, w. of Elmer E.
1529 Bertha G. Humiston.
1530 Oliver N. Judd.
1531 Elizabeth M. (Kitteridge) Hine, w. of Wm. C.
1532 Florence M. Latham.
1533 Albert P. Marsh, .   L 1892
1534 Emily E. Marsh, .   L 1889
1535 John E. McNeil.
1536 Eva Minderlein.
1537 Fannie B. Miller.
1538 Celia B. (Moses) Mix, w. of Edward H.
1539 Mary L. (Nash) Goodrich, w. of Fred. M.
1540 Edward A. Peck,   L 1888
1541 Estelle (DeLamater) Peck,   L 1888
1542 Carrie D. Peck, ...   L 1888
1543 Lucy E. Porter.
1544 Lizzie C. Scheidler.
1545 Frederick O. Schneider.
1546 Amos B. Sheldon,   .   * 1888
1547 Mary Sloan.
1548 Anna M. (Yetter) Smith, w. of Wm. H.
1549 Mary Louisa (Smith) Willard, w. of F. G.
1550 Herman E. Snowman,   .   .   .   D 1891
1551 Clara E. (Spaulding) Warner, w. of W. H.
1552 Katie E. Sperl.
1553 George W. Steele.
1554 Frank L. Stone.
1555 Clara G. Wessell.
1556 Ella E. (White) Baker, w. of Geo. M.
1557 Rosa M. White.
1558 Lena Yetter.
1559 Louisa K. (Yetter) Curdts, wid. of Wm. C. E.
1560 Rosa (Yetter) Buechler, w. of John.
1561 L Clara W. Mingins.
1562 L Charles F. Sheldon.
1563 L Mary E. (Richards) Sheldon,   L 1890
1564 L Marian A. Sheldon.
1565 L Hattie Hendrick, .   L 1891
1566 Jane B. Bassett.
1567 Grace H. Camp.
1568 J. Earnest Cooper.
1569 John Eppler.
1570 Fannie C. Johnson.
1571 Augusta (Wesche) Keller, w. of George.
1572 Harry Killam, ...   L 1888
1573 Frederick H. May.
1574 Edward M. Merwin, .   * 1887
1575 Nellie S. Moses.
1576 Florence G. Parker.
1577 Charles W. Perkins.
1578 Nellie F. Porter.
1579 James M. Relyea.

THE SOUTH CHURCH.

1580 E. Gertrude Rogers.
1581 Bertha K. Scherman,   * 1891
1582 Frederic Scherman.
1583 Sarah E. Seelye.
1584 Edith Smith.
1585 Fannie A. Stratton.
1586 Martha T. Waterman.
1587 Bertha L. Wiard.
1588 Grace L. Wiard.
1589 Bessie Williams.
1590 Margaret N. Williams.
1591 Frederic B. Wood.
1592 Henry N. Wood.
1593 Bertha F. (Revoir) Zimmerman, w. of C F.
1594 Anna (Griffin) Zwick, w. of John.
1595 Augusta G. Burckhardt.
1596 Charles W. Button.
1597 Gertrude L. Chapin.
1598 Caroline A. Clark.
1599 John L. White.
1600 Catharine (Pfercich) Eppler, w. of John.
1601 Annie L. Eppler.
1602 Annie (Gammerdinger) Dow, w. of Chas.
1603 Margaret Horne.
1604 Mary C. Johnson.
1605 Minnie S. Scheiblin.
1606 Mary S. (Clagus) Schneider, w. of F. T.
1607 Lizzie A. Winger.
1608 Casper Yetter,   }   * 1886
1609 Eva M. (Carl) Yetter. }
1610 L Samuel Drysdale,   L. 1890
1611 L Annie (Fleming) Drysdale, .   L. 1890
1612 L Inez B. (Parsons) Henry, w. of William.
1613 L Isaac T. Morris,   }   L. 1889
1614 L Louise B. (Tompkins) Morris, }   L. 1889
1615 Elizabeth Heinzeman.
1616 Emma E. Marsh, .   * 1887
1617 Katharine M. Schmidt.
1618 Louisa A. Bauman,   * 1890
1619 Abbie J. (Seitz) Meisner, w. of Geo.
1620 Lillian (Gammerdinger) Buell, w. of Fred.
1621 Eva B. Relyea.
1622 L Susan (Hinsdale) Lyon, w. of Edwin B.

1887.

1623 L Ralph G. Duvall,   L 1892
1624 Jarvis E. Miller, .   * 1889
1625 Maggie (Sloan) Ellis, w. of Chas. D.
1626 Lena (Gerber) Broadbent, w. of J. J.
1627 L Julia S. (Porter) Case, wid. of Ezra.
1628 L Etta J. Case.
1629 Annie L. Copley.
1630 L Fannie L. (Grant) Hazen, wid. of Jas. A.
1631 L George H. Dyson.
1632 L George S. McLaren,   .   L. 1888

1633 L John Meyer, } . . . L 1887
1634 L Anna (Buebach) Meyer, } . . . L 1887
1635 L Lottie (Wohlfert) Wolfe, w. of Wm. W.
1636   George A. Downs, ... L 1890
1637   Frank Monnier.
1638 L Harriet L. (Buell) Sharp, w. of H. D.
1639 L Abbott G. Butler, } . . . L 1889
1640 L Minna L. (Shaw) Butler, } . . . L 1889

1888.

1641   George M. Baker.
1642   Edward C. Scheiblin.
1643   Grace G. Baird.
1644   Bertha E. Classon.
1645   Grace L. Flint.
1646   Edith A. Martin.
1647   Augusta (Schleicher) Sunburn, w. of John S.
1648   Annie Young.
1649   Emma Zwick.
1650   Allen J. Beaton. }
1651   Mary E. (Boone) Beaton. }
1652 L Wallace J. Case.
1653   Horace C. Deane.
1654   Clarence R. Root.
1655   Lydia A. (Bowman) Steele, w. of Fred. N.
1656 L Elise (Mack) Traut, w. of J. A.
1657   Lucius B. Steele.
1658   Elizabeth B. Bassett.
1659 R Thomas Muir, } . L 1888
1660 R Barbara (Stewart) Muir, } . L 1888
1661 L Eunice W. (Buell) Jenkins.
1662   May Churchill.
1663 L William E. Chapman.
1664 L Charles R. Barrows. }
1665   Josephine (Brown) Barrows. }
1666   Christiana (Scheidler) Vensel, w. of Frank E.
1667   Nellie L. (Corbin) Beers, w. of W. E.
1668   Lillian H. Pierson.
1669   Grace H. Bowers.
1670   Jennie R. Wheeler.
1671 L Florence L. Hart.
1672 L May M. Booth.
1673 L Duncan McArthur. }
1674 L Anna (Hipelins) McArthur. }
1675 L Hannah E. (Pierson) Brockett, w. of Calvin R.

1889.

1676   Edna E. M. Brill.
1677   Elizabeth (Goth) Berg, w. of Frederick.
1678   Lizzie (Gross) Schleicher, wid. of Edward.
1679 L Gustavus H. Samlow. }
1680 L Nettie (Konold) Samlow. }
1681 L Mary (Stone) Hale, wid. of Leonard E.
1682 L Daniel T. Griswold.
1683   Helen L. Bennett.

1684   Orland R. Blair.
1685   Roy N. Buell,   .   L 1890
1686   Margaret O. Fagan.
1687   Jennie S. Fielding.
1688   Bessie A. Gridley.
1689   William B. Grimley,   * 1890
1690   Harry E. Hart.
1691   Maxwell S. Hart.
1692   Henry P. Nothnagle, .   L 1892
1693   William M. Page.
1694   Lena E. Raiss, . .   D 1892
1695   Eliot N. Smith.
1696   Mortimer D. Stanley.
1697   Emily S. White.
1698 L Anna (Hendrick) Stillman, w. of J. A.
1699 L Clarence H. Rockwell.   }
1700 L Hattie M. (Barber) Rockwell.   }
1701 L Frank C. Rockwell.
1702   Pauline K. Luger.
1703   Gastave E. Kurth.
1704   Elbert C. Mead.
1705   Philip Zwick.
1706   Herman Beh.
1707   David C. Rogers.
1708   Stella M. Carroll.
1709 L Robins Fleming.
1710 L Ida B. (Leete) Cotton, w. of Wilbur, .   L 1891
1711 L Minnie (Hall) Rice, w. of Francis W.
1712 L Nira I. (Simmons) House, w. of Wm. A.
1713 L Harriet A. Bosworth.
1714 L Margaret (Wainwright) Glover, w. of Chas.
1715 L Ida M. Glover.

1890.

1716   Albert J. Osgood.
1717   Walter C. Booth.
1718   Ralph C. Correll.   }
1719   Ida M. (Cornwell) Correll. }
1720   Sadie (McLouth) Stanley, w. of T. A.
1721   Mary C. McLouth, ...   L 1892
1722   Grace L. (Crabtree) Smith, w. of Edgar H.
1723   Grace M. Muir.
1724   Christie C. (Eldridge) Judd, w. of Frank.
1725   Carrie I. Smith.
1726   Minnie M. Schilling.
1727   Ida M. Kunz.
1728   Herbert N. Loomis.
1729   Lemuel R. Griffin.
1730 L Mira J. (Kilborn) Bishop, w. of E. R.
1731 L Edgar H. Smith.
1732 L Mary M. Stone.
1733   Selma Eissrig.
1734   Elnora I. Judd.
1735   Eda L. (Collins) Kinyon.
1736 L Sarah J. (McCrumm) Hazlett, wid. of Wm.

1737 Matilda L. Classon.
1738 Jessie M. Beaton.
1739 Cora B. Beaton.
1740 Ida M. Bingham.
1741 Daisy B. Johnson.
1742 John Minderlein.
1743 L Henry H. Clark. }
1744 L Fannie S. (Ventres) Clark. }
1745 L Ventres A. Clark.
1746 L Claude E. Clark.
1747 Samuel B. Bassett.

1891.

1748 L Ada (Goddard) Lester, w. of Harry B.
1749 L Joseph E Marvin.
1750 L Margaret C. Fuller.
1751 Charles E. Gates.
1752 William G. Wagner.
1753 Etheline L. Hart.
1754 Nettie J. (Walter) Lotz, w. of Jacob.
1755 Jessie L. Huntington.
1756 L Timothy E. Hall. }
1757 L Fannie I. (King) Hall. }
1758 Lena (Wilhelmy) Vining, w. of John S.
1759 Florence M. Vining.
1760 Amelia J. Wiegand.
1761 Mary K. Gordon.
1762 L Leon A. Gladding. }
1763 L Aletha (Gilbert) Gladding. }
1764 Mary (Borner) Wagner, wid. of George.
1765 Emma (Landry) Stiquel, w. of L. H.
1766 Edward H. Hart.
1767 Walter H. Hart.
1768 Henry B. Miller.
1769 Henry W. Peck.
1770 Ernest W. Sheldon.
1771 Walter P. Stanley.
1772 Howard H. Wessell.
1773 John B. Wiard.
1774 Carl F. Young.
1775 Minnie L. Smith.
1776 L Ethelbert A. Moore.
1777 L Bessie (Stanley) Hart, w. of Howard S.
1778 L Dwight L. Rogers.
1779 L Betsey (Smith) McNary, w. of Hiram W.
1780 L George M. Dickinson, }
1781 L Mary J. (Knapp) Dickinson. }
1782 L George W. Banning, Jr.
1783 L Edwin W. Schultz.

1892.

1784 Emily (Voglegesang) Kutcher, w. of Louis.
1785 L William L. Hatch. }
1786 L Julia m. (Wetmore) Hatch. }
1787 L Minnie (Gedney) Tuthill, w. of A. C.
1788 L Stephen Morse.

1789   Louisa Kutcher.
1790 L James T. Powell.
1791   Herbert H. Bassett.
1792   C. Irving Bennett.
1793   Carrie L. Bingham.
1794   Rosa E. Birtles.
1795   Cyrus H. Blair.
1796   Nina L. Blair.
1797   Louis L. Cadwell.
1798   William Churchill.
1799   Emma L. Dickinson.
1800   Nellie M. Dickinson.
1801   Helena M. Glover.
1802   Howard S. Humphrey.
1803   Alma Johnson.
1804   Amelia (Vogel) Kurth, w. of William.
1805   Wilfred Kurth.
1806   Mary Lindner.
1807   R. Clifford Merwin.
1808   Hattie A. Mitchell.
1809   Isabel S. Muir.
1810   William H. Peck.
1811   Alphonso B. Porter.
1812   Annie Rehm.
1813   Katie L. Rehm.
1814   John L. Rogers.
1815   D. Miner Rogers.
1816   Francis W. Rice.
1817   Albert H. Rockwell.
1818   Lucy E. Sanford.
1819   Eva Sheldon.
1820   Harry J. Smith.
1821   Nettie E. Snow.
1822   Robert O. Snow.
1823   Mary Scheidler.
1824   Catharine (Scheidler) Slaney, w. of A. A.
1825   Mabel W. Stone.
1826   Oliver M. Wiard.
1827 L Charles A. Blair.   )
1828 L Mary A. (Viets) Blair.)
1829 L Rosa (Tucker) Hibbard, w. of B. H.
1830 L Olive B. (Larrabee) Johnson, w. of Edward.
1831 L John H. Kirkham.
1832 L Thomas Muir.   )
1833 L Barbara (Stewart) Muir.)
1834 L Agnes E. (Whaples) Sanford, w. of James A.
1835 L Lucy A. (Rawlings) Towers, w. of Joseph.
1836   Alice M. (Judson) Brainerd, w. of W. E.
1837   Frank D. Clark.
1838   Frank L. Kieffer.
1839   Rosa B. Langsettle.
1840   George J. Lehman.
1841   Mary A. Lehman.
1842   Emma T. Lindner.

7

1843   Harriet M. (Judd) Parker, w. of Clayton A.
1844   Helen M. (Judd) Parker, w. of Eugene W.
1845   Mary S. Prior.
1846   Charles F. Scott.
1847   Margaret Seipel.
1848   Jennie G. Sloan.
1849   Daniel L. Waddell.   ⎫
1850   Margaret M. (Slavin) Waddell. ⎭
1851   Ernestine J. Wagner.
1852   Annie C. Young.
1853 L Henrietta B. (Weaver) Hinckley, w. of T. H.
1854 L Carrie H. Hinckley.
1855 L Cora W. Hinckley.
1856 L George E. Snow.   ⎫
1857 L Laura M. (Jones) Snow.   ⎭
1858 L William Gemmell.
1859 L Waldemar E. Brainerd.
1860 L Delora J. (French) Boyington, wid. of B. C.
1861 L Carrie H. Conley.
1862   Mary W. Camp.
1863   Rose Churchill.
1864   Harriet Kloss.
1865   Roberta E. Moore.
1866   George Senf.
1867   George Senf, Jr.   ⎫
1868   Helena J. Senf.   ⎭
1869   Elizabeth A. Senf.
1870   William J. Watts.   ⎫
1871   Catharine E. Watts.   ⎭
1872   Willis Whited.   ⎫
1873 L Lizzie C. Whited.   ⎭
1874 L Walter Watkins.
1875 L Florence Marion.
1876 L Andrew Hunter.   ⎫
1877 L Mary A. Hunter. ⎭
1878 L William T. Bissell.
1879 L Frank S. Pierce.
1880 L Jane E. (Fry) Walton, wid. of Thomas C.
1881 L Emma A. Walton.
1882 L Lillian (Somers) Smith, w. of Clarence.
1883 L Henry L. Bissell.
1884 L Samuel W. Irving.

January 1, 1893.

1885   Hattie L. (Smith) Irving, w. of S. W.
1886   William Lambert.
1887   Edith M. Dyson.
1888   Annie Howe.
1889   Theresa Schleicher.

ALPHABETICAL INDEX.

The number following each name refers to the number prefixed to the same name in the Chronological Catalogue. An R prefixed to the name signifies that the relation to the Church has been dissolved; its omission indicates the present membership.

	Name	No.		Name	No.
	Abbe, Edwin W.,	1493	R	Bacon, Chauncey A.,	852
	Agnes J.,	1314	R	Jennie C.,	853
R	Ellen R.,	1225	R	Bailey, Emma A.,	662
	Henry E.,	1465	R	Mary E.,	332
	Emma J.,	1275	R	Mary T.,	241
	Herbert C.,	1504	R	Solomon E.,	660
R	Acker, Sarah D.,	504	R	Anna E.,	661
R	Adler, Adele B.,	916		Baird, Grace G.,	1643
R	Allen, George L.,	984		Baker, George N.,	1641
R	Lewis S.,	808		Ellen E.,	1556
R	Susan C.,	809	R	Baldwin, Julia M.,	1013
	Mary P.,	565		Banning, George W.,	998
	Sarah L.,	934		Ellen W.,	999
	Allis, Anna Y.,	1378		George W., Jr.	1506
	Andrew, Daniel,	1505			1782
R	Christine W.,	665	R	Barclay, John,	722
	George W.,	708	R	Mary A.,	723
R	John R.,	831		Barnard, Caroline G.,	1470
	Marion A.,	709	R	Barnes, Charles D.,	1347
R	Wilford C.,	786	R	Cora B.,	1348
R	Ann E.,	787		Mary A.,	905
R	Andrews, Aaron C.,	16	R	Barnett, James G.,	858
R	Electa B.,	94		Barrett, Edwin,	1505
R	Charles S.,	184		Ellen W.,	1507
R	Clarissa O.,	392		Sophia R.,	988
R	Ellen A.,	185		Barrows, Charles R.,	1664
	Emma P.,	856		Josephine B.,	1665
R	Ethan A.,	147		Bartlett, Annie G.,	1012
R	Lucy C.,	148	R	Ellen F.,	313
R	Ezekiel,	32	R	Ellen S.,	680
R	Sarah E.,	110		John N.,	678
R	Helen M.,	425		Ellen S.,	679
R	Mary,	154		John P.,	902
	Arnold, Emeline B.,	567	R	Bartram, Sarah J.,	857
R	Ashley, Elizabeth J.,	475	R	Bass, Eliza N.,	138
R	Austin, John H.,	835		Bassett, Buell B.,	1466
	Jane B.,	495		Elizabeth E.,	1658
R	Avery, Maria T.,	1009		Franklin E.,	1509
R	Ayer, John R.,	1405		Franklin N. E.,	882
			R	Celia A.,	883

	Bassett, Frederick A.,		1360		Bird, George F., ⎫	1020
	Herbert H.,		1791		Sarah C., ⎭	1021
	Jane B.,		1566	R	Harriet A.,	331
	Lottie B.,		1422		Birtles, Rosa E..	1794
	Margaret A.,		603	R	Bishop, Elizabeth,	676
	Mary S.		81, 522		Mira J.,	1730
	Milton H.,	⎫	354	R	Bissell, Martha J.,	1029
	Prudence M.,	⎭	782		William T.,	1878
R	Ozias B.,	⎫	158		Henry,	1883
	Emeline E.,	⎭	159		Bixby, Josephine S.,	1057
	Samuel B.,		1747		Blair, Charles A., ⎫	961, 1827
R	William,		18		Mary A., ⎭	1828
R	Lois E.,		80		Cyrus H.,	1795
	Bastian, John H.,	⎫	1281		Nina L.,	1796
	Fannie S.,	⎭	909		Orland R.,	1684
R	Bauman, Louisa C.,		1618		William,	1388
	Beard, Samuel H.,	⎫	1260		Blake, Jennie M.,	1111
	Annie B.,	⎭	1282	R	Blakeslee, Chauncey W., ⎫	956
	Beaton, Allen J.,	⎫	1650	R	Merab R., ⎭	854
	Mary E.,	⎭	1651	R	Blakeslee, Mary O.,	457
	Cora B.,		1739		Blinn, Harriet A.,	765
	Jessie M.,		1738		Julia E.,	563
R	Bechstedt, Rosa D.,		1051	R	Boardman, Edward A., ⎫	780
R	Beck, Theresa,		906	R	Nellie L., ⎭	953
R	Beckley, Cornelia H.,		393		Ella M.,	1011
	Bedford, Eunice U.,		986		Martin A., ⎫	538
R	Beers, John W. A.,	⎫	621		Mary S., ⎭	539
	Mary A.,	⎭	622		Bodwell, Emma A.,	1212
	Nellie L.,		1667	R	Boehm, Alfred H.,	1467
	Beh, Herman,		1706		Henry, ⎫	952
	Lizzie R.,		1510		Kate J., ⎭	1023
R	Beinhausen, Frederica W.,		1025	R	Henry, Jr., ⎫	1024
R	Belden, Diodamia C.,		516	R	Nellie L., ⎭	1287
R	James M.,		1252	R	Henry, 2d,	1015
R	Mary R.,		1485	R	Boland, Wesley F., ⎫	810
R	Belknap, Theodore A.,		28	R	Angeline. ⎭	811
	Bennett, C. Irving,		1792		Bollerer, Emily H.,	1286
	Edwin,	⎫	841		Boone, Charlotte,	699
	Ruth M.,	⎭	842	R	Jane,	700
	Helena L.,		1683		Booth, Alice N.,	1398
	Benz, Margaret S.,		1484	R	James,	343
	Berg, Elizabeth G.,		1677	R	Lucius S.,	194
	Berner, Anna S.,		1149	R	Mary J.,	507
	Berre, Hattie H.,		976		May M.,	1672
	Bingham, Carrie L.,		1793	R	Susan M.,	455
	Emily,		496		Walter C,	1717
R	George H.,	⎫	488	R	William S., ⎫	193
	Elizabeth M.,	⎭	863	R	Julia A.,	134
	Ida M.,		1740	R	Fidelia M., ⎭	416
	John C.,		560		Mary E.,	1026
	Mary E.,		948		Bosworth, Harriet A.,	1713
	Sarah F.,		245	R	Bowen, Florence A.,	525
R	Susan P.,		515		Bowers, Annie N.,	543

THE SOUTH CHURCH. 101

Bowers, Bertha M.,	1512	R Buell, Lester P., ⎫	129, 460
Grace H.,	1609	R Louisa M., ⎭	461
Henry C., ⎫	195	Lillian G.,	1620
Augusta M., ⎭	196	R Lydia,	270
Mary C.,	1302	R Roy N.,	1685
William H.,	736	R Bugbee, Julia E.,	540
Boyle, John, ⎫	1283	R Bulkley, Henry C., ⎫	746
Margaret Y., ⎭	1284	Susan B., ⎭	747
Robert W.,	1389	R Bunce, Amelia R.,	352
Boyington, Delora J.,	1339, 1860	R Emily U.,	328
R Brace, Samuel, ⎫	375	Burckhardt, Augusta G.,	1595
R Sarah E., ⎭	60, 376	R Burnham, Mary E.,	1125
R Brainard, James P.,	201	R Burr, Richard M.,	805
Waldemar E., ⎫	1858	R Mary G.,	983
Alice M., ⎭	1836	R Burritt, Ann W.,	68, 272, 584
R Breckenridge, Warren J., ⎫	523	R Butler, Abbott G., ⎫	1639
R Jane E., ⎭	442	R Minna L., ⎭	1640
R Bridgeman, Frederick,	1444	R Elisha H., ⎫	284
R Henry M.,	1445	R Catharine B., ⎭	285
Brill, Edna E. M.,	1676	R Horace, ⎫	27
R Brittain, Almira S.,	372	Orpha H., ⎭	58
Broadbent, Lena G.,	1626	Jane,	636
Brockett, Hannah E.,	1675	Button, Caroline M.,	1513
R Bronson, Mary J.,	414	Charles W.,	1596
Phineas M., ⎫	671	R Butts, Catharine,	440
Sarah M., ⎭	490	R Elizabeth K.,	439
R S. Sophia,	489		
R Brown, Aurelian M.,	748		
Fannie L.,	767	Cadwell, Louis S.,	1797
R Harriet E.,	497	Samuel, ⎫	1033
Harvey G., ⎫	357	Henrietta E., ⎭	720
Amanda F., ⎭	344	Callender, Eda M.,	711
R Horace H., ⎫	690	Ira, ⎫	1036
Harriet S., ⎭	84	R Marilla C., ⎬	101
R James H., ⎫	710	R Maria J., ⎭	279
Ella A., ⎭	1247	R J. Willard,	1034
R Jay H.,	946	Mary M.,	755
Katharine M.,	893	Camp, David N., ⎫	318
Lillie C.,	1322	R Adeline H., ⎭	319
R Maria L.,	544	Ellen R.,	396
R Martin, ⎫	359	R Ellen S.,	210
R Elizabeth C., ⎭	178	R Frances T.,	493
R Minnie L.,	1272	Grace H.,	1567
R William M.,	766	Mary W.,	1862
R Bruemmer, Dietrich, ⎫	1016	Waldo C., ⎫	1514
R Wilhemina S., ⎭	1017	Frances E., ⎭	1502
R Henry A.,	1018	R Campbell, William O., ⎫	658
R William C.,	1019	R Clara P., ⎭	659
Brundin, Ellen V.,	1483	R Carleton, Clara L.,	1295
R Brush, Edward H.,	1022	R Grace M.,	1031
R Buckham, Henry B.,	405	R Isaac N., ⎫	777
Buechler, Rosa Y.,	1560	R Laura T., ⎭	778
R Buell, Ada E.,	607	John W., Jr.,	1425
R Electa S.,	604	Julia M.,	738

R	Carpenter, Joshua,	28	R	Clark, Edward S.,	502
R	Betsey H.,	87	R	Stella E.,	801
R	Samuel W.,	200	R	Emma L.,	1027
	Walter L.,	1354		Frank D.,	1837
	Jennie I.,	1054	R	Frederick A.,	754
	Carroll, Clarence F.,	1438	R	George L.,	901
	Julia W.,	1439	R	Hattie L.,	1176
	Stella N.,	1703		Henry E.,	721
R	Cary, Helen M.,	653		Henry H.,	1743
	Case, Edward H.,	682		Fannie S.,	1744
	Etta J.,	1628	R	Henry M,	248
R	Harriet R.,	226	R	Harriet S.,	249
	Jane E.,	355	R	Isabella A.,	806
	Julia S.,	1627	R	Joseph H.,	1035
	Lucia E.,	1385	R	Joseph H. M.,	1428
R	Nellie J.,	1367	R	Elizabeth F.,	1429
R	Salome B.,	681	R	Julia A.,	231
	Wallace J.,	1652	R	Lucius,	788
R	Cassidy, Clara H.,	221	R	Catharine P.,	789
R	Chaffee, Harriet E.,	1209	R	Mary L.,	641
R	Samuel J.,	1207	R	Polly B.,	46
R	Sarah M.,	1208		Ventres A.,	1745
R	Chamberlain, Anna I.,	789		Classon, Bertha E.,	1644
	Marcia E.,	790		Matilda L.,	1737
	Chapin, Gertrude L.,	1597	R	Clay, Frances B.,	693
	Jennie E.,	1349	R	Clemens, William W.,	316
	Samuel N.,	511	R	Mary,	317
	Emily M.,	512	R	Clement, Nathan S.,	589
	Wilfred H.,	1515	R	Mary J.,	590
	Chapman, William E.,	1663	R	Cody, Martha G.,	350
	Nellie M.,	1306	R	Cole, Lemira H.,	829
R	Charlesworth, Ann W.,	1032		Collins, Augustus P.,	265
R	Cheever, Mary S.,	751	R	Harriet P.,	266
R	Chipman, Harriet E.,	536		Collins, Charles O.,	568
R	Chu, Kai Chong,	1232		Elizabeth A.,	964
R	Chu, Kai You,	1258	R	Comins, Celestia D.,	1010
	Church, Bertha M,	1332	R	Conklin, George A.,	887
R	Churchill, Frederick H.,	1213	R	Sarah D.,	466
	Annie L.,	424	R	Thomas A.,	385
		1214		Martha F.,	386
	May,	1662		Conley, Carrie H.,	1861
	Rose,	1863	R	Cook, Jane M.,	347
R	Selina H.,	98	R	Nathan R.,	52
	William,	1798	R	Lucy B.,	53
R	Clapp, Horace,	151		Cooper, Elisha H.,	1359
R	Sarah W.,	152		J. Earnest,	1568
R	Clark, Abigail,	160		James W.,	1196
R	Ada L.,	703		Ellen H.,	1197
R	Albert,	434		Copley, Annie L.,	1629
R	Mary A.,	435		George D.,	1335
	Alfred H.,	561		Laura S,	1228
	Emma A.,	494	R	Corbin, Charles F.,	891
	Caroline A.,	1598		Frank,	198
	Carrie F.,	756		Mary A.,	289
	Claude E.,	1746	R	George S,	369

THE SOUTH CHURCH. 103

Corbin, Lina K.,	1095	
Mary J.,	327, 949	r
Philip, ⎫	225	
Francina T., ⎬	390	
r William,	368	
r Cornwell, Charles,	1346	
r Chauncey, ⎫	2	
r Mary G., ⎬	69	
r Martha E.,	648	
r Sarah G.,	70	
Correll, Ralph C., ⎫	1718	
Ida M., ⎬	1719	
r Cotton, Ida B.,	1710	
r Cowan, William,	606	
r Cowles, Amy B.,	1326	
Minnie B.,	1461	
Crabtree, Carrie H.,	1352	
George, ⎫	1423	
Lina B., ⎬	1424	
Cryne, George,	1516	
r Cumings, Alvah,	277	
Curdts, Louise K.,	1559	
Curtis, L. Howard,	1517	
r Mary P.,	115	
r Cuyler, Mary T.,	406	
Daniels, Marie A.,	1518	
Davey, Elizabeth J.,	1384	
r Davis, Mary M.,	776	
Watson,	1519	
r Dawson, Hannah F.,	451	
Deane, Horace C.,	1653	
r Deming, Edward L., ⎫	684	
r Elizabeth M., ⎬	685	
r Hulda,	242	
r Newell F., ⎫	619	
r Elizabeth S., ⎬	1361	
r Denison, Laura A.,	473	
r Dewey, Esther,	74	
r George S.,	356	
r Josiah, ⎫	11	
r Lydia S., ⎬	64	
r Dickerson, George H., ⎫	914	
r Mary B., ⎬	915	
r Dickey, Sarah A.,	1377	
Dickinson, Abner W., ⎫	1037	
Fidelia S., ⎬	1038	
r Almeria B.,	1039	
Emma L.,	1799	
George M., ⎫	1780	
Mary J., ⎬	1781	
r Nellie F.,	1041	
Nellie M.,	1800	
Serrilla E.,	1042	
Diehl, Lucinda B.,	701	

Doen, Alice M.,	1291	
r Edward, ⎫	183	
Helen J., ⎬	214	
Edward B.,	1045	
r Louisa I.,	1520	
Nathan M.,	1399	
r Dolan, Henry P., ⎫	880	
r Annie W., ⎬	807	
r Donaldson, James, ⎫	298	
r Anne, ⎬	299	
r Doolittle, Mary J.,	377	
Dow, Annie G.,	1602	
r Dowd, Edward W., ⎫	1049	
r Hattie E., ⎬	940	
r John L.,	627	
r Downs, George A., ⎫	1636	
r Georgia A., ⎬	1421	
r Downton, Anna H.,	874	
r Doyle, Ann,	303	
r Matilda H.,	1255	
r Draper, Abbe L.,	800	
r Drysdale, Samuel, ⎫	1610	
r Annie F., ⎬	1611	
r Dunham, Julia W.,	211, 274	
r Lista W.,	1099	
r Margaret S.,	571	
r Minnie E.,	1364	
Ralph C., ⎫	436	
Charlotte R., ⎬	437	
Ralph C., 2d,	1050	
r Sophia H.,	280	
Sylvester C.,	1048	
r Durgie, Mary A.,	258	
r Dutton, Chloe C.,	269	
Dyson, Edith M.,	1887	
Ellen F.,	1340	
Eliza W.,	1052	
George H., ⎫	1631	
Eliza A., ⎬	1395	
Sarah H.,	1521	
r Eads, Harriet A.,	935	
Eastman, Elizabeth R.,	1226	
Harriet M.,	1004	
Mary D.,	1005	
r Mary R.,	1003	
Eddy, George W.,	1001	
r Mary A.,	132	
Nancy M.,	49	
r Edgar, Harriet B.,	534	
r Edmonson, Julia M.,	1013	
Eger, Carrie,	1189	
Eissrig, Selma,	1733	
Elam, Charles J., ⎫	1523	
Ellen M., ⎬	1524	

Elam, Herbert,	1257	R Fowler, Harriet E.,	452
Ellis, Lydia A.,	617	R Francis, Catharine A.,	120
Maggie S.,	1625	R Dorothy P.,	40
R Mary J.,	908	R Elijah, ⟩	1
R Ely, Cynthia S.,	519	R Jane C., ⟨	54
R Emerson, Frank H.,	836	R Henrietta H.,	133
R Mary C.,	76	R Jennie K.,	993
R Eno, Mary R.,	139	R Romeo, ⟩	47
Ensworth, Jedediah C., ⟩	869	R Catharine A., ⟨	48
Julia A., ⟨	791	Freeman, Mary C.,	666
Eppler, Annie L.,	1601	R Frink, Catharine B.,	234
John, ⟩	1569	R Frisbie, Elnathan B., ⟩	631
Catherine P., ⟨	1600	R Mary E., ⟨	632
R Erwin, Cornelius B., ⟩	370	R Florence E.,	1186
R Maria N., ⟨	93	R Mary E.,	633
R Etzold, Dora M.,	1053	Fuller, Eliza M.,	524
R Evans, Adaline M.,	1406	Margaret C.,	1750
R Sarah L.,	438, 845		
R Evarts, Franklin, ⟩	667	Gamerdinger, Charles H.,	1070
R Mary B., ⟨	668	Mary A.,	1069
R Everest, Ellen A.,	283	Gates, Charles E.,	1751
		R Darius, ⟩	687
		R Anna E., ⟨	688
Fagan, Margaret O.,	1686	R Gaylord, William,	169
R Faichney, David, ⟩	426	Gemmell, William,	1857
R Harriet W., ⟨	341	Georgi, Elizabeth C.,	1344
R Fair, Annie E.,	1028	Gerber, Hermine,	1412
Farnham, Mary H.,	1059	R Giddings, Eliza B.,	288
William,	1065	Frederick W., ⟩	796
Fenn, Ida J.,	629	Mary S., ⟨	1066
R Julius,	628	George W.,	1071
Fenney, Cordelia B.,	1058	William H., ⟩	795
Fenton, Bertha G.,	1067	Geanna L., ⟨	1073
Fielding, Jennie S.,	1687	William W., ⟩ 293, 860	
Nancy S.,	851	Cornelia A., ⟨ 294, 861	
R Finch, Harriet N.,	174	Giesser, Catharine B.,	969
Fish, Adelaide J.,	218, 585	Gifford, Lester F, ⟩	1068
R Adeline F.,	1063	Betsey A., ⟨	503
R Caroline S.,	1064	Gilbert, Lena S.,	1150
R Flagg, Abijah,	14	R Gill, John,	797
Cornelia E.,	243	R Gillett, Richard, ⟩	232
R Honor,	89	R Elizabeth F., ⟨	233
R Louisa H.,	79	R Gillette, Edwin G.,	1370
Fleming, Robins,	1709	R Henry J., ⟩	1375
Flint, Grace L.,	1045	R Rachel M., ⟨	1376
Fodt, Peter, ⟩	1386	R Gladden, Louise S.,	942
Minnie N., ⟨	1387	Mary H.,	816
Forbes, Ellen E.,	719	Gladding, Leon H., ⟩	1762
R Ford, Stephen T.,	141	Althea, ⟨	1763
Foss, John L., ⟩	1061	R Gleason, Frederick G.,	995
Lizzie J., ⟨	1062	Glover, Helena,	1801
R Foster, Charles E.,	549	Ida M.,	1715
R Foulds, Caroline,	1056	Margaret W.,	1714
Lillie M.,	1110	R Goodell, Constans L., ⟩	433
R Fowler, George A.,	1451	R Emily F., ⟨	403

THE SOUTH CHURCH.

	Goodrich, Frederick M., ⟩	1072		Hallbauer, Albert,	1088
	Mary L., ⟨	1538	R	Haman, Martin, ⟨	1305
R	Henry B., ⟩	558		Ann W., ⟨	978
	Laura A., ⟨	559	R	Hamlin, Hezekiah W., ⟩	971
	Mary B.,	1511	R	Catharine C., ⟨	972
	Mary E.,	1427	R	Hand, Louisa A.,	1211
	Goodwin, Albert W., ⟩	1455		Hansel, Minnie W.,	1175
	Amelia D., ⟨	1450	R	Harlow, Catharine T.,	834
R	Gordon, David G., ⟩	1243	R	Harris, Helen E.,	1394
R	Helen H., ⟨	1244	R	Mary J.,	802
	Mary R.,	1761	R	Hart, Abigail B.,	652
R	Graham, Emma L.,	384	R	Anna J.,	752
R	Graves, Ella E.,	533		Anna S.,	1317
	Gridley, Alice M.,	894	R	B. Kellogg, ⟩	1077
	Bessie A.,	1688	R	Olivia C., ⟨	683
	George C., ⟩	410		Charles E., ⟩	763
R	Ellen N., ⟨	367		Jennie W., ⟨	764
R	John,	295	R	Charles W.,	889
R	Mary M.,	113	R	Chester, ⟩	20
R	Solomon D., ⟩	409	R	Elvey W., ⟨	99
R	Dolly S., ⟨	51		Cora A.,	910
	Griffin, Lemuel R.,	1729	R	Cynthia,	155
	Grimley, Caroline,	1494		Edward H.,	1766
	John, ⟩	1525	R	Edward S.,	382
	Ann B., ⟨	1526	R	Elijah, ⟩	12
R	William B.,	1689	R	Louisa W., ⟨	107
	Griswold, Daniel T.,	1682	R	Ellen M.,	349
R	Ida,	1231		Eleanor P.,	1091
R	Thomas F., ⟩	122	R	Ellen W.,	896
	Elizabeth M., ⟨	733		Estelle M.,	1338
	Grocock, Mary J.,	1420		Etheline L.,	1753
	Guenther, Johanna S.,	1829		Florence L.,	1671
			R	Francis,	43
R	Hackett, Jeremiah, ⟩	1076		Frederick D.,	1085
R	Mary A., ⟨	849.	R	Frederick W., ⟩	173
	Hale, Carrie K.,	1383		Jennie M., ⟨	395
R	Chauncey, ⟩	228	R	George, ⟩	17
R	Clara M., ⟨	229	R	Elizabeth F., ⟨	96
	Emma C.,	476	R	Elizabeth E., ⟨	444
R	Israel F., ⟩	236		George P., ⟩	1078
R	Grata R., ⟨	237		Mary J., ⟨	1046
R	Mary E.,	230, 304	R	Georgiana M.,	61
	Mary S.,	1681	R	Hannah J.,	257
R	Sophronia L.,	291	R	Hannah K.,	937
	Hall, Henrietta E.,	1522		Harry E.,	1690
	James, ⟩	870		Howard S., ⟩	1527
	Annie F., ⟨	871		Bessie S., ⟨	1777
	Julia A.,	116, 881		Isaac W., ⟩	383
	Margaret B.,	1468	R	Lucinda L., ⟨	965
R	Sarah M.,	1396	R	J. Henry, ⟩	182
R	Sophia,	649	R	Jane E., ⟨	302
	Thomas S., ⟩	238, 838	R	Josephine P.,	446
	Julia N., ⟨	72, 839		Lillian W.,	1323
	Timothy, ⟩	1756		Louis E.,	1480
	Fannie I., ⟨	1757	R	Lucy J.,	616

	Hart, Mary E.,	672	R	Higby, Rowena J.,	1434
	Maxwell S.,	1691		Hinckley, Carrie H.,	1854
R	Mehitable D.,	106		Cora W.,	1855
R	Ozias,	8		Henrietta B.,	1853
R	Salmon, }	26		Hine, Elizabeth M.,	1531
R	Rosetta N., }	104	R	Hinsdale, Gilman, }	491
	Sarah C.,	166		Sarah M., }	83
	Sarah J.,	417		Hockmuth, Margaret K.,	1209
R	Sarah W.,	112		Hoffman, Elizabeth M.,	1083
R	Samuel, }	5		Julia H.,	1082
R	Orpha N., }	55		Louis,	1084
R	S. Waldo, }	25, 275	R	Hollister, James, }	582
R	Cordelia M., }	189	R	Jane A., }	583
R	Sylvia,	118	R	Hooker, George, }	175
R	Viana P.,	188	R	Sally W., }	176
	Walter H.,	1767	R	Martha C.,	768
	William H., }	360		Horne, Margaret,	1608
	Martha P., }	361		Host, Mary A.,	597
	Hartman, Electa C.,	1368	R	Hotchkiss, Edward F.,	925
	Hatch, William L., }	1785		House, Albert H., }	713
	Julia M., }	1786		Cornelia A., }	1351
R	Hauser, Johanna M.,	1081		Cora L.,	1086
	Hawkins, Emma L.,	1289	R	Truman B., }	656
	Hiram J., }	639		Mary E., }	657
R	Harriet E., }	605		William A., }	1318
R	James B., }	613		Nira I., }	1712
R	Ellen L., }	614	R	Howard, Louisa M.,	373
R	Hawks, Ann E.,	222, 273	R	Howd, Catharine B.,	957
	Hazen, Fannie L.,	1245, 1630	R	Charles B.,	917
	Hazlett, Sarah J.,	1736		Howe, Annie,	1888
	Healey, Chauncey W., }	1498		Hubbard, Reuben L., }	1079
	Amelia A., }	1499		Lucy M., }	1080
R	Heinisch, Frederick H., }	1092	R	William, }	441
R	Anna L., }	1093	R	Elizab'h A., }	564, 924
	Heinzeman, Elizabeth,	1615		Huebner, Catharine B.,	833
	Heisler, Henrietta H.,	875		Hull, Dwight M., }	955
	Lena A.,	1237	R	Lucie K., }	996
R	Hemenway, Fred'k M., }	1266		Humiston, Bertha G.,	1529
R	Helen S., }	941		Luther, }	868
	Hemingway, Allie J.,	1268		Louisa H., }	626
R	Henderson, Adeline E.,	371	R	Rachel P.,	932
R	Grove W., }	412	R	Hummell, Charles, }	1280
R	Elizabeth, }	413	R	Bertha T., }	1330
R	John,	482, 960	R	Humphrey, Augusta C.,	203
R	Hendrick, Edwin L.,	379, 499		Cornelia A.,	992
R	Hattie,	1075, 1565	R	Eliza A.,	186
R	Harriet U.,	167	R	Frederick H., }	1020
R	Jane B.,	500	R	Susan E., }	1248
	Henry, Inez B.,	1612		H. Dayton, }	928
	Herman, Frederick B.,	1087		Harriet C., }	541
R	Hewlett, Abigail A.,	340		Howard S.,	1802
R	Washington K.,	919	R	J. William, }	128
	Hibbard, Rosa M.,	1829	R	Mary F., }	192

THE SOUTH CHURCH. 107

R	Humphrey, Wallace A.,	309		Judd, Elnora I.,	1734
	Hunter, Andrew,)	1876	R	Emeline,	213
	Mary A., }	1877	R	Frederick W.,	334
R	William,)	281, 718	R	Harriet N.,	825
R	Sarah, }	282	R	Hattie E.,	900
R	Huntington, Andrew B.,	1264	R	Henry B.,	255
	Jessie L.,	1755	R	James,)	30
R	Huntley, William H.,)	1277	R	Gunilda, B., }	109
R	Laura P., }	1278		J. Bernard,)	301
				Eliza H., }	333
			R	John,)	13
	Irving, Samuel W.,)	1884	R	Betsey H., }	86
	Hattie L., }	1885		Oliver N.,	1530
R	Isham, David L.,	397	R	Just, William H.,)	1273
R	Sarah A.,	398	R	Alice A., }	850, 1274
R	Ives, Adelaide P.,	453			
			R	Kaempf, Arthur A.,	1098
R	Jackson, Louisa B.,	219	R	Kaupert, Caroline G.,	968
R	James, Adaline L.,	744		Keller, Augusta W.,	1571
	Jenkins, Eunice W.,	794, 1661		Kelley, Erskine H.,	1471
	Jingst, Lizzie M.,	1457	R	Henry R.,)	674
	Johnson, Albert B.,	1400		Sarah J., }	675
	Alice L.,	1528		Sarah E.,	1426
	Alma,	1803		Kelsey, Julia A.,	948
	Anna B.,	1094	R	Lydia B.,	131
	Burr A.,)	1315	R	Maria S.,	947
	Jennie E., }	1316	R	Kennedy, Mary A.,	587
R	Charles H.,	1265		Kibbe, Mary E.,	1430
	Charles H.,)	646, 1478		Kieffer, Frank L.,	1838
	Caroline C., }	647, 1479	R	Kilbourn, Albert G.,	769
	Christine N.,	1321	R	Elizabeth H.,	818
	Daisy B.,)	1741	R	Joseph K.,)	773
	David W., }	1356	R	Jane S., }	774
	Edwin,)	1362	R	T. Woodford,)	464
	Anna M., }	1363	R	Lucy S., }	465
	Fannie C.,	1570	R	Killam, Harry,	1572
R	Herbert E.,	920	R	William,)	846
R	Lucy L.,	532	R	Eunice M., }	847
	Mary C.,	1604	R	Kimball, Anna M.,	1486
	Olive B.,	1830	R	Edwin A.,	779
R	Selma A.,	1310	R	Ella L.,	1055
	Pauline S.,	876	R	King, Henry P.,)	1096
R	Johnston, Agnes H.,	826		Hattie B., }	1097
R	Jones, Ida P.,	975		Kinyon, Eda L.,	1735
	Orville, •)	761		Kirkham, John H.,	1831
	Caroline C., }	762		Kloss, Harriet,	1864
	Jost, Emily,	1358		Knapp, S. Anna,	1044
	Henrietta S.,	1458		Kunz, Ida M.,	1727
R	Juckett, Alfred,)	573		Kurth, Amelia V.,	1804
R	Harriet A., }	574		Gustave E.,	1703
	Judd, Christie C.,	1724		Wilfred,	1805
	David B,)	741	R	Kurtz, Leonard,	1345
R	Ellen J., }	742		Kutcher, Emily V.,	1784
R	Eliza H.,	108		Louisa,	1789

R Lamb, William A., ⎫	599	Lydall, Charles, ⎫	296
R Elizabeth T., ⎭	600	Margaret R., ⎭	297
Lambert, William, ⎫	1886	Kate N.,	1123
Sarah G., ⎭	1229	Olive J.,	912
R Landers, Catharine P.,	137	Lyman, Edwin H., ⎫	650, 1372
Charles S., ⎫	562	R Mary J., ⎬	651
Grace H., ⎭	781	Effie M., ⎭	1373
Landgren, Joseph, ⎫	1365	R Eveline U.,	329
Charlotte, ⎭	1366	R Lyon, Charlotte S.,	1223
Langsettle, Rosa B.,	1839	Edwin B., ⎫	634
Latham, Florence M.,	1532	R Charlotte W., ⎬	635
William E., ⎫	715	R Emily A., ⎪	1101
Henrietta B., ⎭	388	Susan H., ⎭	1622
R Latimer, Emily,	859	Mary W.,	1296
Law, Jane E.,	824	R Sabra A.,	686
R Lawrence, Marcellus,	706		
Learned, Fannie M.,	1800	R Macomber, Albert W.,	918
Lettie H.,	1301	R Maguire, Addison, ⎫	325
R Lee, Abigail B.,	207	R Cornelia C., ⎭	326
R Esther M.,	37	Mallory, Harriet L.,	1331
R Isaac S., ⎫	775	Marion, Florence,	1875
R Julia E., ⎭	542	R Marsh, Albert P.,	1533
Jane B.,	259	R Emma E.,	1616
R William H.,	735	R Emily E.,	1534
Lehman, George J.,	1840	John, ⎫	1187
Mary A.,	1841	Johannah B., ⎭	1188
R Leonard, Ira E.,	286	R Mary P.,	1119
Lester, Ada G.,	1748	R Marshall, Eliza A.,	31
Lewis, Caroline M.,	1201	R Martin, Annie H.,	938
R Charles M., ⎫	45	Catharine M.,	1417
Cornelia W., ⎭	1198	Edith A.,	1646
R Harriet M.,	267	Marvin, Joseph E.,	1749
R Jane A.,	330	R Massey, Ellen F.,	346
R Jane E.,	140	R Mary N.,	345
R Lillian L.,	535	Mather, George, ⎫	1114
R Lucy P.,	172	R Mary C., ⎭	1115
R Margaret M.,	252	R Matthewson, Nettie S.,	1230
Lindner, Emma T.,	1842	May, Frederick H.,	1753
Mary,	1806	McArthur, Duncan, ⎫	1673
Lindgren, Sophia W.,	1199	Anna H, ⎭	1674
R Lloyd, Jane B.,	700	R McConnor, William,	931
Loomis, Emma J.,	1152	R McCormick, Edward, ⎫	419
R Flora W.,	696	R Grace A., ⎭	420
R Grove W.,	324	R Leontine J. S.,	1100
Herbert N.,	1728	R McKinley, L. Ann,	235
Sarah J.,	673	R McLaren, George S,	1632
R Long, Caroline R.,	485	R McLean, Arthur E.,	640
Lotz, Nettie J.,	1754	R Clarence T.,	758
R Luce, Leverett H., ⎫	427	R Phebe C.,	278
R B. Elvira, ⎭	428	R McLouth, Mary C.,	1721
Luddington, Harriet A.,	1433	McNary, Betsey S.,	1779
Luger, Pauline K.,	1702	R McNaughton, Janet,	1217
R Lukey, Thomas E.,	877	McNeil, Daniel, ⎫	1104
R Lum, Charles H., ⎫	483	Jane P., ⎬	1105
R Jane B., ⎭	484	John E.,	1535

THE SOUTH CHURCH.

R	Mead, Alice E.,	498		Ethelbert A., ⎫	1776
R	Charles L., ⎫	663		Martha E., ⎭	1327
R	Isabella M., ⎭	664		Grace R.,	1298
	Elbert C.,	1704		Jane P.,	1107
R	Helen,	518	R	Perry, ⎫	726
R	Meigs, Elizabeth H.,	156	R	Lovica S., ⎭	505
	Meisner, Abbie J..	1619		Roberta E.,	1865
	Hannah L.,	1190	R	Samuel,	467
R	Merriman, Alanson H., ⎫	513	R	Morris, Ella G.,	911
R	Ellen A., ⎭	514	R	Isaac T., ⎫	1613
R	Merwin, Edward M.,	1574	R	Louese B., ⎭	1614
	Harriet N.,	1369		Morse, Stephen,	1788
R	James B,	197		Moses, Louisa M.,	1313
	R. Clifford,	1807		Nellie S,	1575
R	Meylert, Asa P., ⎫	771	R	Mudford, Mary,	268, 321
R	Harriet E., ⎭	772		Muir, Agnes C.,	1393
R	Meyer, John, ⎫	1633		David,	1391
R	Anna B., ⎭	1634	R	Elizabeth A.,	1195
	Middlemas, Mary W.,	1204		Grace M.,	1723
	William, ⎫	1270	R	Hugh M., ⎫	1392
	Susan C., ⎭	895		Jane C., ⎭	462
R	Mildrum, Willis W.. ⎫	1116		Isabel S.,	1809
R	Anna S., ⎭	1117	R	James A.,	1435
R	Miller, Edward J.,	1624	R	James S.,	592
	Emile H.,	1448		James T.,	1390
	Fannie B.,	1537	R	Jane S.,	547
	Henry B.,	1768		Robertson B., ⎫	591
R	Jarvis,	885	R	Jane A., ⎭	506
R	Stephen, ⎫	1102		Samuel, ⎫	1112
R	Christina B., ⎭	1103		Margaret P., ⎭	1113
R	Thrza C.,	950		Thomas, ⎫	548, 1659, 1832
	William, ⎫	1407		Barbara S., ⎭	823, 1660, 1833
R	Hannah E., ⎭	1408	R	Muller, Louisa S.,	1147
	Mills, Dwight P., ⎫	697	R	Mumford, Mary E.,	353
	Sarah A., ⎭	698	R	Munger, Nancy N..	958
R	Roger H., ⎫	311	R	Wallace T., ⎫	843
R	Harriet A., ⎭	312	R	Emma D., ⎭	844
	Susan G.,	904	R	Murray, Pascal D.,	670
	Minderlein, Catherine H.,	595			
	Eva,	1536			
	John,	1742		Nash, Emma H,	1328
	Mingins, Clara W.,	1561		Henry,	1411
	Mitchell, Hattie A.,	1808		Isabella J.,	743
R	Jennie P.,	1126	R	Newell, Emma J.,	1419
	Reuben, ⎫	1108	R	Lydia,	310, 991
	Jane C., ⎭	1109	R	Nichols, Charles, ⎫	471
	Mix, Celia B.,	1538	R	Louisa, ⎭	472
R	Molender, Carl A., ⎫	1309	R	Lethiel E, ⎫	812
R	Josephine J., ⎭	1311		Caroline M., ⎭	813
	Monnier, Frank,	1637		William,	1121
	Montague, Bertha F.,	1297	R	Noble, Abigail M.,	1227
	Lucy M.,	1294	R	Susan M.,	575
	Moore, Alice A,	449		Norman, Mary L.,	1256
	Charles L.,	1118	R	North, Alvin, ⎫	4
	Moore, Ella M.,	907	R	Clarissa B., ⎭	65

R	North, Caroline,	215	R	Parsons, Mary E.,	1216
R	Charles F.,	749	R	Payne, John,	637
R	Cordelia B.,	422	R	Jane T.,	638
R	Emily A.,	351	R	Pearl, Eliza H.,	374
R	Frederic H.,	227	R	Pease, Emma M.,	819
R	Mary E.,	217	R	Peck, Abram,	244
R	Grace E.,	750		Carolyn,	1303
R	Henry,	7	R	Carrie D.,	1542
R	Lauretta S.,	56		Charles,	199, 271
R	Hubert F.,	190		Mary F.,	314
R	Jane M.,	168	R	Edward A.,	1540
R	Oren S.,	689	R	Estelle D.,	1541
R	Sarah C.,	67	R	Edward F.,	1128
R	Sarah A.,	262	R	Mary A.,	1014
R	Sarah B.,	77	R	Elizabeth A.,	209
R	Seth J.,	3	R	Elnathan,	33
R	Elizabeth S.,	66	R	Mary D.,	73
R	Northend, Charles A.,	644		Henry W.,	1769
R	Martha M.,	645		John H.,	526
R	Mary E.,	1043	R	Harriet B.,	527
R	Northrop, Elizabeth M.,	323		Sarah F.,	1006
R	Norton, Jane A.,	177	R	L. Sophia,	300
R	Louise G.,	939	R	William E.,	888
R	Nothnagle, Henry P.,	1092		William H.,	1810
				Penfield, Henry N.,	1475
				Harriet B.,	1476
R	Oldershaw, Fanny,	418			
	Ordway, Fannie M.,	867	R	Rhoda C.,	486
R	Ortiz, Elizabeth C.,	220		Perkins, Charles W.,	1577
R	Osborne, Ella S.,	820	R	Perry, Roxy A.,	884
	Osgood, Albert J.,	1716		Petry, Joanna B.,	1357
	Ervin E.,	1436	R	Phillippi, Sarah S.,	1137
	Helen M.,	1336	R	Piatt, Eliza S.,	1136
R	Otis, Orrin M.,	1124		Pierce, Frank S.,	1879
R	Alice M.,	1271	R	Erastus W.,	336
R	Oviatt, Joshua N.,	520	R	Flora M.,	337
R	Martha A.,	521	R	Gertrude M.,	1353
				Pierson, Lillian H.,	1668
R	Padelford, Cromwell,	1453	R	Pillard, Ellen S.,	1200
R	Anna E.,	1454		Pilz, Louisa N.,	1120
	Page, Spencer C.,	1134	R	Piper, Samuel P.,	714
	William M.,	1693	R	Platt, Frederick,	287
	Paine, Arabella G.,	1202	R	Plumley, Henrietta A.,	445
R	Palmer, Charlotte W.,	1127		Polson, George,	1132
R	Kate A.,	921		Ann W.,	1133
R	Mary A.,	39		Pond, Elizabeth,	862
R	Park, Catharine,	387		Porter, Alphonso B.,	1811
	Parker, Clayton A.,	1472	R	Betsey C.,	146, 415
	Harriet M.,	1843	R	Charles H.,	792
	Eugene W.,	1472	R	Eva M.,	793
	Helen M.,	1844	R	Eli H.,	729
	Florence G.,	1576		Ella M.,	730
R	Julia,	290	R	Jane A.,	320
	Luther A.,	1241		J. Elizabeth,	954
	Nancy E.,	1242		Lucy E.,	1543
R	Lydia D.,	164		Mary S.,	705

THE SOUTH CHURCH. 111

	Porter, Nellie F.,	1578	R	Roberts, Ruth A.,	481
	Sarah H.,	985	R	Roby, Julia P.,	1140
R	Post, Elizabeth L.,	202		Rockwell, Albert H.,	1817
R	Elizabeth S.,	143		Clarence H.,	1699
R	Potter, Andrew P.,	10		Hattie M.,	1700
R	Isaac H.,	127	R	Elizabeth E.,	365
R	Mary E.,	926		Frank C.,	1701
R	Powell, Annette,	240	R	George P.,	362
	James T.,	1790	R	Eliza S.,	363
R	Pratt, Caroline E.,	208	R	Clara H.,	962
R	Henry,	1130	R	Samuel,	654
R	Mary C.,	1131	R	Charlotte N.,	59
R	Philo,	307	R	S. Willis,	892
R	Sarah L.,	308	R	Anna M.,	1374
R	Prentice, Caroline H.,	480		Rogers, Daniel M.,	611
R	Preston, Arthur D.,	1138	R	Philena H.,	612
R	Clara F.,	1129		Daniel O.,	695
	Elbert H.,	759		Emma J.,	704
	Emma I.,	760		David C.,	1707
	Wilfred E.,	1443		D. Miner,	1815
	Bessie S.,	1290		Dwight L.,	1778
				Fannie L.,	1236
	Prior, Edward L.,	669		Emma Gertrude,	1580
	Mary A.,	1437		John L.,	1814
	Mary S.,	1845		Mary Harriet,	944
R	Purple, Norman E.,	429	R	Noah C.,	945
R	Mary C.,	430	R	Anna N.,	1193
R	Raiss, Lena E.,	1694		Sarah P.,	1139
	Ralph, Hannah M.,	757		Root, Clarence R.,	1654
R	Rand, Carrie F.,	579		George C.,	865
R	George D.,	401, 580		Mary P.,	866
R	Martha J.,	402, 581		G. Ernest,	1254
R	Mary,	578	R	Hannah E.,	97
R	Philander,	576	R	Rosangran, Alida J.,	1812
R	Mary F.,	577	R	Ross, Maria S.,	740
R	Raymond, William F.,	153		Rossetter, Mary E.,	477
R	Reed, Elizabeth N.,	1141	R	Rowe, Celia A.,	447
	Rehm, Annie,	1812	R	Rowland, Emma D.,	1469
	Katie L.,	1813	R	Royden, Thomas,	239
	Relay, Ellen A.,	959		Rundlett, Carrie B.,	1324
	Relyea, Eva B.,	1621	R	Russell, Elizabeth R.,	1304
	James M.,	1579			
	Reynolds, Arthur J.,	1415	R	Sage, Frederick E.,	1151
	Loraine E.,	1416	R	Mary E.,	1292
R	Robert M.,	492	R	Samlow, Edward C.,	1144
	Rice, Francis W.,	1816		Gustave H.,	1145,1679
	Minnie H.,	1711		Nettie R.,	1285,1680
	Helen K.,	1047		Sanford, Agnes E.,	1834
R	Wilfred B.,	927		Lucy E.,	1818
R	Richardson, Anna S.,	872		Sargent, Emma N.,	1122
R	Jessie,	463		Scheiblin, Augusta H.,	1320
R	Richmond, Helen C.,	555		Edward C.,	1642
R	Richmyer, George E.,	967		Emma C.,	1319
R	Riecker, Edward C.,	1224	R	John,	1191
R	Risley, Sarah A.,	391		Louisa W.,	1192

	Scheiblin, Minnie S.,	1665	R	Seymour, Arisoma F.,	1007
	Scheidler, Andrew A.,	1446	R	Harriet G.,	450
	Libette,	979	R	Orson H., }	135
	Lizzie C.,	1544	R	Maria S.,	71
	Mary,	1828	R	Shaffer, Anna K.,	963
R	Pauline E.,	1842		Sharp, Harriet L.,	1638
R	Scherman, Bertha K.,	1581	R	Sheldon, Amos B.,	1546
	Frederick,	1582		Charles F., }	1562
	Henry, }	1159	R	Mary E.,	1563
R	Elizabeth B.,	1160		Earnest W.,	1770
	Schilling, Minnie M.,	1726		Eva,	1819
	Schleicher, Lizzie G.,	1678		Lena,	1490
	Theresa,	1889		L. Gay, }	1495
	Schmallfuss, Ada H.,	1074		Sarah M.,	1496
	Schmidt, Anna F.,	1163		Marian A.,	1564
	Bertha M.,	1308		Shepard, Elizabeth C.,	745
	Katharine M.,	1617	R	Josiah, }	569
	Susanna C.,	1460	R	H. Clarissa, }	125, 570
	Schneider, Frederick O.,	1545	R	Jane M.,	923
	Mary S.,	1606		Harriet O.,	454
	William T.,	1262	R	Sarah J.,	857
	Scholes, Thomas, }	1481	R	William N.,	994
	Ann S.,	1482	R	Sherman, Anna B.,	1276
	Schultz, Edwin W.,	1783	R	Horace E.,	855
R	Mary,	1157		Shipman, Ann Eliza,	1410
	Schutz, Edward F.,	1158		Siering, Catharine C.,	977
R	Frank, }	973	R	Simpkins, Mary,	551
R	Dora E.,	974		Slaney, Catharine S.,	1824
	Louisa P.,	997	R	Slate, Emily M.,	899
	Scott, Charles F.,	1846	R	Genevieve M.,	785
R	George,	315	R	Helen,	572
	William, }	873	R	James D.,	702
	Mary E.,	864	R	John J.,	625
	William W., }	608	R	Julia A.,	601
R	Adaline F.,	936	R	Orin, }	783
	Scoville, Laura J.,	1155	R	Catharine W.,	784
R	Scribner, Louisa F.,	1060	R	Slater, Burnham S.,	191
	Searle, Ellen J.,	1379	R	Elam, }	126
R	Frederick A.,	1401	R	Matilda W.,	50
	Seelye, Helen M.,	1341	R	William B.,	1205
	Sarah E.,	1583		Sloan, Jennie G.,	1848
	Seipel, Anna H.,	596		John, }	1220
	Margaret,	1847		Mary K.,	1221
R	Selden, Joseph, }	1142		John Jr., }	1253
R	Emma F.,	1143		Jennie M.,	1106
	Senf, Elizabeth A.,	1869		Mary,	1547
	George, }	1866	R	Smedley, George,	1161
	Eva M.,	1418		Smith, Alice C.,	1444
	George Jr., }	1867		Anna M.,	1548
	Helena J.,	1868		Antoinette R.,	1397
	Sengle, Mary H.,	1371		Carrie I.,	1725
R	Seymour, Abigail H.,	38		Edgar H., }	1731
R	Albert P.,	1167		Grace L.,	1722
R	Alfred K., }	990		Edith,	1584
R	Margaretta J.,	1166		Eliot N.,	1695

R Smith,	Elizabeth A.,	85	R Stanley,	Harriet A.,	95
	Elizabeth A.,	1288	R	Henry, }	34
	Elisabeth U.,	737	R	Catharine A., }	35
	Elisabeth W.,	508	R	John, }	338
	Francis H., }	509	R	Martha J., }	339
	Ruth A., }	510	R	John P.,	550
R	Frederick E.,	1148		Katharine A.,	832
	Harry J.,	1820		Mary J.,	304
R	Henry K., }	1164		Mary L.,	443
	Leontine S., }	1165		* Mortimer D.,	1696
R	James D., }	588	R	Oliver, }	130
R	Mary T., }	707	R	Cordelia H., }	206
R	Jane E.,	224, 408		Robert H.,	1403
	John B., }	1233	R	Theodore A.,	366
	Lucy F., }	474, 1234		Theodore A., }	1261
R	Julia A.,	187		Sadie M., }	1720
	Laura C.,	1350		Walter P.,	1771
R	Levi O., }	691	R	William B.,	44
R	Elizabeth S., }	223	R Starr,	Caroline C.,	1441
	Lilian S.,	1882	R Stebbins,	Laura M.,	1206
R	Lucretia M.,	82	Steele,	Alice H.,	1492
	Lucy W.,	212	R	Amelia A.,	1491
	Mary G.,	1488	R	Caroline M.,	556
	Mary Julia,	1235		Charles E., }	487, 1382
	Minnie L.,	1777		Emma B., }	1497
R	Roswell, }	179	R	Daniel, }	618
R	Mariva K., }	180	R	Delia W., }	655
R	Sidney,	181	R	Dwight N.,	552
R	William H., }	19	R	Edmund, }	22
	Lucinda H., }	63	R	Lucy N., }	100
Snow,	George E., }	1856		Ella C.,	1503
	Laura M., }	1859		Frederick N., }	553
	Nettie E.,	1821		Lydia A., }	1655
	Robert O.,	1822		George W.,	1553
R Snowman,	Herman, }	1550		Harriet A.,	557
	Rosa M., }	1343		Jefferson W., }	1153
Spaulding,	William A., }	530		Mary N., }	1154
	Anna A., }	531		Lucius B.,	1657
Sperl,	Katie E.,	1552	R	Maria W.,	105
R Sprague,	Homer B.,	620	R	Mary W.,	1146
Spring,	Fannie,	1459		Sarah M.,	933
R Stanley,	Abigail L.,	92	R	Selah, }	170
	Alice S.,	903	R	Phebe B., }	171
R	Alonzo,	15		Walter P., }	554
R	Amzi,	145		Ida A., }	1263
	Arabella D.,	124	R Stephens,	Henry C., }	642
	Carrie L.,	922	R	Eleanor B., }	643
R	Chloe A.,	91	R	Annie C., }	799
	Edward N., }	890	R	Joseph H.,	260
	Mary T., }	1452	R Stephenson,	Alf'd W., }	380, 431
	Emily L.,	364	R	Rhoda S., }	381, 432
R	Frederick T., }	692	Stevens,	Celia S.,	1040
R	Melvina C., }	90		Emily B.,	1194
R	Gad, }	121	Stillman,	H. Anna,	348, 1698
R	Fannie L., }	822	R Stino,	Mary,	980

R Stino, William,	814	R Thurston, Charles H., 1380
R Adora M.,	815	R Carrie A., 1381
Stiquel, Emma L.,	1765	R Frank W., 1402
Stone, Frank L.,	1554	R Tibbals, George L., 21
Jay S.,	727	Timbrell, Ann S., 837
R Anna E.,	728	R Tomlinson, Charlotte A., 586
Rebecca D.,	1219	Towers, Lucy A., 1835
Lizzie J.,	1156	R Towle, Thomas D., 716
Mabel W.,	1825	R Annie S., 717
Mary W.,	1732	R Townsend, Julia C., 517
R Timothy D. P.,	263	Traut, Elise M., 1656
R Phebe,	264	Tuck, Alice C., 817
William S.,	1334	R J. Warren, 724
R Story, Frank,	1489	R Phronia N., 725
Stoughton, John W.,	1238	Marie L., 1168
Sarah B.,	1239	R Tuller, Jannette E., 1210
Stratton, Fannie A.,	1585	Tuthill, Minnie G., 1787
R Strickland, George W.,	149	R Tyler, George L., 1169
R Jane B.,	142	R Ann O., 456
R Henry C.,	528	
R Mary E.,	529	R Unwin, George, 985
R Strong, Anna E.,	1251	R Joseph, 987
Seymour,	1249	R Upson, Marietta C., 292
R Ellen W.,	1250	R Russell, 161
R Strout, Harriet A.,	848	R Adeline T., 162
Styles, Lydia A.,	1487	R Samuel, 163
R Sugden, Ellen F.,	1240	R Theron, 358, 407
Sunburn, Augusta S.,	1647	
R Sutherland, Mary M.,	840	Vensel, Christina S., 1666
Swasey, Hope S.,	1477	Vile, Fannie G., 1307
R Sweet, Dennis,	9	Vining, Florence M., 1759
Caroline U.,	75	Lena W., 1768
R Sweetland, Sarah H.,	205	R Vishno, Charles, 623
		R Delina O., 624
Talcott, Caroline T.,	598, 1267	
R Charles T.,	250	Waddell, Daniel N., 1849
R Jerusha G.,	251	Margaret M., 1850
R Ellen J.,	898	R George D., 1203
George S.,	1404	Wagner, Ernestine J., 1851
John B.,	305	Mary B., 1764
R Jane C.,	306	William G., 1752
Fannie H.,	1246	Wainwright, Jane S., 1355
R John C.,	897	R Waldo, Horatio, 157
Tatem, Joseph,	970	Walton, Jane E., 1880
R Taylor, Charles,	803	Emma A., 1881
R Frances A.,	804	R Ward, Alexander M., 342
Jane G.,	886	R Louisa B., 62
R Virgil C.,	150	R Laura A., 378
R Thomas, Sarah R.,	566	R John, 1170
Thompson, Anna S.,	1162	R Warner, Charles A., 24
R James H.,	1449	R Matilda C., 102
R Alida I.,	1450	Clara E., 1551
Thomson, Mary L.,	753	R Edmund, 41
R Thorpe, Virginia E.,	602	R Elizabeth W., 42
Thrall, Lena W.,	1089	R Warren, Almira W., 103

THE SOUTH CHURCH. 115

R	Warren, Catharine L.,	448		Whiting, Mary,	649
R	Herbert W.,	734		W. Howard,	1172
R	Maria A.,	615		Wiard, Albert L., ⟩	501
R	Mortimer A.,	335		Ella A., ⟨	712
	Waterman, Frank N., ⟩	1333		Bertha L.,	1587
	Anna L., ⟨	1293		Grace L.,	1588
	Martha T.,	1586		John, ⟩	458
	Watkins, Walter,	1874		Jennette R., ⟨	459
	Watts, William J., ⟩	1870		John B.,	1773
	Catherine E., ⟨	1871		Martin S., ⟩	469
R	Webster, Charles,	966		Louisa F., ⟨	630
	John, ⟩	1500		Oliver N.,	1826
	Lydia F., ⟨	1501		Wiegand, Amelia S.,	1760
	Welles, Chauncey W., ⟩	821		Wilbor, Thomas W., ⟩	1279
	Anna A., ⟨	822		Grace S., ⟨	1440
	Elizabeth W.,	1337		Wilhelmy, George, ⟩	1180
	Frank N., ⟩	1431	R	Mary M., ⟨	1181
R	Fannie C., ⟨	1432		Leonard, ⟩	609
	Mary L.,	1325		Catharine B., ⟨	610
	Wells, Levi W., ⟩	276		Willard, Mary L.,	1549
	Adeline H., ⟨	389		Williams, Bessie,	1589
	Wesche, Amelia G.,	1414		Cornelia R.,	830
	Wessell, Clara G.,	1555	R	Ellen R.,	913
	Frederick, ⟩	1173		Margaret N.,	1590
	Mary F., ⟨	537	R	Mary E.,	1135
	Howard H.,	1772	R	Robert G., ⟩	29
R	Westover, Elizabeth B.,	216	R	Amelia S., ⟨	57
.	Wetmore, Charles E., ⟩	1299	R	William C.,	⟩ 731
	Estelle S., ⟨	1030	R	Geraldine V. S., ⟨ 732	
R	Marietta H.,	261	R	Wilson, Henry, ⟩	1177
	Wetzel, Emma G.,	1413	R	Jessie M., ⟨	594
R	Whaples, Curtis, ⟩	36		Margaret M.,	593
	Elizabeth C., ⟨	136	R	Winchell, Lucy H.,	114
	Isabella E.,	546		Winger, Amelia,	1222
	Meigs H.,	545		Lizzie A.,	1607
R	Wheeler, Emeline H.,	981	R	Winston, Jane E.,	478
.	Henry J., ⟩	1002	R	Winton, Frederick D.,	468
	Mary E., ⟨	1178	R	Wise, James H., ⟩	878
	Herbert H.,	1474	R	Lucy M., ⟨	879
R	Jennie E.,	982	R	Wolcott, Lizzie D.,	1409
	Jennie R.,	1672	R	Wolfe, August,	1442
R	William, ⟩	399		Lottie W.,	1635
R	Sarah J., ⟨	400, 1215		Wood, Frederick B.,	1591
	White, Elizabeth H.,	1218		Henry N.,	1592
	Emily S.,	698		Spencer H., ⟩	827, 1184
	John, ⟩	1463		Melissa B., ⟨	828, 1185
	Mary A., ⟨	1464	R	Woodruff, Alma,	88
	John L.,	1599		Arthur L.,	1174
	Rosa M.,	1557	R	Eliza B.,	1000
	Whited, Willis, ⟩	1872	R	Franklin, ⟩ 144, 929	
	Lizzie C., ⟨	1873	R	Elizab'h A., ⟨	930
	Whiten, Sarah A.,	423	R	Lucius, ⟩	246
	Whiting, Amelia T.,	951	R	Harriet L., ⟨	247
	Estelle A.,	1171		Mary L.,	770
	Henry W., ⟩	123	R	Norman. ⟩	6
. R	Sarah K., ⟨	111	R	Abigail B., ⟨	78

R	Woodruff, Sarah B.,	204, 677	R Yetter, Casper, ⎱		1608
	Sarah T.,	421	Eva M., ⎰		1609
R	Simeon,	479	Lena,		1558
R	Wealthy A.,	411	Young, Annie,		1648
	Woods, Margaret H.,	1179	Annie C.,		1852
R	Mary A.,	1008	Carl F.,		1774
R	Woodworth, Amy A.,	404	Elizabeth,		1182
	Elizabeth R.,	470	Jacob, Jr.,		1183
R	Wright, Dorothy H.,	165			
R	Henry, ⎱	253	Zimmerman, Charles F., ⎱		798
R	Sarah L., ⎰	254	Bertha F., ⎰		1593
R	Hercelia A.,	256	Margaret B.,		1462
R	Laura C.,	1259	Zwick, Anna,		1594
R	Lucy,	117	Emma,		1649
	Olive B.,	119	Philip,		1705

SUMMARY.

Withdrew from First Congregational Church in New Britain to constitute this Church,		120
Admitted on confession of their faith,		1,073
Admitted by letters from other churches,		692
Restored,		4
Total names on Register,		1,889
Deceased,	325	
Dismissed to other churches,	574	
† Removed by discipline,	85 —	984
Membership January 1, 1893,		905

† Under this head are included all whose names have been dropped from the roll on account of long absence or residence unknown.

1842—1892

Semi-Centennial Celebration.

REPORT OF SERVICES

COMMEMORATING THE

SEMI-CENTENNIAL OF THE CHURCH,

AS HELD

SUNDAY AND MONDAY, November 27 and 28, 1892.

SEMI-CENTENNIAL SERVICES.

At a church meeting held April 15, 1892, the Standing Committee made a report to the church, recommending that the church should publish a memorial volume embracing a complete history of the church during the fifty years since its organization and including a church manual. The committee also suggested, as a further commemoration of the semi-centennial of the church, that a day be selected some time in the next autumn, upon which exercises appropriate to the occasion should be held.

On motion of Deacon David N. Camp, it was voted to publish the memorial volume and hold the commemorative services, as recommended by the committee. On motion of Rev. Charles E. Steele, it was voted that the Standing Committee shall have charge of, and make arrangements for these commemorative services, including the publishing of the memorial volume.

The days selected for the semi-centennial services were November 27th and 28th; the Sunday and Monday following Thanksgiving. A large committee of arrangements was appointed from among the ladies and gentlemen of the church and congregation, and the work of preparation divided among them. Invitations were sent to friends of the church and former and absent members. Entertainment was provided for visiting friends and for an anniversary social reunion. The church was elaborately decorated in green and gold, and an interesting collection of portraits and mementoes of former days was exhibited.

The programme of exercises for the two days was as follows:

SUNDAY MORNING.

ORGAN MEDITATION.
SENTENCES AND RESPONSES.
DOXOLOGY — "Praise God from whom all blessings flow."
INVOCATION AND LORD'S PRAYER.
TE DEUM LAUDAMUS.
SCRIPTURE LESSON AND RESPONSES.
PRAYERS.
HYMN — "Glorious things of thee are spoken."
OFFERINGS.
CHOIR HYMN — "Denmark," "Before Jehovah's awful throne."
SERMON BY THE PASTOR — Text, Romans 11: 18.
PRAYER.
HYMN — "I love thy Kingdom, Lord."
BENEDICTION.

SUNDAY-SCHOOL.

JUBILATE DEO.
PRAYER.
HYMN — "O God of Bethel, by whose hand."
PAPERS —
    Facts and Figures for Fifty Years,   *John Wiard.*
    Old Days and Former Leaders,   *Charles Peck.*
    Our Primary Department,   *Mrs. Charles Peck.*
HYMN — "Onward, Christian soldiers."
PAPERS —
    Our Teachers,   *John H. Peck.*
    The Sunday-School Library,   *Miss Alice C. Tuck.*
    The Church in the School,   *Edwin B. Lyon.*
HYMN — "I love to tell the story."
BENEDICTION.

SUNDAY EVENING.

ORGAN PRELUDE.
THE MAGNIFICAT.
SENTENCES, RESPONSES, AND PRAYER.
HYMN — "Let saints below in concert sing."

ADDRESSES —
    The Organization, Life, and Growth of the Church,
                                                   David N. Camp.
    Financial Statements and their Lessons,
                    E. N. Stanley, W. H. Hart, J. B. Talcott.
CHOIR HYMN — "Jerusalem, my glorious home."
ADDRESSES —
    The Service of Song, ... *John P. Bartlett.*
    Woman's Work in the Church, . . . *John N. Bartlett.*
    The Young People and the Future, . *Rev. Charles E. Steele.*
HYMN — "How firm a foundation."
BENEDICTION.

MONDAY AFTERNOON.

CHOIR HYMN — "Come, my beloved, haste away."
SCRIPTURE LESSON AND PRAYER.
HYMN — "The church's one foundation."
ADDRESSES —
    The Mother Church, . . *Rev. G. H. Sandwell.*
    The Sister Churches, . *Rev. I. F. Stidham, Ph.D.*
SOLO — "Come unto Me."
ADDRESSES —
    Co-Workers of Former Days,   *Rev. D. M. Seward, D.D.*
                                                 Mrs. C. L. Goodell.
                                                      C. L. Mead.
ANTHEM — "Strike the Cymbals."
ADDRESS — "Our Friends." . . . *Rev. A. W. Hazen, D.D.*
HYMN — "Blest be the tie that binds."
BENEDICTION.

MONDAY EVENING.

ANNIVERSARY SOCIAL REUNION IN THE PARISH CHAPEL.
SUPPER, served from 5 to 8 o'clock.
CLOSING EXERCISES, from 8 to 10 o'clock; consisting of music and song, informal addresses, original poems, and letters from absent friends.

All these services were conducted by the pastor.

The service of song was under the direction of Mr. Richmond P. Paine, organist and choir master, with a quartet and chorus choir.

SUNDAY MORNING SERMON.

By the Pastor, Rev. James W. Cooper, D.D.

But if thou boast, thou bearest not the root, but the root thee. — *Romans* xi., 18.

The church of Christ is an organism. Its successive generations are not separate links welded together in a chain; they are new branches put forth by a growing tree. The kingdom of God is a kingdom of life. The originating and directive force in the Christian church is a principle of life, which shapes its character and gives it productive power. This life principle is the indwelling Spirit of the risen Christ.

Whenever a company of Christian believers are drawn together by the Holy Spirit and united in a church fellowship, the result is more than an aggregation of individuals; it is the creation of a new unity. An organization has come into being which has a separate individuality and corporate life, with qualities and powers all its own. Henceforth it exists in its own character, to develop its own personality, and fulfill its peculiar mission in the world.

The first appeal of Christianity is, indeed, to individual men. One by one human hearts are converted to God and baptized by His Spirit. Souls must be regenerated, before a Church can be formed. But when these believing souls are united in a covenant of grace and fused together by the fire of their common faith, then we have the genuine and living unity of a Christian church — a church which draws into itself the qualities of all its members, but which, as a whole, is different from any one of them — a living, worshiping, working church, which is more permanent, more wise, more efficient in its corporate life, than any or all of those who compose it, in their separate lives.

Fifty years ago, this South Congregational Church, into which so many of us here present have put ourselves, was first brought into being. Its history covers less than two generations. There are those still with us who had a part in its organization. The honored and beloved Mother Church, from whom we came, continues by our side in intimate and loving fellowship — first in the dignity of years, strong in faith, vigorous in service. Other sister churches are around us, with some of whom we have been long allied in delightful Christian intercourse. All these churches have existed for a common purpose. We have stood in this community for the common faith. We have preached the same gospel, and have been led by the same Spirit. But, as members of a family have their separate identity and peculiar characteristics, so it has been here. Our church has a character of its own, and it has lived long enough to have a personal history.

The Spirit of God works out results in this world, on the basis of our humanity. The divine and human are inextricably mingled. The laws of heredity and environment are operated upon by spiritual forces. We are not, therefore, to make this anniversary, in any sense, an occasion for boasting. Self-glorification at such a time as this would be as irreverent as it would be unseemly. But we may, with profound gratitude, acknowledge our indebtedness to those who have lived before us — recount their toils and sacrifices, their sagacity, patience, faith, and courage — while we recognize the good hand of the Lord which has led us as a church through this half a century.

Few churches have, in so brief a period, undergone a more complete change in membership. The personnel of the church is not at all now what it was at its organization. Of the 1,879 names which have been upon our register, 895 remain in our fellowship to day. Of this 895 only nine were charter members, and only sixty-three are the descendants of charter members; 823 of those now in the Church came into it from without. Our human bodies are continually passing through processes of waste and reparation whereby their constituent parts are changed, but a man of fifty has scarcely undergone a more thorough transformation in his various members than have we.

And yet we are the same Church that began its life in 1842. We have grown; there have been added to our number of such as are being saved; new experiences have come to us; new surroundings are about us; new work has been given us to do. But the conditions which shaped the character of the church at the beginning, the spirit and purpose of the men and women who formed it, have influenced us to the present hour. As "the child is the father of the man," so the original body of disciples who founded this church gave permanent direction to its life. And whether we, who are here to-day, have grown up with the church, or have, as the apostle says, been "graffed in" upon it, we have all alike entered into the original inheritance, and are together sharers in the inspirations of the past. "Thou bearest not the root, but the root thee!"

The soil out of which this root developed gave promise of a vigorous growth.

New Britain had not, at that time, attained to the dignity of a separate town government. It was a part of Berlin; a retired and rather out-of-the-way place, just passing from the quiet of a country parish into the condition of a stirring manufacturing village. Its population did not number as many hundreds then as it does thousands now.

But it was a God-fearing and church-going community. The old "North Church," as it was called, had stood for nearly a century, presided over for more than half that time by one of the ablest and most energetic of the old New England divines. "All business arrangements were shaped to favor the moral and religious welfare of the place." Young men of promise were encouraged, by the gift of land and by financial assistance, to come and assist in the development of its industries. Workmen were urged and expected to attend public worship, "and those loose and demoralizing habits which too often characterize manufacturing towns were openly discouraged."

It was a homogeneous community. Almost without exception the inhabitants were of New England stock, and dwelt together in the good old-fashioned way of simple and hearty neighborliness — finding no place for those marked social divisions which the inequalities of our modern life have since developed. Employer and laboring man toiled together at the same work. There was a community of interests, a common acquaintance, a simplicity of life, which have been swept away by the complex conditions of a prosperous and advancing age.

It is sometimes questioned whether the old days were not, in some particulars at least, better than these in which we live. Life is fuller now than it was then — fuller of conveniences, of luxuries, of engagements, pleasures, religious activities, and perhaps also of benevolences. "But," as Bishop Potter has recently suggested, "whether life is really fuller, in the sense that it is richer and more worthily intelligent and more generally aspiring, is a very different question." Our possessions are greater, our resources are more varied, our numbers have increased, the range of our living has been immeasurably widened, and we spread ourselves over a vaster field; but we may still learn from the past, lessons of virtue and equity, of righteousness and purity, both in private and in public life, and pause to ask ourselves whether, with our larger experience and greater wealth and wider influence, we have made a corresponding advance in the nobility of our aims and the sincerity of our devotions.

And, moreover, we shall make a great mistake if we suppose that the life of fifty years ago was uneventful and monotonous. On the contrary, there has been no decade in the present century so prolific in influences affecting the social conditions of our national life as the decade immediately preceding the organization of this Church. It was a generative and an originating period — a period pregnant with new ideas, fruitful in new enterprises, excited, restless, ambitious, effervescing — a kind of hot-bed period, when the germs of a new social order were energetically nourished and forced forward into rapid expansion.

Our political institutions had, by that time, become well established. Our struggle for independence and recognition among the nations of the earth had come to a successful issue. We had won the respect of the world. It was natural, therefore, that attention should be given to domestic affairs and to the development of our internal life. The thought of the people turned upon themselves, and the spirit of the times was that of enterprise and self-improvement.

The introduction of steam power and new inventions in machinery was just then beginning to revolutionize the industries of the land. Railroads were being started. The road from Hartford to New Haven was finished in 1839, but was not extended to New York until 1848. The locomotive whistle was heard for the first time in this village in 1850. No telegraph line existed till 1844; and none for us till several years after that. The influence of these marvelous discoveries and inventions has been often discoursed upon, and cannot well be exaggerated.

But before this material progress was inaugurated, the people were being profoundly moved by important intellectual, moral, and religious questions. Great subjects were agitated. The great modern reforms were looming up majestically on the horizon. The attention of every one was drawn to them. The minds of the most serious were busy with them. The problems were vital and pressing. Men had conflicting opinions concerning them. Families, churches, towns, and the nation itself, were divided, over the methods proposed for their solution.

These agitations were commenced and followed up, with most intense earnestness and devoted zeal, during the few years immediately preceding the birth of this church.

Take the matter of popular education. The two names most highly honored in connection with the development of the common school system of New England are Horace Mann and Henry Barnard. Mr. Mann began his work in 1837; Dr. Barnard, in 1838. Educational reforms were not really adopted in those days, and the controversy was warm. But the men of New Britain were awake to the situation. As early as 1832 they began the formation of new school districts and the building of new schoolhouses, and in 1839 they had subscribed $4,000 to found a training school for teachers, one of the earliest movements of the kind in America, which finally resulted in the establishment of our State Normal School in 1850.

This was also the inaugural period of public lectures, libraries, and lyceums. The "New Britain Lyceum" was started in 1836, and was afterwards succeeded by the "New Britain Institute." In 1841, our distinguished fellow citizen, Elihu Burritt, made his first appearance as a lecturer, presenting the characteristic subject, "Application and Genius," and emphasizing the possibilities of self-culture and the need of it.

These may also be called the birth years of our American literature. Whittier's first volume was issued in 1831, Longfellow's in '33, Bancroft's in '34, Emerson's in '36, Holmes's, Hawthorne's, and Prescott's in '37, Motley's in '39, Lowell's in '41. The first cheap newspaper, the New York *Sun*, was issued is 1833, the New York *Herald* in 1834, and Horace Greeley's *Tribune* in 1841.

The most absorbing and distracting of all the great moral reforms was that which resulted twenty years later in the abolition of human slavery. Garrison began the publication of the "Liberator," in 1831. The first national "Anti-Slavery Convention" was held in '33. The mobs in Philadelphia and Boston occurred in '35. Lovejoy was murdered in '37; and the matchless eloquence of Wendell Phillips was then for the first time heard in Faneuil Hall.

The temperance reformation rose to the importance of a national movement during these same years. Societies were formed; speeches made; the total abstinence pledge was discussed with an interest excited by its novelty, and only after long and serious debate was it finally adopted as the basis of the reform. The first national temperance convention met in 1833. Dr. Cheever went to jail for writing his irritating tract, on "Deacon Giles's Distillery," in 1835. The phenomenal Washingtonian movement, — the first concerted effort for reclaiming drunkards, — was organized in 1841.

Those were, indeed, exciting times. Is it any wonder that the blood was not always cool, nor the head always clear? In that first shock of the great social onset, can we be surprised that there were exhibitions of extravagance and fanaticism, that indignation against wrong rose at times into wholesale denunciation, that men were not always wise, nor their tempers serene? Even good men found it difficult to agree. Society was in a ferment. Great issues were at stake. Conscience was at work. Men had convictions in those days; and they acted upon them, fearlessly and decisively.

There were also religious agitations. The Unitarian controversy had originated in the previous generation, but the battle still went on, and moved forward to new positions. Emerson withdrew from the Unitarian church in 1832. The "Transcendental Club" was formed in Boston in 1837. Theodore Parker began his ministry in Roxbury in 1837. George Ripley started the "Brook Farm" experiment in 1841. The "Book of Mormon" was published to the world in 1830, and in 1842 Joseph Smith was at the height of his prosperity. Mormon missionaries ranged through our Connecticut towns. Wilford Woodruff, the present president of the Mormon Church, left his home in Farmington and was ordained to the priesthood in 1833.

Doubtless these things did not greatly move the fathers of this church. They were too well grounded in the faith for that. But there were old and new schools in theology, then as now. Dr. Taylor of New Haven was teaching a modified form of Calvinism, and Dr. Tyler of East Windsor was defending the traditional faith, and Taylorism and Tylerism were the theme of anxious and eager discussions in all our Connecticut churches.

It was out of this animated and prolific soil that this church sprang into life. It had its birth in the midst of these varied, conflicting, and exciting interests. It was the child of religious devotion and zealous faith, the product of profound intellectual and moral convictions.

The newly-awakened spirit of enterprise entered into it. Its founders were gifted with a kind of prophetic foresight. They believed in the future. They had hope and aspiration, and the courage of men with a good conscience. They were ready to undertake a new and difficult work. They were generous men. They had faith in God. Religion was to them a supreme matter; their own personal hopes were centered in it, and they believed that apart from it nothing could insure the advancement of society and the solid prosperity of the community where they lived.

Their attitude toward the great questions of the day was that of progressive conservatism. They were not radicals; they were moderate men. But their faces were toward the sun-rising; their hearts were open to divine influences, and their hands were trained to a ready and willing obedience.

So it came to pass that when the time seemed ripe for the institution of a new church of Jesus Christ in this then southern portion of the town, they first purchased the land, built and paid for a house of worship, and then they were organized into a church;—and "the number of names together were about an hundred and twenty."

I should be glad, if I were able, to give you a realistic picture of that little company — both for the sake of the pardonable interest we may be expected to have in it, and also as an illustration of a substantial and worthy family church of two generations ago. All ages were there, from the youth of seventeen and the little girl just entering her teens to the grave and venerable man of more than fourscore. All classes were there — so far as there were classes in that equal social state of fifty years ago — the rich and poor, the wise and simple, the strong and weak, together.

Let us venture to take the first seven names that appear upon the church list, and say of each a single word. I am only sorry that no woman appears among them.

At the head of the roll stands most fittingly the name of Deacon Elijah Francis. He was a venerable man, with an interesting history. Born in New Britain in 1760, he did not become a Christian until he was fifty-seven years old, when he joined the church under Dr. Smalley — "a remarkable instance of the renewing and regenerating grace of God." He had been a deacon in the First Church for more than a score of years, and was eighty-two years of age when this church was formed. He had served as a soldier in the revolutionary war; had been a frequent representative in the legislature; was a man of great sobriety of character; seldom spoke in the meetings of the church; but is remembered to this day by some here present for his remarkable gift in prayer.

The second name is that of good Deacon Cornwell. He was a much younger man than his associate, though for several years he had served in the diaconate of the old church. Deacon Cornwell was a manufacturer, and one of those constant, faithful, Christian men who gave substantial weight and character to our old New England churches.

Then comes the name of Seth J. North. Major North has often been called the "founder of New Britain." He was the leading business man of the town, a man of wealth and influence, a man of large and comprehensive views, public-spirited, generous, efficient, no less interested in the educational, moral, and religious advancement of the community than in its business affairs — the leader of the new church enterprise.

Alvin North comes next, and Henry North follows close after. These three were brothers, all over fifty years of age — strong, substantial, earnest men. Alvin North was a positive man, clear-headed, tenacious, and generous withal — the man with a conscience. He was the theologian of the company, a well-read man, and a Bible Christian. It was his custom to read the Bible through, in course, three times every year!

Henry North is spoken of by Deacon Andrews as "the man without an enemy." Mr. Rockwell describes him as "an Israelite, indeed, in whom there is no guile." He was a man of the most scrupulous integrity, and the spirit of kindness and good will added the grace of a beneficent life.

Dr. Samuel Hart was the beloved physician of the village. From his youth up he had been a Christian, and now at fifty-six, in the full maturity of a well-rounded character, he was at the height of his influence in the community and in the church. Intelligent, skillful, sympathetic, and faithful in his profession and in every duty, a man of deeds rather than of words, he was respected and trusted by all.

Norman Woodruff's is the seventh name — a plain and unassuming business man, serious, scrupulously honest, intelligent, and generous.

So I might go on if there were time; but these seven must suffice, as indicating something of the composition and character of that original South Church — forty men and eighty women — which has given direction and force to our history for the past fifty years. This history it is not my purpose to rehearse. That will be done by brethren of the church in the other services of the day.

From that vigorous beginning, which was sanctified by prayer and offerings, and sealed with the Holy Spirit's blessing, the great Head of the Church has maintained us in life until this present. The fathers have all passed away. Not a man remains of the original forty. But through the unanticipated growth of our city the church has been increased, and its field of work has been enlarged, until the fondest hopes of its founders must have been more than realized.

That the church has been thus able, in some measure, to perpetuate the spirit of the fathers, and to meet the new emergencies which have arisen, we give thanks to Almighty God, through whose grace all blessings have been received.

Among these blessings I should do violence to my convictions if I neglected to refer to the three faithful and successful pastors who have followed one another here in the ministry of Jesus Christ. Their names will ever be held in remembrance with grateful praise.

It was a good providence that sent the Rev. Samuel Rockwell to this flock in 1843. Mr. Rockwell was not a magnetic man; he never strove for oratorical effect; but he was one of the truest and purest of men, and one of the most faithful and sympathetic pastors that ever served a church. He was a wise leader, a good preacher, a judicious adviser, an efficient helper in every good work. He was just the man for the time and place.

And when he laid down his office, after more than fifteen years of service, it was God's hand that brought to this spot young Constans L. Goodell, and made him to be your minister for fourteen happy, eventful, prosperous years. "The Model Pastor of Connecticut," he was called, and he was in every way worthy of the distinction. Ardent, devoted, spiritual, full of the love of God and the love of souls, how joyously he worked, and how marvelously the church was blest!

Both these grand men have entered into the triumphs of their heavenly reward. The one, as the memorial window reads, has been received "into the joy of his Lord"; the other, passing "through the gates into the city," has joined the throng that greet each other there, himself to welcome those whom he has led into the Saviour's love, and to rejoice forever in the presence of the King!

It was our exceeding great desire that the sole surviving pastor of this church, the Rev. Henry L. Griffin, might be with us to-day, to share the pleasures of this anniversary. We are glad to have messages from him, which will be read at the service to-morrow afternoon. Mr. Griffin's ministry was a short one, but it was abundantly fruitful. Two hundred and thirty-eight received to the church fellowship in four years, is the record of this eminently evangelistic pastorate. In many a regenerated home in this parish the name of the young minister will long be cherished with reverence and affection.

And now we stand upon the threshold of a new half century! Our circumstances, our work, our outlook, are all very different from what they were fifty years ago. The theological atmosphere has changed.

The old-time discussions of the "governmental theory" and "natural and moral inability," are no longer of interest to us. The famous old "New England Theology" has had its day, and fills an honored place in the history of Christian doctrine. There has been an advance out of the speculative into the biblical and spiritual conceptions of truth. The logical school has been supplanted by the intuitional school of thought. Philosophical systems have given place to biblical theologies. The attention of the church has been directed more exclusively to the Person of our Lord Jesus Christ. All those "Lives of Christ," found in our libraries and in your homes, have been written within the past fifty years. Theologic thought has become Christo-centric. And as men have concentrated their attention upon Him, they have forgotten those minor differences that separated them from one another, or have remembered them only as furnishing opportunity for tolerance and Christian charity.

The Christian world has thus been drawn together in fraternal sympathy and co-operative service. We have felt the pressure of the world's great needs. We have stimulated each other to multiplied forms of Christian activity. Our hands are full of work. The appeals of missionary enterprise are constant and clamorous. Abroad the nations wait for His law. At home the nations are at our very doors to receive the ministry of His love.

It is good to live in such a time as this! the past so full of inspiration; the present, so crowded with opportunity; the future, so rich in promise!

"Wherefore," my brethren, "seeing that we also are compassed about with so great a cloud of witnesses, let us lay aside every weight, and the sin which doth so easily beset us, and let us run with patience the race that is set before us, looking unto Jesus the author and finisher of our faith."

SUNDAY-SCHOOL SERVICE.

This service was held in the main audience room of the church immediately after the morning worship, the three departments of the Sunday-school uniting together. After the *Jubilate Deo* by the choir, prayer was offered by Deacon David N. Camp.

The following historical papers or addresses were then given in the order named:

FACTS AND FIGURES FOR FIFTY YEARS.

DEACON JOHN WIARD, *Superintendent of the School.*

When the godly company of one hundred and twenty men and women who formed this South Church fifty years ago would lay well the foundations for its future growth and spiritual success, I believe they acted wisely and under the divine guidance, when, only four days after the church was organized and before any other business was transacted, they met and instituted this Sunday-school. The entire management of the school, including the annual appointment of its officers, has continued under the control of the church to the present time.

Eleven persons have received the appointment of superintendent and have served as follows: David N. Camp, John B. Talcott, George D. Rand, and Isaac N. Carleton, each one year; Horatio Waldo and Hubert F. North, each two years; Ozias B. Bassett and Henry C. Bowers, each four years; Lucius Woodruff, five years; Orson H. Seymour, six years; John Wiard, twenty-three and one-half years. The growth of the school has been continuous, and the membership, by decades, has been as follows: 1842, 130; 1852, 175; 1862, 213; 1872, 649; 1882, 975; 1892, 1,348, including the home department.

Some years ago the question of organizing branch or mission schools was discussed by our people, but inasmuch as our parish territory is not large, it was decided better to concentrate our efforts upon one time and place, and unite all classes and ages in one organization and under one roof. No questionable means or devices have ever been adopted to increase our membership. Other and much more satisfactory reasons can be given for the results attained, some of which I will mention and others will be referred to by those who follow me.

All four of the pastors who have served the church have been thoroughly interested and efficient helpers in our work. May 9, 1869, a class was formed of our most prominent men, with Rev. Samuel Rockwell, who had been our first pastor, as teacher. There were present the first Sunday, eighteen persons, including such men as C. B. Erwin, Philip Corbin, F. T. Stanley, William H. Smith, Horace H. Brown, Henry W. Whiting, Horace Butler, A. P. Collins, T. A. Conklin, Gilman Hinsdale, Levi O. Smith, and other leading business men. Thirty identified themselves with the class during the year. Of these, twenty-three, including the teacher, have already passed away. Mr. Rockwell resigned his position on account of his health in 1870, and was followed successively by A. P. Meylert, John B. Talcott, Philip Corbin, and John N. Bartlett. The last named has led the class for the past fifteen years.

Our present pastor, Rev. Dr. Cooper, has now, for nearly fifteen years, been exceedingly helpful to the school in all practical ways, at times leading our teachers in weekly preparation for teaching the lessons, and for thirteen years past conducting a large class of prominent young business men.

In regard to our list of teachers, I am sure no one will question the statement that all through our history a very large proportion of the most devoted Christian activity as well as the best educational talent in the church, has been enlisted in the instruction of our people, young and old, in God's word. My yearly records for the last twenty-four years include the names of nearly 350 members of the church who have served for a longer or shorter time in this capacity. This list in April, 1868, when I became superintendent, was thirty; of whom eleven have died, twelve have left town, and five are now teaching, though only two have taught continuously since that time, viz.: David N. Camp and John H. Peck. The present number of teachers is ninety-three. We have had from forty to sixty per cent. of the resident members of our church connected with the school for the past twenty-four years at least. In the early years of our history comparatively few adults were in the school as learners; but our theory for a long time has been, no limitations of age for the reception of members and no graduating point encouraged for the retirement of any who are able to reach the house of God.

The ages of those now members of the school range from three to eighty-seven years. It is indeed delightful to know that our revered mother, Mrs. O. B. Bassett, who for nearly seventy-five years has been in the line of Bible study in this and the Sunday-school of her youth, is still able to be frequently present with us, while among her six great-grandchildren, little Marjory Hart, only four years old, may be found in the primary department taking her first Sunday-school lessons from God's word.

I cannot report the aggregate amount of contributions in the school for the whole fifty years, but for the last twenty-four years they have been as follows:

For benevolence,	$9,058.25
For supplies, quarterlies, etc., since 1882,	881.04
For new chapel expenses since 1888,	833.20
Total,	$10,772.49

I wish I could tell you, in conclusion, just how many of the 1,068 persons who have been added by confession of faith to the original 120 members of our church during the fifty years were received from this institution. It certainly is a very large proportion. I can say, however, that since my appointment as superintendent in 1868, nearly twenty-five years ago, not a year has passed but that some from the school have publicly confessed Christ. The number thus received to the church was in 1869, 48; in 1872, 43; in 1876, 38; in 1877, 75; in 1886, 93; in 1892, 58. And altogether during the last twenty-five years more than 600 have been received, making an average of twenty-four for each year. For which, and for the many other evidences of the divine approval manifested in all our history, let us be devoutly grateful as we review the past to-day.

OLD DAYS AND FORMER LEADERS.

Deacon Charles Peck, *Superintendent of Senior Department.*

I am asked to speak of the "Old Days and the Former Leaders," I suppose, because I am a young man; or, to put it in another form, because those who made up the active working element of the Church and Sunday-school in those early days are not here to speak for themselves. Out of the original one hundred and twenty, not one of the male members is here to-day.

Our Sunday-school sessions were in those days held in the basement of the old church, at the close of the morning worship. The old church stood a little east of the present edifice. An inner stairway led from the front vestibule to the hall below. At the easterly end of this hall there was a door from the outside, so that persons could enter direct, and it was the practice of the small boys to make a rush at the close of service, going down the front steps and entering by this side door. From the hall we passed through a central doorway upon a platform, and then down a few steps to the level of the well-sanded floor of the Sunday-school room. The walls being partially below ground, made the room damp and chilly in summer, and in winter it was smoky, owing to a defective draught; while for seats, we had hard uncomfortable settees. But in spite of these discomforts there was good cheer and a general unanimity of interest to promote the common welfare of the school. I recall those sessions with pleasure. A small room in the southeast corner was partitioned off for a prayer-meeting room and in later years was used for the infant department. The corresponding room on the opposite side was used for the ladies' sewing room, leaving a space for the entire Sunday-school about half the size of that now occupied by our junior department.

Listen as I recall the names of some of those who were active workers in the Sunday-school fifty years ago, as nearly as I can remember them. Horatio Waldo, superintendent; Deacon Chauncey Cornwell, assistant superintendent; R. G. Williams and Charles M. Lewis, librarians; teachers, Prof. E. A. Andrews, Alvin North, Horace Butler, O. B. Bassett, Francis Hart, Wm. H. Smith, H. F. North, Henry Stanley, Dr. Samuel Hart, Josiah Dewey, Mrs. Samuel Rockwell, Mrs. Dr. Samuel Hart, Mrs. Chester Hart, Mrs. Wm. H. Smith, Mrs. Gilman Hinsdale, Mrs. Horace H. Brown, Mrs. G. M. Landers, Mrs. C. B. Erwin, Mrs. Mary C. Emerson, Mrs. F. T. Stanley, Mrs. C. A. Warner, Miss Elizabeth Smith, Mrs. Sarah North Brace, Mrs. Levi W. Hart, and Miss Lucy Wright.

The sessions were called to order by a bell, followed by singing, reading of the Scriptures, and prayer. Plenty of time was always given to the strangers present to talk to the school, and about an hour was allowed for the entire session, as the afternoon service began at half past one or two o'clock.

On the right of the platform, Mr. Horace Butler had a class of young men, among whom I remember the names of Wm. S. Booth, Philip Corbin, Henry F. Peck, Hubert North, Frank Corbin, Thomas Smith, Sherman Steele, Edward Doen, Charles W. Whaples, H. C. Bowers, Lester P. Buell, and John E. Woodruff. An interesting class of girls also came from the mother church, Louisa Hart, Julia A. North, Caroline North, Cordelia Smith, Clara North, Julia Cornwell, Eliza Seymour, Julia Belknap, and others.

We had no book of song as now, but sang the words from our regular church hymn book. For some time we had no instrument to lead our music, but later a new interest was given to the singing by Virgil C. Taylor, who opened a singing school, at which the scholars were thoroughly instructed in the rudiments of music.

We had no uniform system of lesson-study at that time. The international system of lessons had not been born. The younger classes generally used a question book. I recall the "Topical Question Book" as one, also "Questions on the Miracles and Parables of Christ and the Acts of the Apostles." The older classes studied the book of Romans. The scholars were expected to answer the questions from memory and to recite the Bible references as far as possible. I think the lessons were generally studied faithfully by the scholars, many of whom later became efficient teachers in the school. Sunday-school concerts of prayer, for the growth and success of the school, were held monthly. Later our pastor, the Rev. Samuel Rockwell, introduced a new feature, making it the occasion for diffusing missionary intelligence. We had maps showing us the field, with the dark spots where heathenism prevailed. In this and other ways he sought to cultivate a missionary spirit, and thus prepared the way for us to become interested in the monthly missionary concert. There were no young people's meetings in those days, and the Christian Endeavor Society was a thing undreamed of.

Of the old leaders who have passed away I have only time to refer to a few, beginning with the first superintendent, Horatio Waldo. He will be remembered by many as the teacher of a select school in the old academy building near the site of the present Burritt school. He was a man of liberal education and an earnest Christian. Deacon Cornwell was a warm-hearted Christian and did much to uphold the prayer-meetings of the church at a time when there were but few to bear an active part. Ozias B. Bassett was superintendent four years, followed by Deacon Orson H. Seymour, who will be remembered pleasantly by the young men, in whom he always manifested a hearty interest. Lucius Woodruff was superintendent of the Sunday-school from 1858 until 1861 and was always its ardent supporter and friend. He did much to promote the growth and efficiency of the school, bringing to it good business tact and ability. His gift of the fund for the library will ever serve to keep his name in remembrance. Alvin North was an interested worker in the church and Sunday-school from the date of its organization. He was for many years chairman of the standing committee, a man of sterling integrity and great influence in the community. He had great love for the Bible and was exceedingly pat in quoting passages of Scripture on every occasion. It used to be a marvel to me how he could retain so much in his memory, and I always looked up to him with great awe and respect. I must not fail to speak also of Horace Butler, who taught the large class of young men referred to, and held them for many years. His fervent prayer that the "young men might be led to ponder the path of their feet and choose the path of wisdom, which in mercy grant," will not be forgotten.

Of the lady teachers, mention should be made of Mrs. Orpha Hart, who successfuly led a class of elderly ladies, many of them older than herself. Her influence here, as well as in the mothers' meetings, still abides with us as a sweet and precious perfume. Her saintly face, and that of Mrs. Chester Hart who taught a class of young ladies, will be remembered with gratitude.

Before closing let me refer briefly to Mrs. C. B. Erwin and Mrs. G. M. Landers, whose work and labors of love in the church and kindly deeds of charity in the community will ever live in our memory. If I were to express my feelings in regard to these workers in one word I should say, they were faithful, and as such I believe they have received the reward of those to whom it was said by our Saviour, "Well done, thou good and faithful servant: thou hast been faithful over a few things, I will make thee ruler over many things: enter thou into the joy of thy Lord."

THE PRIMARY CLASS.

Mrs. Charles Peck, *Superintendent of Primary Department.*

The primary class connected with this Sunday-school was first formed about 1858 by Miss Mary Bassett, now Mrs. Mumford, of Philadelphia.

In response to a letter, asking for information concerning those early days, Mrs. Mumford writes: "The infant class was organized and held its sessions, as long as I was connected with it, in a forlorn little room in the southwest corner of the basement of the old South church. I remember quite well a number of little German faces in that first group, but recall the name of only one, Willie Siering, — this because he was a restless little fellow, I suppose. Poor little things! I am afraid they did not learn much from their inexperienced and irresponsible teacher, and their surroundings could not suggest much of earthly or heavenly comfort. We taught them Bible verses and hymns, and gave them attendance tickets and picture cards; and I have no doubt they were very glad when it was all over and they were allowed to go home. The kindergarten light had not dawned upon us then, and the new South church, with all its lovely incentives, was but a dream." Some of Mrs. Mumford's pupils still retain pleasant memories of her sunny face and kindly ways, and did not find the sessions as tedious as she represents.

Soon after, Mrs. Frederick North became the teacher, the class numbering about twenty. Mrs. North was eminently fitted for this work, her personal charms and winsome manners making her most attractive to the little folks under her charge. Every Christmas she invited the children to her own beautiful home, beginning with a party of twenty-two and increasing each year, till even her spacious parlors could not accommodate her guests, and she was obliged to hold her Christmas gatherings in the chapel. In Deacon Wiard's report, at the semi-centennial of the "Sunday-school Union," he says of her: "By her great love for children, her tender sympathy with the poor and neglected, her abundant ministries to their physical as well as spiritual necessities, large numbers were drawn under an influence of refinement and spiritual culture, and the results can never be measured, save in the light of eternity." Our distinguished townsman, Elihu Burritt, in recognition of Mrs. North's work for the young, dedicates to her his little book, "The Children of the Bible," in these words: "To Mrs. Frederick H. North, who first suggested its character and object, this little book, the first published in New Britain, is inscribed by the compiler, in the most sincere appreciation of her generous devotion to the religious instruction of the young as the principal of the largest infant Sunday-school in the town." By reason of impaired health Mrs. North was compelled, though with great reluctance, to relinquish her trust in 1872, leaving about 200 little ones to the care of her successor. Mrs. North was ably assisted by her sister, Miss Cordelia B. North, and at Christmas time both Mr. and Mrs. Pillard always lent a helping hand.

In 1873, Mrs. A. P. Meylert, with Mrs. Hendrick as assistant, was chosen superintendent of this department, which position she filled with great acceptance till her removal from the city in 1875. Mrs. Josiah Shepard was appointed her successor, with Mrs. Hattie Butler-Dowd and Mrs. Edward L. Prior as her assistants.

In the autumn of 1877 Mrs. Shepard, much to the regret of her pupils, was obliged to give up her charge, and Mrs. Charles Peck was appointed to fill her place, and continues superintendent of this department. During these fifteen years valuable assistance has been rendered by several young ladies of the church, till each in turn received a louder call to another sphere of action.

After removing to the new church the sessions of this class were held many years in the west room of the chapel till it outgrew its quarters. On pleasant Sabbaths in the spring and autumn it was a discouraging task to find seats for the waiting children. Not only was every available chair and settee filled, but the platform was so crowded with the little ones that much care had to be exercised not to tread upon them. Two hundred and seventy were several times thus packed into these close quarters. The lack of proper ventilation was another serious objection to this room. It was, therefore, a cause of great rejoicing to the friends of the school when our new parish chapel was finished, with a large sunny room on the ground floor for the use of this department. The first session in the new quarters was held the last Sabbath in June, 1889. Then a long-desired change was made and the school was divided into classes, each with its own teacher, thus permitting a better acquaintance with the little ones and a closer sympathy between teacher and pupils.

The church has generously continued the Christmas festival which

Mrs. North provided at her own expense. The children at this season also contribute, from their own supplies, books, toys, and pictures, which are sent to more needy schools in the West or South, and so they experience the blessedness of giving as well as receiving.

The international lessons have been used in this department, with the exception of the Sundays from Christmas to Easter, the past year, when a life of Christ, prepared by our pastor, was studied with profit.

The primary department now numbers 323 scholars and 30 teachers. The officers, besides the superintendent, are Mrs. H. Dayton Humphrey and Mrs. George D. Copley, assistants; Miss Nettie Smith, secretary, and Miss Lillian Hart, organist.

OUR TEACHERS.

Deacon John H. Peck.

The growth and development of a large, well-ordered Sunday-school is an interesting study. The office of such a school is two-fold. It is to train up the children of the church in the truths of religion and to foster the general study of the Bible: it is also to reach out in a missionary spirit to the children of the poor, the neglectful, the godless, and bring them within the sphere of religious influence and instruction. A great and successful school sometimes gathers about an individual of uncommon energy and magnetic influence, and its power becomes immense; the employment of new and ingenious devices to attract attention; or of novel methods of instruction, sometimes creates a temporary popularity and apparent success; but the steady normal growth of any school depends upon the efficiency of its teachers. It is to the teachers of this school, their faithfulness, their consecration, their *esprit du corps*, that its phenomenal growth is mainly due.

To speak of all, or even of many, of these teachers in the few minutes allowed to me would be manifestly impossible, but it will be pleasant to recall the work of a few.

The older ladies, as they sit here, are thinking of Squire Bassett, who year after year sat among them and unfolded in his quiet way, the comforting truths of God's word. Those women never tired of being Sunday-school scholars. The venerable Mrs. Eno, when nearly ninety years of age, was still a regular member of the class, though unable to hear what was said. When Mr. Bassett was called from his work on earth, his place was well filled by the Rev. Mr. Nichols. This faithful and conscientious teacher was wont to begin his preparation of the lesson on Sunday afternoon and continue it through the week. On the last Sunday of his life he was with his class, and after his death, which occurred on the following day, notes prepared for the next lesson were found in his desk.

Dr. Woodruff was the teacher of a class of young ladies for many years, and his constant attention to this duty to the end of his life is no less a monument to his Christian devotion than the generous gift which he left for the support of the library. These classes of ladies were gradually gathered into one, the largest, I suppose, in our school, of which Prof. Camp, the veteran Sunday-school teacher in our ranks, has been for many years in charge.

Of other business men of the church who have given themselves to the work of teaching, time permits the mention of but one, that able and original thinker, Dr. Meylert, who during his short stay in New Britain was the leader of the business men's class.

The Sunday-school, no less than other departments of church work, must depend greatly upon the women of the church. Of those women who have been greatly successful as teachers, it is hard to desist from mentioning many names, especially of some who are still engaged in faithful service. One, whose name is among those of the original members of our church, Mrs. Horace Brown, has bound to herself in bonds of loyal attachment, a large class of young men. One by one she has seen them drafted for duty, for which her years of faithful labor have greatly served to fit them, but a remnant still remains studying with her the same precious truths.

The Swedes of this community, especially those of our sister church, will always and justly feel a debt of gratitude to the late Mrs. Lyon. This gifted lady gathered nearly a hundred young men and women of this nationality into her class, strangers to our country and our language, and not only on Sundays, but during many an evening, with painstaking care, helped them in the way they most needed. Her labors, so sadly and suddenly interrupted, have been continued with no less perseverance and success by Miss Ellen Camp.

A large number of those here present are remembering to-day the warm friend they once had in Mrs. Tuck. Perhaps to no one more than to this earnest worker is due the inception of that most successful and helpful organization, the "Young Women's Christian League."

Every well-managed class in the Senior department should be, and is, a training class for teachers, but mention may be made notably of the class which Dr. Lyon called his "Normal Class." This class, which occupied the choir gallery for many years, furnished 73 teachers to our Sunday-school, and some 25 more to other schools.

Our school has always owed much to the hearty coöperation of the pastors of the church. Though I am warned of the lapse of time, I cannot refrain from alluding to the work done and the example shown by our present pastor. For years he has carried on his heart the young business men's class, labored to build it up, and to interest the men of this church in the careful study of the word of God; and this in addition to his exhausting work as our minister. The church can never duly estimate their obligation to our pastor for all this, nor for the valuable aid which in past years he has given to the teachers in the evening class.

How would those teachers of twenty-five, forty, and fifty years ago think of the school of to-day? They would see a corps of teachers as large as the ordinary Sunday-school of those days, with aids to biblical study such as they never dreamed of; a school about equal in size to the entire population of New Britain when the school was organized. Those early teachers would see here the fruits of their planting. Would they have any words, had they the privilege of addressing us to-day, respecting self-denial or generous self-sacrifice? No! No! They would only speak of the privilege and the joy of Christian service. It is our privilege, fellow teachers, to enter into their joy.

OUR SUNDAY-SCHOOL LIBRARY.

Miss Alice C. Tuck, *of the Library Committee.*

The history of our Sunday school would indeed be incomplete without reference to the library which has been a strong factor in its working force ever since the organization of the school.

One of the first expenditures of the church was for a few Sunday-school books. From the beginning great care has been exercised in the selection of appropriate and worthy books. They have been sifted again and again, their number has been as often increased, and the school has been kept closely in touch with the best Sunday-school literature.

As early as 1844 it was voted that the officers of the school be a comtee to reject from the library such books as they judged "unfit for use," and to make suitable addition.

In 1846 a committee was appointed consisting of Mr. Rockwell, Prof. E. A. Andrews, Horatio Waldo, and O. B. Bassett, to examine the library and see what new books were needed, and, for they were a progressive people — whether some of a "higher order" might not be useful. It is of interest now to note the wide range of their selection, including as they did in the six hundred volumes, histories by Macaulay, Prescott, and Abbott, many of Irving's writings, the "letters" of Abigail Adams, several of Carlyle's works, a fine edition of the "Spectator," and Webster's speeches in three volumes. After this part of the library had filled an important place in the parish for some years, it was thought best to place it in the New Britain Institute, in order that access to it might be more general, and it might become more widely useful.

In 1869 Dr. Lucius Woodruff, for several years superintendent of the school, presented to the teachers a valuable reference library of one hundred and fifty volumes. This included choice works on church history and theology, together with commentaries on all parts of the Bible. Important additions to this collection have recently been made, so that it now numbers about four hundred and fifty volumes. It has also been recently rearranged and newly catalogued. On the death of Dr. Woodruff in 1872, the Sunday-school came into possession of $5,000. This generous bequest is to be kept as a permanent fund, its income being used for the benefit of the libraries for teachers and scholars.

In considering the general library of some two thousand books, it is needful that we remind ourselves of the promiscuous character of our school, which represents wide differences of intelligence, culture, and spiritual need. The books, which some of the scholars most appreciate and enjoy, often do not appeal to others, and since tastes and opinions differ regarding Sunday-school books, as other things, our large membership compels a varied supply in order to meet the many demands.

Your present committee has very nearly completed its task of renovating the library. Some of the oldest books have been put aside. Many have been rebound, and others duplicated. New books have been added, new cards and catalogues provided, and now it remains for the library to be used.

The standard of the church for the library has been "books which inculcate, directly or indirectly, moral or religious truth, and also those which contribute towards a knowledge of church history, or minister to the upbuilding of character." This year an attempt has been made to extend its usefulness along these lines by the addition of good poetry and literary criticism, such as would tend to the Christian culture of our people; and also such books on patriotism, as those of Samuel Adams Drake, John Esten Cooke, Brander Matthews, "Poems of American Patriotism," and the "Makers of America" series. Prof. Broadus has said: "We may help young children not a little by deepening their interest in any impressive natural objects within the reach of their vision, by striving to interpret for them, in sympathetic fashion, the meanings of nature." The committee has hoped to lead our children "through nature up to nature's God," by giving them books like Olive Thorne Miller's "In Nesting Time," "Star-land" by Sir Robert Ball, and the pleasant science lessons from the "Sunshine," by Amy Johnson. Some of the old stories have been retained and others added, for it has seemed that in our school the story has not outlived its usefulness as an educative power in Sunday-school work. It has been found that the girls who, eight years ago, when the library was last made over, were reading its simpler stories, are now drawing the historical stories, Christian Endeavor literature, and helpful biographies.

The committee has also seriously considered whether our school has not a direct commission to place in the hands of the young other books, which have been a delight and help in our own homes, although they may lack direct religious teaching. On the new catalogue will be found the titles of books by Mrs. Whitney, Miss Alcott, and Thomas Knox, which it is expected will prove suggestive and helpful, as well as entertaining.

But there are many stronger books upon the shelves which are especially recommended to be read on Sunday, for Sunday should stand apart from the rest of the week in its reading, as in its work. These are books of a higher order, such as "Culture and Religion," "The Evidence of Christian Experience," and the "Incarnation of the Son of God." In most cases these books will go unread if not drawn for Sunday reading, as time is seldom taken for them in the midst of the busy week.

The appeal is for aid in bringing the right book to the right scholar. We need co-operation, the helpful interest of teachers, parents, scholars and officers. The work is not too small for which to ask so much. There are infinite possibilities before a Sunday-school library wisely used. Ours has been selected with great painstaking. It is large and varied. The services of wise and good men and women have been freely given to it for many years. We owe a special debt of gratitude to our senior deacon, who has been chairman of the committee for more than twenty years, and to those who were associated with him.

While we point with pride to the record of this unusually rich Sunday-school library, we of to-day may claim for ourselves very little of its honor. For we are only trying to keep up the high standard and follow on the broad basis of the library as planned and begun by the thoughtful men and women of fifty years ago. Can we not unite in making our Sunday-school library in the future of even greater service than in the past?

THE CHURCH IN THE SCHOOL.

Edwin B. Lyon, M.D.

Much as I would like to be mentioned among the ancient worthies of this church and Sunday-school in these semi-centennial commemorations, I am debarred by limitations of time, it being only a quarter of a century this month since I accepted an invitation to make this city my home.

This house was then just receiving its finishing touches, and a few weeks later myself and family were welcomed to accommodations which we had not builded, to worship with a church we had no part in forming, and to work with a Sunday-school we had nothing to do in organizing.

When first introduced to the Sunday-school I thought the appointments admirable, the rooms adequate, and the organization of the senior department in particular remarkable, inasmuch as it embraced an unusually large proportion of the adult members of the church and congregation arranged in Bible classes, and led by the men who, in educational and business affairs, had made the town illustrious.

The apartments were supposed to be ample for many years of growth, and would have been, measured by ordinary estimates. But the phenomenal growth of the primary and senior departments soon called for more room, and the call grew louder and longer until our new building was planned, constructed, and occupied by the largest primary and senior departments in the State, and one of the largest in New England. The senior department — "The Church in the School" — is divided into twenty Bible classes of young gentlemen and ladies, occupying the main assembly room of the parish chapel, while the seventeen side rooms opening into it are occupied by large spectacled classes of aged men and women, large classes of business men and women, large classes of working men and women, large classes of young gentlemen and ladies, a large class of Normal school pupils, and a large class of young Swedes, of both sexes; in all nearly four hundred adults, well officered and taught by devoted and skillful Bible-class leaders.

It is the main work of the primary department to find and gather in the lambs, the junior department folds and keeps them, while the legitimate and important work of this senior department is to feed and lead out into green pastures and beside still waters those who in turn shall leave the ninety and nine safe ones and go out into the mountains for the lost, or to the highways and hedges for the wanderers. This supplements the pastor's teaching, and the Church cannot do its best work without this right arm of service.

Auxiliary to this department, we have organized a large home department (about two hundred and fifty), embracing adults and others who, for various reasons, cannot come to us. Availing themselves of the Sunday-school lesson-helps and Sunday-school library, they form home and neighborhood classes, and through these means of communication and inspiration they are changed from passive members into active Christians engaged in the work of the church.

10

In view of the fact that we have such organizations and such rare facilities for the work, and that there are still many adults out of the Sunday-school, we can see our opportunities and responsibilities. How shall these be met?

> Men of hearts must pray for it,
> Men of hands must work for it,
> Men of brains must plan for it,
> Men of means must pay for it —

and the good work will go on. God will bless human instrumentality in the future as He has always in the past.

The Sunday-school offerings were here received for a Christian school among the negroes of the South, and after song the benediction was pronounced by the pastor.

SUNDAY EVENING SERVICE.

The service opened with an impressive rendering of the *Magnificat:*

> "My soul doth magnify the Lord,
> And my spirit hath rejoiced in God my Saviour."

The sentences were read and prayer was offered by the pastor, and the responses were by the pastor and choir.

The Historical addresses were given by members of the church and were as follows: —

ORGANIZATION, LIFE, AND GROWTH.
Deacon David N. Camp.

It may be thought strange that while the civilized world is preparing to celebrate the four hundredth anniversary of the discovery of America, we should turn aside from our accustomed exercises to commemorate the semi-centennial of a single church. But events, scarcely noticed by the busy world, may become important links in the chain of God's providences.

We were this morning directed to the thought that, "thou bearest not the root, but the root thee." If we are to look for the root from whence this church sprung we must turn to the First Church in Hartford, which was organized at (Cambridge) Newtown, Mass., about 1632, or 140 years after Columbus discovered America.

In 1633, Rev. Thomas Hooker became its pastor; and in June, 1636, the church, pastor, and people came across the wilderness with their little ones, their flocks and herds and household goods to Hartford. In less than three years, a part of this church had asked for an "enlargement of accommodation at Tunxis." This was granted by the General Court and a settlement was made. In 1645 the town was incorporated and named Farmington, and in 1652 the church was organized with seven pillars, a part of whom were ancestors of members of this church.

The church and town of Farmington, and at that time church and town were nearly synonymous, were remarkable in their constitution and history. Among the owners of house lots were Governors Haynes, Hopkins, Welles, Webster, four of the first five Governors of the colony; and Samuel Wyllys, son of the fifth; John Steele, the secretary, and John Talcott, treasurer of the colony, and a number of other officers of the General Court. The church and town were also remarkable in their growth. Three years after the church was formed there were but forty-six ratable persons in the town, while at that time there were one hundred and seventy-seven in Hartford. One hundred years later Farmington had seven hundred more inhabitants than Hartford, and in 1774, its population exceeded that of Hartford by more than a thousand, and it had become, with one exception, the town with the greatest number of inhabitants in the state.

The Farmington church has been a mother of churches and of foreign missions. About twenty-five years after the church was organized, a colony went out to Mattatuck, and finally became the First Church of Waterbury, from which at least a dozen other Congregational churches have sprung, and as many more in other directions have sprung from the mother church. Among these are the three largest Congregational churches in the state. The enterprise, or unrest, which led to the founding of some of these churches led to the peopling of the east and west parts of New Britain, as far as Christian Lane and Great Swamp.

In 1705, the southeastern part of the town was incorporated into a new society called Great Swamp. A meeting-house was soon erected at Christian Lane, and a church formed. The parish extended from Smalley street, New Britain, to the Blue Hills near Meriden, or Southington. In less than twenty years, an effort was made to build a new meeting-house. After much disagreement, failing to unite on a location, the General Assembly at last ordered one to be built, sent out a committee from Hartford to erect and finish it, and taxed the people to pay for it. This house was more than a mile to the southeast of the other, and so much further from the families in the north part of the parish. These families petitioned for the privilege of having worship nearer their homes for four of the winter months each year on account of the distance, bad weather, and bad roads, and to be excused from paying for the support of worship at the Kensington Church for that part of the year. The petition was not granted at the time, but after fifteen years of frequent petitioning, their prayer was answered, and a new ecclesiastical society was incorporated in 1754, named New Britain. In 1758 a church was organized, and Rev. John Smalley was installed pastor. A plain meeting-house had been erected, and for some years the church was harmonious in action. The houses were then in Stanley Quarter, on East street, and in Hart Quarter, there being but four near the center or within a half mile of the present churches.

After a time there was a difference in sentiment. Some of the ministers in this part of the state became dissatisfied with the theological teachings at Yale, and instituted a separate theological school at

East Windsor. The successor of Mr. Jones, Dr. Coggswell, the fourth pastor of the church, became a professor in this institution. The anti-slavery question was discussed with much warmth. Different views were held, differing as to methods more than principles. Other moral questions were prominent. Local questions also probably had an influence, and a portion of the church petitioned for separation. The matter was referred to the Hartford South Consociation, and this body, after mature deliberation, decided that a division of the church was wise, and proceeded to organize one hundred and twenty members into a new church, to be called the South Church in New Britain.

This was July 5, 1842. The church was all ready for work. The Ecclesiastical Society had been organized under the laws of the state nearly two months before. A new meeting-house had been finished and dedicated. The Ladies' Benevolent Society had been organized and engaged in active work several months. Four days after the church was organized and at its first business meeting, the clerk of the church and officers of the Sunday-school were appointed, and a few days later two deacons.

In October Rev. Samuel Rockwell began to preach here, and December 5th, five months after the church was organized, he accepted a call to settle, and was installed pastor, Jan. 4, 1843. He was at the time fifty years of age, on his father's side a direct descendant of Deacon William Rockwell of the Congregational church, originally organized at Plymouth, Eng., and on his mother's side, the eighth generation in descent of Governor William Bradford of the Plymouth Colony. So that this church of the Puritans had a pastor of Pilgrim descent, who wisely guided it in the first years of its history. The house of worship where he officiated was a plain wooden structure. The little basement room, where prayer and conference meetings were held, was sometimes dark and dingy, but was brightened with triumphant faith and Christian hope.

A church prayer meeting was held every Friday afternoon, and a conference meeting every Friday evening, and both were well attended. The monthly concert of prayer for Foreign Missions, established soon after the organization of the church, was held regularly every month, with almost constant interest and full attendance. The pastor was able to visit all the families with considerable regularity; but in addition, members of the church, two by two, were accustomed at the request of the pastor, or by appointment, not infrequently to go through the whole parish visiting each family and extending the welcome hand and loving heart of Christian fellowship to each member of the church. The only strictly church societies for the first fifteen years were the Ladies' Benevolent Society and the Maternal Association, but at the weekly church meeting held in the daytime, the various projects for advancing Christ's kingdom were freely discussed, and the final action was the result of the concurrent judgment of all, or of the majority.

After a ministry with this church of fifteen and a half years, Mr. Rockwell was dismissed at his own request, June 20, 1858. During his pastorate, 137 were received on confession of faith, and 133 by letter, in all 270. There were dismissed to other churches by letter, 93, and 53 were removed by death, and 5 by discipline, total, 150, leaving the net gain 119, or nearly one hundred per cent. Mr. Rockwell still resided in New Britain, and occasionally preached in his accustomed place, but Rev. Constans L. Goodell, who had been preaching at the First Church, Hartford, in the summer and early autumn of 1858 was invited to preach here, and was ordained February 2, 1859. Mr. Goodell's pastorate began in the years of excitement preceding the civil war. The attention of the community was largely absorbed in the events which preceded the outbreak, and this church partook of that interest. The first war meeting in the state was held in New Britain, presided over by the first pastor of this church. The captain of the first company which went from New Britain to the army was a member of this church. Young men and men in mature life were enlisting and going to the front.

When Mr. Goodell was installed there were 227 members of the church, but at the close of the year there were but 220, and his first five years of service closed with the same number. After the war closed, society gradually resumed its normal condition, and an advance in church work was inaugurated. Active and efficient efforts were put forth to bring the gospel to the neglected. Large additions were made to the church, and for nine years in succession, there were net gains in membership every year. During this period over five hundred united with the church, and the net gain over losses by death, dismission, and discipline, was 322, or one hundred and forty-six per cent., and the church from being one of the smaller in the state, had become the largest outside of the city of New Haven. The Sunday-school during this decade had more than trebled in numbers. This church edifice had been erected and dedicated. Though during this decade more than $200,000 had been raised for church building and parish expenses, benevolent contributions had largely increased. Two or three missionary societies and the "Young People's Meeting" were established, and 501 members were added to the church, during Mr. Goodell's pastorate. On account of the health of his family, he was dismissed at his own request, November 18, 1872.

Rev. Henry L. Griffin was ordained and installed pastor, October 1, 1873. A powerful revival occurred during his ministry, and in 1876, in a single year, 178 members united with the church, 157 on confession of faith, and 21 by letter, and the net gain for the year was 156, the largest in the history of the church. The Ladies' Foreign Missionary Society, two of the mission circles of young people, and the Society of Christian Brotherhood were established during Mr. Griffin's pastorate. The attendance at the Young People's meeting was largely increased, and the church had increased in numbers until its membership was larger by more than one hundred than any other Congregational church in the State.

On the 23d of September, 1877, Mr. Griffin read a communication to the church, in which he said that, "For the purpose of seeking rest by a prolonged season of travel abroad and study in a foreign university, in accordance with previously formed plans, he tendered his resignation." The church was loth to part with him, and unanimously passed resolutions rehearsing the prominent events of his pastorate and requesting him to withdraw his resignation. After due consideration, he returned an answer in which he most affectionately and lovingly spoke of his relations to the church, but his plans were so far matured that he did not deem it his duty to withdraw his resignation, and he was dismissed by council December 20, 1877.

In three months the church was again supplied with a pastor, by the installation of Rev. James W. Cooper, March 20, 1878. Three years after, or March 1, 1881, Deacon Wiard was employed to give his whole time to the duties of his office as superintendent of the Sunday-school and assistant to the pastor in pastoral work, with a salary for his services.

Those who have been with the church during these fifty years, or for any considerable part of it, cannot but exalt the overruling providence of God, and recognize His signal blessings in giving a succession of gifted, faithful pastors, all unlike, but each adapted to the special needs of the church, in preserving it from dissensions and divisions, in providing for it so beautiful and convenient a church edifice and appliances, in blessing our families, in sanctifying our homes, in prospering our interests, in raising up a succession of men and women for service in His kingdom, and in casting our lot in the green pastures and by the still waters of His salvation.

Standing here between the past and the future, looking backward, we are led to exclaim, "The fathers! Where are they?" Not one of the men who helped to found the church and was on its first roll of members is living. The fifty who were banded together two months before the church was organized, to constitute the Ecclesiastical Society, are nearly all passed over the river.

Looking forward, with our faces toward Zion, by faith we behold brighter scenes and richer joys than earth can ever give, where we shall soon meet the sainted ones who have gone before.

FINANCIAL STATEMENTS AND THEIR LESSONS.

Financial statements were here made, in behalf of the Ecclesiastical Society, covering home expenses, and in behalf of the church, covering benevolent contributions. These statements were given by the respective treasurers, and were immediately followed with remarks by Deacon Talcott.

THE ECCLESIASTICAL SOCIETY.
Mr. Edward N. Stanley.

The period covered by this financial report of the South Congregational Society is from May 9, 1842, the date of the organization of the society, to the close of the last fiscal year, January 11, 1892 — a period of fifty fiscal years.

Within this time eight different persons have held the office of treasurer, namely: Henry North, from 1842 to 1849; Charles M. Lewis, from 1849 to 1852; Thomas S. Hall, from 1852 to 1854; Charles Peck, from 1854 to 1855; Walter H. Stanley, from 1855 to 1859; Henry W. Whiting, from 1859 to 1875; Oliver Stanley, from 1875 to 1890, and Edward N. Stanley, from November 3, 1890. Although Oliver Stanley was not elected treasurer until January 11, 1875, the accounts of the treasurer were kept by him from May 12, 1862. He was also the treasurer of the church building funds from May 9, 1864.

The thorough and systematic manner in which all the treasurer's accounts have been kept by my predecessors, and the care with which they have all been preserved, has made the task of the preparation of this report a comparatively easy one.

In reporting the receipts of this society, all moneys received as the proceeds of loans have been omitted, it being the object of this report to present a statement of the amount of money received by this society during the past fifty years from the members of this church and congregation for building up and maintaining the work of the Master, and for providing adequate facilities for its constant growth and extension; and also to indicate in what ways this money has been expended.

The receipts and expenditures have been as follows:

STATEMENT OF TREASURER'S ACCOUNTS — 1842–1892.
RECEIPTS.

From slip rents, ...	$172,580.64
Subscriptions for church buildings, etc.,	203,751.48

Ladies' Benevolent Society, the proceeds of fairs and other entertainments given under their auspices,	2,830.78
Contributions, pledge funds, etc.,	2,993.45
Sale of parsonage property,	9,500.00
Bequest of Cornelius B. Erwin for parish chapel,	12,500.00
All other other sources,	13,166.05
Total,	$417,322.40

EXPENDITURES.

For current expenses, including repairs,	$174,183.09
Church edifice, including parish chapel and furnishing,	179,257.22
Interest on indebtedness,	44,596.23
Insurance,	8,006.44
Parsonage property,	11,124.34
Total,	417,167.32
Cash on hand January 11, 1892,	155.08
	417,322.40

In addition to these receipts there should be reported the sum of $8,000, which is the amount contributed for the original church edifice, but which does not appear in the accounts of the treasurer, the church having been built and entirely paid for during the year preceding the organization of the society. Also the sum of $4,100, representing the value of the plot of land formerly owned by the Union Hall Company, on a part of which the parish chapel now stands, received by the society as a gift from the late Cornelius B. Erwin. Including these items the total receipts of the society, from all sources, except loans, during the past fifty years have been $429,422.40, an average of $8,588.45 per year.

The receipts from pew rents the first year were $773.12, and the expenditures for current expenses $774.99. From 1842 to January, 1868, or during the time the first church edifice was occupied, the receipts from pew rents were $34,637.62, an average of $1,332.22 per year, and the expenditures for current expenses were $37,542.10, an average of $1,443.93 per year. From 1868 to 1892, the period that the present church edifice has been in use, the receipts from pew rent were $137,943.02, an average of $5,747.63 per year; and the expenditures for current expenses were $136,640.99, an average of $5,693.37 per year. In 1871 the largest amount was realized from the sale of pews, namely, $8,003.02. For current expenses the expenditure was the largest in 1890, amounting in that year to $6,877.84.

During the period from 1864, the year the present church edifice was begun, to 1880, the year the last of the indebtedness was paid, a period of seventeen years, the average annual receipts of this society from the members of this church and congregation were $16,832.28 — the total being $286,148.82.

From the date of the completion of this building, when the indebtedness of the society was a little over $60,000, to January, 1881, this society was heavily encumbered with debt. In November of 1880, by what might almost be termed a spontaneous subscription, amounting to twenty thousand dollars, provision was made for canceling the last of this indebtedness, and in January, 1881, I notice an entry, on the cash account of the treasurer, of a payment of $1,500 to the Savings Bank of New Britain, and interlined with it are these words, "which is the last indebtedness." And so it has proved in a double sense thus far, for since that time the society has had no debt.

For the erection and furnishing of this building, and the parish chapel, and for canceling the indebtedness, there have been six subscriptions, as follows: The first in February, 1864, amounting to $60,334, to which there were seventy-eight subscribers; the second in January, 1867, amounting to $52,278.24; to this there were forty-two subscribers; the third in November, 1874, amounting to $47,300, to which there were one hundred and eight subscribers; the fourth in November, 1880, amounting to $20,241, to this there were one hundred and seventeen subscribers; the fifth in February, 1887, amounting to $5,371; this subscription was for building the parish chapel and had eighty-five subscribers; the sixth and last in December, 1888, for furnishing the parish chapel, amounted to $1,432.48, to which there were one hundred and eleven subscribers, mainly ladies of the church.

The original cost of the present house of worship, including the organ and furnishing, was $143,170.77. The building committee, which had the care of its construction, was appointed March 17, 1864, as follows: C. B. Erwin, F. H. North, Henry Stanley, Oliver Stanley, H. H. Brown, Philip Corbin, and Lucius Woodruff. Mr. Erwin was appointed chairman, but resigned in March, 1865, and was succeeded by Mr. Henry Stanley. Oliver Stanley was appointed agent and superintendent of building, and when the statement is made that the whole edifice from foundation to pinnacle was built by day labor, it is hardly necessary to add that it occupied a very large part of his time and thought during the three years of its construction.

The cost of the parish chapel, including furnishing, was $27,533.37. The building committee having this work in charge was Oliver Stanley, A. P. Collins, Dr. E. B. Lyon, D. O. Rogers, and T. W. Wilbor. D. O. Rogers was appointed secretary, and Mr. Rogers and Oliver Stanley were appointed a sub-committee to superintend the erection of the chapel. Under their careful attention and wise direction the chapel was completed within the sum appropriated for that object, Mr. Rogers especially giving a great part of his time and thought to it.

The society has received by bequest from the late Cornelius B. Erwin, to be by it held in trust, the beautiful parsonage property on Washington street (his former residence), and a fund of $25,000 to assist in its maintenance. The trustees of this fund are Deacons David N. Camp, John B. Talcott, and Mr. Philip Corbin.

Such in brief has been the financial history of this society during its first fifty years, a review of which impresses one with the broad-minded, generous spirit which has been characteristic of its dealings, its high conception and liberal execution, and the faithful meeting of individual responsibilities by those who have been its contributors.

OUR BENEVOLENT CONTRIBUTIONS.

Mr. William H. Hart.

It is my privilege to report the contributions of the South Church for benevolence during the past fifty years. I have prepared a statement showing the amounts contributed to each of the great missionary societies of our Congregational Churches and for other objects, for each year, which may be valuable for future reference; but I will only report the aggregate for each decade.

The records show for the first decade items amounting to $7,370; the second decade, $12,800; third $66,000; fourth, $60,200; fifth, $78,300; making a total for the fifty years of $224,213.07.

This sum is exclusive of the bequests of Dr. Lucius Woodruff, Rev. Charles Nichols, and Cornelius B. Erwin. Dr. Woodruff, in addition to his bequests to the South Church ($10,000 to the Church and $5,000 to the Sabbath-school), bequeathed to the New Britain Institute $10,000, and Rev. Charles Nichols to the American Missionary Association, Berea College, etc., $2,200. The bequests of Mr. Cornelius B. Erwin for Home Missions and Educational work and for various benevolent objects already amount to $866,419. His residuary estate, not yet divided, is to be given in equal shares to five Christian colleges, four Western and one Southern.

LESSONS FROM THE FINANCIAL STATEMENTS.

Deacon John B. Talcott.

The statements you have just heard show more clearly than can any words of mine how dear to the hearts of this people are the church and its institutions. Nor are these statements made in any spirit of boasting — but rather of grateful thanksgiving for having been permitted to do so much for the cause of religion at home and abroad. Nor has any contributor to these amounts any other regret, I am sure, than that he has not been able to do more; for, large as they are, they have already been returned ten-fold in blessings on ourselves and our community.

Every day we are taught that it is only by giving up a part of what we call our own that we can enjoy the full benefit of the rest. Society, the state, the community in which we live, all demand something of us, and all pay back double in return. They open the way for public and private prosperity, and for those social enjoyments and privileges, which are at once the aim and the joy of our lives. How true this is, is seen more clearly from a glance at our national history. What but anarchy, civil war, and final ruin would have been the fate of our American colonies after the Revolution, if they had clung each to their own individual right, and not yielded up the part necessary to constitute this now glorious Union. What, too, but the consciousness of its priceless value made the North ready as one man to sacrifice property and life in its defense.

It is one of the axioms of Euclid, as every school-boy knows, that the whole is greater than any of its parts, and school-boys used to be willing to admit Euclid's conclusions without the test of demonstration. But a pagan living two thousand years ago could not reasonably be expected to be abreast of the wisdom of this, the wisest of all the centuries. Observation daily proves the part to be often infinitely greater and more valuable than the whole, and the whole to be valueless except for the possible separation.

In these days of prosperity and wealth, we are not apt to fully realize the sacrifice and self-denial that the founders of this Church were called upon to endure. All did their part, encouraged by the splendid liberality of one of their number, who, ever as bold as he was farsighted, saw in the church an institution, adding value to everything around it, and for which no present sacrifice could be too great. Later on we saw that same man, when other men of larger means in different parts of the state were hesitating, with the courage of deep conviction, coming boldly forward, and with the aid of his friends, securing for New Britain the State Normal school, of which we all are so justly proud. The church and the school, the two great moral forces in the community, making home and property and life itself doubly blessed. Think you these men were the poorer for these sacrifices? Nay, even, were they not a thousand times richer, not merely in the consciousness of noble deeds, but even in material resources. What banker after that was not more ready to furnish them any needed aid? Character as well as enterprise gave them capital. From that time on a higher spirit has pervaded our entire community. Education and religion, labor and culture have joined hands in achieving the noble results visible all around us.

Our city has grown up under such influences; small it may be, but of a moral power, great and far-reaching; nor more famed for successful business enterprise than for its philanthropic and liberal spirit.

We justly admire the foresight and liberality of our fathers. Yet they builded better than they knew. Like those who framed the constitution of our Union, they had no conception of the grand results which should follow their work. They saw not even in imagination this great congregation, and this beautiful church building, which their sons and successors have erected, hardly daring to count the cost, but resolved in imitation of them to build a sanctuary, itself a continual song of praise and thanksgiving, which, as it lifted itself heavenward, should lift up the whole community with it, speaking in language which all could understand of God's love for man, and man's gratitude to God; and as one noble deed inspires another, so the church inspired the chapel, together making one grand symphony of gratitude for unnumbered unmerited blessings.

Nor should we fail at this time to call to mind among the many benefactors of this church him especially who provided so liberally for our church library, and for aiding in the support of the poor among us. Fountains of continual usefulness are those funds, the perennial streams from which refresh and gladden wherever they flow. Nor him again, whose liberality could be confined within no denominational limit, but reached to adorn and bless our community on every side, and not ours only, but colleges and religious institutions in the far off West and South, but of whose truly Christlike charity, the Erwin Home will ever remain among us the most fitting memorial. Nor him, perhaps above all, who for so many years so successfully managed our financial affairs, not only himself fruitful in good works, but the constant occasion of them in others.

These all rest from their labors, but their works remain for our example and inspiration. We may not be called upon to repeat just what they did, but the field of active Christian benevolence daily widens, and humanity on every side reaches out for aid and encouragement. But not more for their sacrifices and self-denial do we honor those who have gone before us, than for the spirit which prompted them, making of them not a burden but a blessing. Another fifty years, and in its softened light the beauty of their lives will appear even more glorious. Not on the wealth of our community then do we boast but on the use made of it. Our churches, our schools, our libraries, our Christian associations, our private benefactions, our sacrifices and self-denials, to make the life around us richer and nobler. Not what we have, but what we have given up for the sake of others, that is our glory, that our most enduring possession.

They tell of St. Martin, how on the way to church in the cold and storm, meeting an almost naked beggar, and having nothing else to give him, he gave him half of his cloak; and how the same night Christ appeared to St. Martin, wearing the beggar's cloak now all radiant with divine glory. Infinitely more precious henceforth than the whole was the part that remained to St. Martin. If in our lives we exhibit a like spirit, we may be sure of a like reward.

The old anthem, so dear to our fathers, commencing

> "Jerusalem, my glorious home.
> Name ever dear to me,"

was sung by the choir, after which the history of the Church in detail was continued in the addresses following.

THE SERVICE OF SONG.

John P. Bartlett, Esq.

One who had noticed the printed announcement that I was to speak to-night on our "Service of Song," asked what I knew about it,—if I ever sang a song. Before that, my ignorance of the subject was recognized, so that the suggestion was not novel, and the situation has not improved in my own mind as this hour has approached. It is said that "no lawyer can plead his own cause"; perhaps on that theory the committee thought no singer could sing his own song, and so commissioned me to speak to you of the service of song during the first fifty years of the life of this church.

It is understood that the person who wrote

> "A drop of ink
> Makes millions think,"

added,

> "A musical ring
> Makes millions sing."

While we may not agree with the exaggeration poetic license permits, still, relatively speaking, we recognize the truth in the rhyme. Although but few actually sing, these few touch responsive notes in the relative "millions" who sing in sympathy. And so it is that the consideration of our service of song becomes important and its history inseparably linked with the history of the whole church.

In the early days of the life of this church the music was furnished by a choir led by a chorister and accompanied by instruments. These instruments were the "double bass," played by Edward Doen, the 'cello, or "single bass," as it was called, played by Wm. S. Booth, the violin, by Sherman Steele and Charles Dickinson, and the flute, played by (now Deacon) Charles Peck. It was quite an event when, about 1860, the first key-board instrument was used. It was a melodeon, and was played by John E. Woodruff and George Booth.

The choristers for the fifty years, naming them as nearly as may be in order, have been James F. Lewis, Sherman Steele, Charles Dickinson, J. M. Potter, John E. Woodruff, Eli Porter, Wm. S. Booth, John H. Peck, Dr. J. G. Barnett, Frederic G. Gleason, Dr. Barnett (his second engagement), A. W. Kibbe, R. O. Phelps, A. W. Kibbe (again), and our present chorister, Mr. R. P. Paine. Dr. Barnett was the first chorister in the new church, and was also organist, as have been all since then.

In the choir in the old church there was no paid quartette, though the chorister generally received some compensation. Among those who frequently sang solos in those early days were Miss Martha Peck (now Mrs. Wm H. Hart), Miss Louisa Hart, afterwards the wife of Rev. Dr. Flagg, and Miss Julia E. Smith. In this new church the sopranos' have been Mrs. Emma Watson Doty, Miss Minnie Eldridge, Miss Anna Woodford, Miss Amelia Staumn, Miss Alice Wetmore (now Mrs. Wm. W. Smith), Miss Lillian Woodhouse, Miss Grace Robbins (now Mrs. A. J. Pickett-Moore), Mrs. J. P. Francis, Mrs. Oliver Stanley (now Mrs. Moore), Miss Adams (now Mrs. Clark), Miss Jessie Leigh, Miss Carrie Louise St. John, Miss Leigh ; the altos, Mrs. E. L. Hendrick, Miss Emma Lawrence (now Mrs. J. A. Pickett), Miss Minnie Haslam (Mrs. Hartman), Miss Catlin, Miss Mary S. Fox (Mrs. Pierson), Mrs. O. Stanley ; the tenors, Prof. John H. Peck, Max Kastner, W. B. Roberts, W. H. Gladden, and Charles E. Wetmore ; the basses, Wm. S. Booth, S. Willis Rockwell, Richard Follett, Robert H. Stanley, Mr. Mallory.

Among those who sang in the choir in the old church were Philip Corbin, George M. Landers, Elnathan Peck, Deacon Charles Peck, Henry F. Peck, Lucius Booth, Henry C. Bowers, James P. Merwin, Thos. A. Conklin, Zenas Rainey, Col. Samuel Moore, Dr. R. C. Dunham, Louisa Hart, Julia E. Smith, Martha Peck, Mrs. Philip Corbin, Mrs. Geo. M. Landers, Mrs. Levi O. Smith, Mrs. H. H. Brown, Mrs. G. Hinsdale, Mrs. Loren F. Judd, Mrs. C. B. Erwin, Mrs. V. B. Chamberlain, Mrs. E. Doen, Mrs. H. C. Bowers, Mrs. T. S. Hall, Mrs. T. A. Conklin, Kate Francis, Mary Jane Stanley, and Sarah Cornwell.

The first quartette in the new church (Dr. Barnett organist), was Miss Emma Watson (Mrs. Doty), Mrs. Edwin Hendrick, John H. Peck, and Wm. S. Booth; the quartette in the "centennial year," 1876 (Mr. Gleason organist), was Miss Grace Robbins, Miss Emma Lawrence, W. B. Roberts, William S. Booth. Philip Corbin and Wm. S. Booth sang side by side in our choir for twenty-five years, the latter continuing for a much longer period.

Lack of time forbids the mention of many important events in the history of our song service, the introduction of the melodeon and the exit of the stringed instruments, the change to the pipe organ, first used in the new church, the introduction to this town of the special evening praise service by Dr. Barnett, etc., etc. The organ was dedicated by a concert on the evening before the dedication of the new church. It was then played by the now famous Dudley Buck. At the dedication of this church the music was under the direction of Mr. George Henry Mitchell, of Bristol, with a quartette of Bristol singers, Miss Atkins soprano. The farewell service of Dr. Goodell stands out in the memory,— the church crowded in every part, the last loving benediction pronounced, and the congregation standing with heads not yet raised, when the organ's soft notes float out over the church, and the sweet melody, bearing tender words of affection and well wishing, is sung, sending the beloved pastor away with a farewell of song ringing in his ears.

We should be false to our trust should we fail to pay our tribute of acknowledgment and appreciation to all those who have, and do now, so effectively aid us in this part of our service. While we recall the past, we acknowledge our pleasure in the present; and as we contrast the scant equipment of early days with the splendid organ, gifted chorister, and trained choir of this, our day, we realize that the present outshines the past, brilliant as we find it.

Such, in barest outline, is the sketch of our service of song. Would that time permitted to touch in the colors and give life to the picture. What associations, what a wealth of incident, even the bare recital of the singers' names suggests! That old choir was a feature in the life of that day. One old member, of whom I made inquiries, remarked that "about all our fun in those days was at choir and prayer meeting"; and one notices that the last vestiges of the use of those institutions as sources of amusement have not entirely faded away even in our time. What a misleader of the future careers of its prominent members that old choir life often was! No doubt they of that day, as the Hon. Geo. M. Landers led the choir at the old North church, and sang in the old South church, looked forward to him as to be no less than the conductor of some state musical festival, or the composer of Te Deums to the praise of God, little anticipating him as a politician who should enroll his name on the list of the nation's legislators at Washington, or, like his fellow singer, Mr. Corbin, as a manufacturer, give name and fame to the products of New Britain skill and industry.

That early choir life, too, affords an incident typical of the wonderful possibilities of that community. A youth from a neighboring town just over our line, not distantly related to the Hon. Philip Corbin, found employment here. He loved to sing, and he made his way one Saturday night up the stairs of the old church to the gallery, where the choir was rehearsing. A single suit of clothes was all he possessed. As they were soiled and worn from his work, he had waited for this visit to the choir and church until cold weather came, and he could wear his overcoat. A stranger, he took a seat at the end under a light. His voice and singing attracted the leader. He was invited to a seat near the center, gladly vacated by Elnathan Peck, then of advanced years. His clothes were forgotten in the pleasure of his position. He was constant and punctual in attendance, found his wife there, climbed on and on till within even the swift, brief sweep of our day and generation we see him close to the top round on the ladder of success, influential in state, and trade, and church.

May not this retrospect, inadequate as it is, still be profitable to us? As the harmonies of voice and organ roll forth through these familiar arches, may not our hearts be attuned to worship, and be to us a foretaste of joys in praise during that eternity toward which we all are involuntarily drifting, and in that heavenly home into which may the passing years bring us every one!

WOMAN'S WORK IN THE CHURCH.
Deacon John N. Bartlett.

The nature of woman's work in the church may be inferred from her position in the Christian home, where she sits on her throne of love, its tender watchfulness and patient endurance, the center and soul of its affections. Remove from home the wife and mother, the daughter and sister, and the hearthstone is *desolate*. Take from our church life what woman is doing in it, and you rob it of its symmetry, its beauty, and much of its efficiency. The historian of the occasion and others who have preceded me have, of necessity, covered much of the ground pertaining to my theme; and what has been well said need not be repeated.

It remains for me to admire the picture already presented.

Look at our large and prosperous Sabbath-school and remember that of its 115 officers and teachers, 83 are women, and that its Infant Department has always been under the instruction of devoted women, who have counted it a joy to tell little children of the love of Jesus. Look at the Ladies' Benevolent Society, dating from 1841, older than the church. It has clothed the missionary and his family, and has kept our hearts in sympathy with the Master's work in the far West;

and besides, it has never tired of inviting us to its well-spread tables, and to enjoy a social hour enlivened by song and speech.

Think of the Maternal Associations, dating, one of them, from 1846, the other from 1883, where many a mother, anxious for the salvation of loved ones at home, has brought her burden to cast it upon the Lord in the presence of kindred souls, who would help her to lift her prayer.

How many, think you, have come into the fold of this church in answer to these prayers? The history of these mothers' meetings is intensely interesting. One of them originated in the parlor of the sainted Mrs. Rockwell, and had its home there for thirty-five years. Under her fostering care it increased continually. We cannot overestimate the value and importance of these mothers' meetings. They bring, in one hand, the heart of the home, and in the other, the heart of the church, and they lay both upon the heart of Christ.

The Ladies' Foreign Missionary Society, dating from 1874, is a branch of the great organization that undertakes to carry the Gospel into all lands. The missionary intelligence and world-wide benevolence that have come to this church, and the prayerful interest and generous contributions that have gone from this church in consequence of the existence of this society are known and remembered by Him who gave Himself to save the world. The Young Ladies' Missionary Society, dating from 1883, shows that the spirit of the Gospel which goes beyond our own surroundings is not confined to women of mature years.

The Young Women's Christian League, dating from 1882, and first known as the "Class Union"— inseparably connected with the memory of Mrs. Tuck, is a club which interests many in self-improvement, who are occupied during the day with the stern problems of self-support, and gives instruction in a variety of useful and practical industries, also in the principles of economy and frugality, as well as in the broader fields of Christian benevolence.

The Mission Circles, dating from 1887, are all under the guidance of women of the church. What better work has been done for the spread of the Gospel than this of enlisting our children in missionary work, helping them to plant their missionary seed in heathen lands, and then, with the faith of little children, to watch for the harvest. This age offers no sight more inspiring than the hosts of children and youth, led by woman's hand, marshaling under the banners of the church for Christian service. The sight of their loyal ranks prompts veterans to exclaim with Simeon, "Mine eyes have seen thy salvation."

The songs of the sanctuary that lift us heavenward on pinions of ecstatic joy send out their loftiest, sweetest notes from woman's voice and soul. The Board of Ladies for Home Work systematically watches over the whole parish, visiting those in affliction and sorrow, feeding the hungry, clothing the destitute, and carrying the Gospel balm in hands of Christian sympathy into many homes, and comforting many hearts.

I am unwilling to close my brief paper without alluding to important work done by the women of this church associated with other women of the city. When the war of the Rebellion burst upon us, men willing to defend the country seized their muskets, anxious to march to the conflict; but neither the state nor the city could clothe an army in a day. The emergency was fearful. The flag had been dishonored; bombarded Sumter had fallen; the "Plug-uglies" of Baltimore were resisting the passage of troops. The uniforms must be had immediately, and the women of the South Church, together with other women of the city, left the dough unbaked at home, and worked day and night, with an earnestness that inspired the men who were to wear these uniforms into the "jaws of death." Mrs. Erwin's parlor was one of the tailoring shops, her piano was one of the cutting boards. And so the first company of volunteers from New Britain hastened away in uniforms made by the patriotic women of the city.

The New Britain Tract Society, in which the women of this church were conspicuous, during the years of its existence accomplished a work of Christian benevolence that has not been surpassed in the history of the town. It included the Evangelical churches of the place, but did not aim to build up any one of them. It was *gospel* in the widest sense. It undertook to visit every family monthly, regardless of nationality and faith. It relieved the distressed, watched at the bedside of the sick and dying. It left a Bible or a tract in every home, and carried the Gospel with its help and sympathy to many burdened hearts. Among its conspicuous workers are names that are redolent of the atmosphere of Heaven; names which the Master will call with the plaudit "Well done." Some have answered the call, and have heard the plaudit — Mrs. William A. Churchill, Mrs. Virgil Cornish — while others equally deserving still linger and labor among us.

Woman's work in our church has ever been what we might expect from that class of redeemed humanity that "lingered latest at the cross, and gathered earliest at the sepulchre."

THE YOUNG PEOPLE AND THE FUTURE.
Rev. Charles E. Steele.

The religious life of the young people of our church has been so intimately connected with the Young People's meetings during recent years that we are led to inquire how they originated.

About the beginning of December, 1864, Dr. Goodell invited the young people to meet at his house. Although the religious interest was not so marked this first winter as in the following, many who attended these meetings came to regard them as the most attractive of all their social engagements. It has been said that they were started to counteract the influence of worldly amusements, in which some were getting absorbed. However this may be, Dr. Goodell did not desire to antagonize the young people in their amusement. He was far too wise for that. He realized the truth which Dr. Bushnell has so finely expressed, that too much of even innocent amusement ceases to be innocent and becomes the vice of dissipation. His method was to overcome evil with good, and in this aim he was signally successful. Several conversions followed the first series of meetings, and when they were resumed the next winter the interest became very marked. During that winter, some who have become foremost in the business life of this and other communities stood up to testify to their new-found love for Christ. Mrs. Goodell contributed greatly to the interest in leading the singing, often starting a hymn that exactly voiced the common feeling.

The last young people's meeting was held in Dr. Goodell's house May 1, 1866, the attendance having outgrown the accommodations there. Then for a time while the new church was building they were held in Thomson's Block. Later they were held for many years in the primary class room of the new church. Dr. Goodell's tact in developing the latent interest that he knew existed was remarkable. A single incident will illustrate this. In an after-meeting in the ladies' parlor, an expression of interest was called for. There was no response. The trouble was that those present did not know just how to take the first step. Dr. Goodell took a piece of chalk and drew a line on the carpet, and asked all who really wished to accept Christ and be on the Lord's side to step over that line. Then they saw it, and in gladly taking this step they found it was only a step to Jesus.

Very vividly I recall the thrilling scenes of those years, the joy, surpassing all other earthly joy, of seeing one and another committing themselves to the service of Christ. I recall the faces of many who contributed by their constant attendance and words to the helpfulness of these meetings. There were Lamb, and Murray, and Seymour, and Lee, and

Otis, and others not now residing here, some of whom have been called to the nobler service above.

From the beginning the young people have had most inspiring help from their pastors in the conduct of these meetings. Religion never could seem a joyless and forbidding thing to those who in those first years saw the radiance that lightened Dr. Goodell's face, and later during the great revival of 1876, the face of our young pastor, Mr. Griffin. They seemed to speak as though they saw Heaven opened as they unfolded the attractiveness, the riches of the spiritual life. Then Dr. Cooper, with his practical wisdom and organizing power, welded our highest spiritual fervors to the experiences and duties of our every-day life.

After Mr. Moody's and Mr. Sayford's work in 1885, the primary class room was outgrown and the meetings were held in the chapel room. A covenant of Christian service, involving in the main the obligation of the Young People's Society of Christian Endeavor pledge, was introduced, and about a year later our young people formed themselves into a Christian Endeavor Society. Greater possibilities for good seem open to them now than have been presented in the past. The influences now working will surely lead to great improvements in our church life and in the tone of our community.

Much as we have reason to thank God for the inheritance of the past, there is very much room for improvement. The definite obligations taken for Christian service, and with God's help lived up to, will surely prevent the disproportion between the male and female membership of our church. Only just one-third of the original one hundred and twenty members were males, and the proportion of the nearly nine hundred members to-day is still less. This surely cannot be the fact in the near future, when the Christian men of our community realize that the obligations of church membership and church work are just as vital to the interests of this city as any business engagements possibly can be. With a population more cosmopolitan than that of any other city in the state; with the ends of the earth coming to us, if the moral and spiritual tone given to this community by the good men and women who have lived here in the past is to be maintained, the young men of this city will be forced to see that they must take their true place and do loyal service for Christ and the church.

But we should not be satisfied in holding the ground merely. The increased responsibilities of living in these times under different circumstances bring vastly greater opportunities for service and for personal development in the graces of the Christian life. The watchword of our young people should be, and I am sure it is, "Strive after the best gifts," and with all their strength they should seek to impart to others the Christlike love with which their own souls have been blessed.

A fitting close to this historical review of fifty delightful and prosperous years of church life, with its inspiring suggestions for future activity and devotion, was found in the singing by the whole congregation of the hymn,

> "How firm a foundation, ye saints of the Lord,
> Is laid for your faith in His excellent word!"

after which the benediction was pronounced by the pastor, and the choir added its solemn "Amen."

MONDAY AFTERNOON SERVICE.

On Monday afternoon at half-past two o'clock the congregation assembled in the audience room of the church to receive the fraternal greetings of old friends of the church, representatives of sister churches, and former members. The service opened with an old-time anthem by the choir, "Come, my beloved, haste away," and during the progress of the service still another one of the sacred songs of former days, "Strike the cymbals! Sound the timbrels!" was also sung.

The Scripture lesson was read from the 145th Psalm by the Rev. Magee Pratt, pastor of the Kensington Church. Prayer was offered by Rev. Thomas Clayton, pastor of the Church in Berlin.

It is to be regretted that full reports of all the addresses delivered at this service have not been preserved and cannot be obtained for this memorial volume.

THE MOTHER CHURCH.

Rev. George Henry Sandwell, pastor of the First Church in this city, extended the greetings of the "Mother Church" in a most felicitous and friendly manner. He expressed his very great pleasure to be present on this occasion, and remarked upon the cordial and kindly relations of the mother and the daughter church. He said that when he was about to come to this town, he heard much of the generous spirit of fellowship existing among the Christian people here, but his expectations had been more than realized. He had never lived in a place where there was such good feeling and kind-heartedness as was shown in New Britain. He congratulated the South Church on its marvelous growth and prosperity, and hoped that it would continue to increase and abound in every good work, and that the bonds of Christian affection might be strengthened, until we all were gathered in the eternal fellowship of the family of God in heaven.

OUR SISTER CHURCHES.

Rev. Dr. I. F. Stidham, pastor of the Baptist Church in New Britain, was introduced by the pastor as representing what might be called the eldest daughter of the First Church, its organization antedating that of the South Church by many years, and its original membership being drawn largely from the old church.

Dr. Stidham, in behalf of the "Sister Churches," congratulated the South Church on its fiftieth anniversary and on its continued prosperity to the present time. He said that its many facilities enabled it to do large service, not only for itself, but in the wider field of home and missionary effort. The other churches in the city were stimulated to greater and more earnest endeavor in emulation of the work done here. He commended the church in a sympathetic manner for the work it has done and is now doing among the foreign portion of the city's population, and expressed himself emphatically, that our churches should not live unto themselves, but exist for the uplifting and saving of the whole community in the midst of which they were placed. Such sacrificial service is the very essence of the Gospel of Jesus Christ. He good-naturedly insisted that the Baptist denomination was, in its church polity, a little more congregational than the Congregationalists themselves, and closed his fraternal address with hearty congratulations and an earnest "God-speed."

A solo, "Come unto me," was sung by Mr. Robert H. Stanley, a member of this church, now resident in New York city.

CO-WORKERS OF FORMER DAYS.

It was a great disappointment to the church that its only former pastor now living, the Rev. Henry L. Griffin of Bangor, Maine, was unavoidably detained from attendance upon this semi-centennial celebration. Several letters were, however, received from him, selections from which were read at this service.

Mr. Griffin says:

"In reply to your kind invitation to make an address at your coming celebration, I would say that, owing to private and local reasons, I shall not be present. I trust it is not necessary for me to assure you of my affection for the dear church of my first love and the splendid people who constitute its membership. It would give me great pleasure to grasp them by the hand and look them in the face. It gives me pleasure to think that my presence would be gratifying to you. I shall eagerly await the report of the gathering."

"Please give my love to the church, and express for me my hearty interest in the dear church, whose signal prosperity under its present splendid administration would, by itself, imperatively call for such a celebration. May you receive an added impulse and blessing as a result of your rejoicings."

This church has had fourteen deacons, seven of whom are still in its service. Of the remaining seven, four died in office and one after removing from the town. But two former deacons of the church are now living: Mr. George P. Rockwell, a son of the first pastor of the church, and Prof. Isaac N. Carleton, formerly principal of the Connecticut State Normal School. Deacon Rockwell writes from Denver, Colorado, his present home:

"My family and I thank you for so kindly remembering us with an invitation to the fiftieth anniversary of the organization of *your* church, I suppose I must say, although it would seem more natural and pleasant to say *our* church. It would give us great pleasure to be with you on that occasion, but distance prevents. It is pleasant to look back over the years to the time when my father was installed the first pastor of the church, and recall the memories of his own and of the pastorates since. I can almost see the pleasant faces of Dr. and Mrs. Goodell, and of Mr. Griffin, who came to us a young man full of zeal, and of the present beloved pastor and his family.

"The old home feeling is strong, and the desire to be with you exceeding great, but while we may not be present in person we will be with you in spirit."

Deacon Carleton writes from Bradford, Mass.:

"It is a great disappointment to Mrs. Carleton and myself not to be able to accept your invitation, but we feel that we must deny ourselves the pleasure of taking part personally in the glad observances of your joyous semi-centennial. It is with grateful hearts that we recall what the South Church has been to us. To our souls, this beloved church was the medium of blessings untold, and our love for her will ever be deep and fervid. May her favored membership ever enjoy the sanctities of a pure communion and the blessings of God's abounding grace."

The Rev. Dwight M. Seward, D.D., was pastor of the old North Church, the mother church, during the six years immediately preceding the organization of the South Church, from 1836 to 1842. In the summer of 1886 the two churches united in a service commemorative of the fiftieth anniversary of his ordination. It was a pleasure to have him with us again on another semi-centennial occasion, and listen to his bright, strong, hopeful words.

Dr. Seward opened his remarks with an allusion to a previous speaker, who had acknowledged a shrinking from the coming on of old age. He observed that age with its confessed drawbacks and disabilities had a bright and redeeming side. He affirmed the necessity of grouping the years together in order to get a truthful estimate of life. He then proceeded to exhibit some of the lessons of the last fifty years.

"So far as we can learn from tradition and history, they contain more of radical change and revolution, of rapid progress and great events, than any half century before them. They show more vividly and dramatically than any other fifty years in the annals of time, that life is a term of ever alternating light and dark, of gladness and grief, of victory and defeat. While these years have brought wide changes in creeds and changes in the themes of theological discussion and controversy, they have attested the vitality, the freshness, the unabated power of old and fundamental truths. They have carried away some things that should have stayed and taken root for succeeding centuries. They have brought in many things, in the material and religious realms, that add to the beauty and the significance of life.

"These years have borne into another temple and another world the original members and the organizers of this church. But the faith and energy of these honored founders were a prophecy of growth and vigor which has come to ripe fulfillment. The advance, the successes, the resources of this church, are a marvelous record of religious history and of the blessings of God, Only fifty years old, and the peer of the strongest churches in this goodly commonwealth."

Dr. Seward alluded, with grateful acknowledgment of the grace of the Head of the church, to the strength and increasing prosperity of the mother church, and of the delightful and unmarred harmony between the churches. He drew a brief picture of the possible and brilliant future in secular and religious spheres, and maintained that the deep and perpetual longing for something better and richer and diviner was an intimation of another larger and immortal life. He gave some personal incidents in his early ministry, and concluded with some fitting stanzas of an autobiographical quality, on the building and the coming in of the ship of life.

For fourteen joyful and prosperous years the Rev. Constans L. Goodell, D.D., was pastor of this church. He was ordained here, and here he brought his young bride in the year 1859. It was with peculiar appreciation and gratitude that the church welcomed Mrs. Goodell to its semi-centennial, and listened to her graceful and tender reminiscences.

PERSONAL REMINISCENCES.

Mrs. C. L. Goodell.

I should do injustice to myself no less than to you, if I disregarded your courteous invitation to me, to contribute a little to this hour of mutual congratulation and reminiscence. It is an occasion which stirs many of the most precious memories of my life, and thrills my very soul with praise and thanksgiving to God.

As I attempt to give utterance to some of the overflowings of my own heart, I feel, that in some sense, I am speaking not only for myself, but also for *one other* whose lips are now silent, but whose quick sympathies, during his pastorate here, were wont to reach out toward you in tender and strong ways, and whose affection for each member of his flock never afterwards diminished during the years of his absence from you. I would have you believe he is now a privileged and sincere beholder of your joys and triumphs, from the "great cloud of witnesses" by which you are "compassed about."

If his voice could be heard to-day, it would give no uncertain utterance touching his love to you all, and his deep and earnest desires for your spiritual welfare, and if his prayers for you were unceasing while he was yet with you, how much more, now he is nearer the Father's ear and beholding His glory?

I doubt not he is saying, even now, "I thank my God upon every remembrance of you"—the people of my first love—"always in every supplication of mine, on behalf of you all, making my supplication with joy for your fellowship in furtherance of the Gospel from the first day, ... being confident of this very thing, that He which began a good work in you, will perfect it until the day of Jesus Christ; even as it is right for me to be thus minded on behalf of you all, because I have you in my heart."

It was a little over thirty-three years ago that the Lord directed our way to this beautiful town, and to this church who received the young pastor with his bride to their homes and hearts. A generation has passed since then, and in the place of the fathers are the children now occupying the posts of honor and responsibility in this Zion. Oh, the unwritten history of those years! How pregnant with anticipations and hopes realized! Of this church the words of the prophecy have already proved true, "A little one shall become a thousand, and a small one a strong nation."

But of the blessed years of our sojourn among you, it is my privilege to speak more particularly just now. The joyous spring was opening in beauty and loveliness when we came; the apple blossoms perfumed the air and gave promise of abundant fruitage—a happy symbol of the sphere of spiritual seed-sowing and harvesting of souls which was opening to earnest hearts.

The hospitable home of one of your esteemed members, on the hill, which overlooked the other homes of the parish, received and sheltered us for about ten months. The kindness and considerateness with which that dear family ministered to us can never be forgotten. And in all the years that followed, not only they, but many other loyal and true friends endeared themselves to us by their timely assistance in the new and untried experiences, and by their loving sympathy and counsel in planning for the good of all. In our hearts, as well as in God's book of remembrance, their names are written, and can never be effaced.

It was in that home, in those first months, that we gained our early impressions of this people, as they came and went in their visits to the new pastor; no doubt they, in turn, were getting *their* impressions too! But impressions, on our part, soon deepened into a settled conviction, that our lines had indeed fallen to us in pleasant places, and that this church embodied a choice membership of God's dear people, with whom it was an ever increasing delight to dwell and mingle in Christian ways, a conviction which continued to grow stronger with the years.

During the first twelve months, a beautiful and commodious house was built for a parsonage. Here we lived for more than thirteen years.

It was a proud day when we found ourselves at the head of a household! I remember well the surprise given us the first day of our occupancy, when a grocer's wagon backed up to our side door, and unloaded a wealth of good things for our larder — a generous outfit to begin life with! No clew could ever be found to the source of this benefaction, so delicately was it bestowed; it was only one instance out of very many, of the thoughtfulness of the people, which took shape in acts of helpfulness to the minister's family, and were oft repeated so long as we remained here.

It was a happy home through all the years. There was our "family altar," and the "Pastor's study," bright and sunny, a sacred spot. There was the "Chamber of Peace," for friends and guests who favored us from time to time with their presence and benediction; the parlor, where the members of the church and congregation always received a warm welcome, and left a blessing. Oh! what could those walls speak, of personal conferences concerning the better life, and earnest prayers for souls seeking the light! There were the sitting-room, and dining-room, and front hall, which at times echoed the songs and prayers of the young people of the church in some revival prayer-meeting. Hardly a room in the house but what was devoted to some such use in behalf of the interests of the church.

Around the table in our dining-room, which held our working materials, were gathered, on Saturday afternoons, for several successive winters, a circle of bright, interesting girls, "The Juvenile Mite Society." There they sewed and listened to attractive reading, and joined in prayer and song, and learned useful lessons of benevolence. Although this Society was composed entirely of female members, in one of the later seasons, lo! a bright, cheerful baby-boy might have been seen sitting in his little high-chair, in the midst of the group; if not the inspirer of work, the unconscious cause, at least, of merry-making and play. And who shall say that he really hindered any of the diligent workers?

Yes, in this home I first tasted the sweet joys of motherhood, and consecrated to God the children He gave us. It was in this church they were baptized, and trained in the life-habit of public worship and attendance at Sabbath-school. It will always be a cherished thought to me, that some of you still include these children of mine in your prayers.

If I seem to linger long on the happy memories of the home which was *our first home*, it is not that my thought does not also go out to the many other homes of this parish, where we mingled with you in joyous festivities, and shared the confidences of your every day family life, coming closer to you still in tender and loving sympathy during the darker days of sorrow and bereavement, drawing mutual comfort from God's precious word and communion with Him, while we felt His brooding presence and strengthening grace.

If time would permit, what pleasure it would give me once more to re-visit every home, even though I came alone, and recall personally the pleasant visits of the past, when as yet my own fireside was unbroken, and your former beloved pastor walked by my side. This may never be, but the time is coming, when, in our Father's house above, we shall review His gracious dealings with us all, and no change shall separate us there.

The Ladies' Benevolent Society is an organization which, I am told, has held its unwavering existence through the years, growing in usefulness and efficiency, and blessing hundreds of worthy missionaries in the far-away home-land, who stand as God's messengers on the frontier. God bless this venerable Society! and continue to raise up friends who shall perpetuate the noble work it has carried on so long! It was a memorable day for me when, as pastor's wife, I was made president of it. I shall never forget the first time I occupied the honored chair in the presence of my elders. In my youthful embarrassment and ignorance of parliamentary rules, I looked imploringly to my constituency for their leniency and help. On one occasion, during the transaction of business, as I attempted to guide this ship of state, dear Mrs. Erwin, who long since went to her reward, quietly suggested to me the proper time to put a question to vote, which waited for action, and thus saved me from a threatened failure. But she was not the only one who sought to cover and shield my imperfect attempts at duty in those early years. Many helpers surrounded me, who certainly were not critical, and to whose loving encouragement I owed more than they knew. Together we walked in counsel and in service until our hearts and aspirations were as one; and together we shared our mutual failures and triumphs.

The Church Sociable which then followed the afternoon meeting, was the crowning joy of the day. The pastor and deacons and members of the congregation came upon the scene in the evening, and entered sympathetically into the efforts and aims of the Society. The honorary membership fee of a dollar from the brethren, if I remember correctly, was a much-appreciated addition to our treasury, and it reacted most delightfully upon those who thus became silent partners with us in the glorious work of Home Missions, binding their hearts to the same cause.

It is around this dear church, after all, that our most sacred memories dwell, and within whose walls our choicest hours were spent. As oft as the familiar Sabbath bell called us hither, we loved to come. The hush and calm of the holy day was upon us as we entered these courts, and as the anthem, "Lo, God is here," was rendered by the choir, accompanied by the rich, solemn tones of the organ, which seemed almost to utter the very words, we knew or felt we were in the presence of the King, and all bowed in praise and adoration and worship. Here we brought our empty hearts to be filled. Here we laid our burdens down and bore a song away. Here we listened for God's voice to us through the utterances of the pastor, and voiced our vows and petitions and praises back to our Father in heaven through his lips. Here we sat in the hallowed communion seasons at the table of our Lord, one with Him in love and faith, and renewedly pledged to Him our loyalty and trust. And here too, we had the joy of welcoming to the fold hundreds who rose to confess Jesus as their Lord and Saviour, some of whom now walk in white amid the redeemed throng in heaven. Who does not recall with sincere gratitude and praise special seasons of this kind, when they felt they were indeed sitting in heavenly places in Christ Jesus, and were ready to exclaim with the disciple of old, "Lord, it is good for us to be here."

The Sunday-school, as I remember it, could hardly be called the nursery of the church, if that term suggests an assembly of babes alone. The infant class, to be sure, so long under the happy leadership of Mrs. Frederick North, was an institution almost by itself, so far as loving care and devotion in that mother-heart could make it. She drew in the children from many homes less favored than her own, and by her sweet and graceful presence won every child to herself and to her Saviour, who said, "Let the little ones come unto Me." But the older classes included a large number of youth as well as those of riper years, who had learned long ago to love their bibles, and count the hours sweet that were spent in studying its blessed truths.

I have still among my treasures an album containing the photographs, twelve in number, of the young ladies of my own class. Some are not, for God has taken them. Many of them are teachers themselves now, and mothers — I am not sure but some are grandmothers, so rapid is the flight of time, and so surely are we all moving on. I shall never cease to love those young ladies, though gray hairs may crown their heads, and never forget the sessions we were together in profitable bible study.

The Young Ladies' Missionary Circle that for a time met in our parlor; the Mother's Meeting in the home of our beloved Mrs. Rockwell; the Tract Society, although not confined to this church, yet claiming many active workers from its membership — these, and other channels still, of Christian enterprise, enlisted my sympathies and prayers and efforts, and served to enrich my own spiritual life. Though much has intervened between then and now to absorb my attention, they are yet classed among my cherished memories of our life here.

In striking contrast to all the pleasant experiences among you, there came a time I do not like to remember. It was the day the Lord led us out from you to make our home in another city; it was a sad one indeed to us. We seemed to be leaving all the good people in the world behind us, and to be facing a land of strangers. Our sun set in clouds and darkness, and we could only follow by faith the hand that was guiding us. Though the skies brightened as time went on, I can never recall our separation from you without a pang! The homesickness and heart-sickness that we both endured can never be told. We came, however, to realize it was a part of the discipline of our lives, which, in the end, would result in the greater good of us all.

The years that followed were too greatly filled with blessing, both in this church and our own in the West, to leave cause for lasting regret that the ties which bound us so closely together had to be sundered.

A true love still binds our hearts together in Christ, and the blessed hope of a reunion in heaven, with one another, and with those who have gone before, cheers us and sustains us amid the changing scenes of our later years.

I am not unmindful that another church exists here now, in place of the one that was here when our home was in this city; and that all I have said will interest very lightly the younger portion of those present to-day. My hope is, however, that this memorable occasion will furnish me the opportunity for a closer touch with those I used to know, and who knew me and mine, and that together we may recount gratefully all the way the Lord has led us, and mingle our praises and thanksgivings for His manifold mercies to us.

The day is hastening with us all when these scenes will close to our earthly vision, and our opportunities for service here will be over. What an incentive this for renewed efforts in behalf of others who need us, and for coveting earnestly the best gifts, in order to work the works of Him who sent us!

I rejoice and shall rejoice in the continued prosperity of this dear church, and in the welfare and extending influence of her present beloved pastor and members; and shall continue my prayers that, in the days and years to come, she may enjoy the blessing and abiding presence and benediction of the Master she serves; and, too, that hundreds of souls may be born here, who shall, in turn, become shining lights in this community, to the praise of Him who loved us and gave Himself for us.

"Blessed are they that do his commandments, that they may have right to the tree of life, and may enter in through the gates into the city."

Mr. Charles L. Mead of New York city was the last speaker among the "Co-workers of Former Days," representing that large number of former members of the church who have gone from us to other places and other work.

After some pleasing opening remarks, Mr. Mead went on to say :

"In coming to New Britain twenty-five years or more ago, this building in which we now sit was just ready to be occupied ; and the first religious service I attended in this city was the dedication of this noble edifice. The wisdom of the men who founded this town, in making such liberal provision for succeeding generations in the matter of churches and schoolhouses cannot be overestimated. The devoted and able men who have in succession ministered to this church, have given to the plans of the early fathers their fullest value. It has been my great privilege to know well all the ministers who have thus far served the South Church.

"Just outside of strictly church work, an abiding impression was received here by me in witnessing and participating in the remarkable temperance revival which came to this whole community about the year 1870. Wonderful results appeared in the reclaiming of confirmed drunkards, and in educating a whole generation of men and youth in the principles and practice of sobriety; and all this was done in a short time with the simplest possible organization, and with only the informal meetings of the 'Good Samaritans,' so called.

"An instructive incident to me in church life here, and one that has always remained fresh in my memory, was that of over-hearing a conversation between two poorly-clad urchins who had evidently been attracted to the door of the Sunday-school concert one evening, and had there hesitated as to the propriety of entering, or as to their being welcomed if they did so. The remark of one to the other was, "If we can see Goodrich, it will be all right." A little inquiry, later, satisfied me that Goodrich was one of those helpful persons, though but a boy, who could be relied on to see that all his comrades had a share in every good thing that came within his reach. A very 'doorkeeper in the house of the Lord.'

"After less than four years of agreeable and profitable church life in New Britain, through a business necessity, I became a *tramp*. With the true instinct of a tramp who always knows where he is likely to be well fed, I often came around of a Sunday to listen to Dr. Goodell, in St. Louis. Only two years ago that other trait of the tramp, stealing, developed in me; and with others I attempted to steal your present pastor (Dr. Cooper) for a vacant secretaryship in a national society, but unsuccessfully, as you already know.

"In returning to-day to celebrate with you the semi-centennial anniversary of this church, we may well remember with profound gratitude, that with all of material improvement made in this community and others in the past fifty years, no improvement has been made or can be made in the way back to free acceptance with our Heavenly Father. This is and always will be through the merit and mediation of His Only Son. Although tongues cease which once spake unto us the word of God, 'Jesus Christ is the same yesterday and to-day, yea, and forever.' And the gates of death have not prevailed against this branch of His Church, its membership numbering now more than at any previous time. May there never lack here a goodly company continually coming forward to fill the places made vacant from inevitable causes, and to still further increase the membership of this beloved church."

This church is rich in its friends. Several neighboring pastors were present during the services, besides those who took part in the exercises, among whom may be named the Rev. Horace Winslow, formerly pastor of the First Church, Rev. Asher Anderson and Rev. John C. Wilson of Meriden, Rev. F. G. Woodworth, D.D., of Mississippi. Letters were received from Rev. Burdett Hart, D.D., Rev. E. P. Parker, D.D., Rev. President Timothy Dwight, D.D., Rev. C. R. Palmer, D.D., Rev. Lewellyn Pratt, D.D., Rev. Prof. G. B. Stevens, D.D., Rev. J. W. Backus, Rev. W. R. Eastman, and others.

In behalf of these and many other friends, and of neighboring churches long in fellowship with us, the Rev. A. W. Hazen, D.D., pastor of the First Church in Middletown, made the following address:

OUR FRIENDS.

Rev. A. W. Hazen, D.D.

I bring you the cordial salutations of a church that is nearly two hundred and twenty-five years old; one that had lived a century and three-fourths when you were born. But we cherish a kindly feeling toward our younger sisters, and rejoice in their prosperity. We most sincerely congratulate you on this auspicious semi-centennial, in view of your remarkable history and your inspiring outlook.

It is not always true that

> "Memory locks her chaff in bins,
> And throws away the grain."

For what multitudes of hallowed associations fill and flood our minds to-day. I regret that time will allow me to glance at only a very few of these freighted with precious meaning as they are to myself, as well as to many of you.

I do not permit any man, unless he is stronger than I am, to call me old, yet I have had the pleasure of knowing all the pastors of this church. One of them, the second, was a beloved elder brother to me in my early ministry. In those years of inexperience and self-distrust I owed more to Dr. Goodell than to any other of my associates. It was, indeed, his presence here and his influence that decided me to come to Hartford as a student of theology. Ever after that year, 1865, while his home was here, it was a place of manifold attractions for me, from which came choice counsels and kindling incentives. Mrs. Goodell, whose life was so exquisitely intertwined with that of her husband in all its emotions and its activities, also gave me tender sympathy and priceless help. What grace, what pathos, what sacred reminiscence, what lofty consecration, in her charming paper read to us this afternoon! Did not the spirit of him whom she seemed to impersonate on this occasion breathe through its every line?

I well remember a meeting for prayer which I attended in 1866 in your former house of worship. We all sat in the pews near the entrance, and the pastor spoke from one of them. What a contrast this, to your present commodious chapels, parlors, rooms for the Sunday-school, and other complete appointments.

Dr. Goodell was a member of the council at my ordination, with Dea. W. H. Smith as delegate. He gave a characteristic charge to my people which they have not yet forgotten.

A year or two after, when I was somewhat in doubt concerning methods and fruitage of work, he sat in my study and told me with tears of gladness how the Holy Spirit was repeating among you the scenes of the Acts of the Apostles.

But I must not prolong this strain of to me most fascinating recollection. For I want a moment in which to speak of these later years of large expansion and ingathering. Your present pastor was my classmate for a year at Andover, and he has been ever among my valued friends. The relations between our churches have not been as close as in earlier days, because of the formation of the Middlesex Conference. Yet I have not ceased to admire the steady growth of this noble organization along all lines of Christian effort. That the last decade of your history has surpassed in not a few of its results its third decade, is ample witness to the skill and the fidelity of him in whose ministrations you have now rejoiced for almost fifteen years.

"Better fifty years of Europe than a cycle of Cathay," sang the lamented Tennyson. Better fifty years of such a royal church as this than a cycle of some of the venerable institutions of the Old World, strong though they are in alliance with the state, and rich as they are in wealth of traditions and in grandeur of imposing liturgies. This church has grown by prayer in all its departments. But for its ceaseless petitions, its labors would not have been so abundant nor so fruitful.

It was my privilege to extend to your pastor the right hand of fellowship when he entered upon his successful ministry here. I wish now to repeat the welcome and the good wishes of that happy inauguration. Long may his bow abide in its strength for the Master's service! And may he, too,

> "See his Pilot face to face,
> When he has crossed the bar."

Take this right hand, my brother, and ever be of good cheer.

> " For still we hope
> That in a world of larger scope,
> What here is faithfully begun
> Will be completed, not undone."

The pastor received this right hand of fellowship, so unexpectedly given, both for himself and for the church, grateful beyond expression for these cheering and stimulating fraternal greetings.

After singing "Blest be the tie that binds," the benediction was pronounced by the Rev. Horace Winslow of Simsbury.

ANNIVERSARY SOCIAL REUNION.

The Monday afternoon service of fraternal greeting merged itself very naturally into the Anniversary Social Reunion, which followed immediately afterward. The people passed from the church to the chapels and were constantly being reinforced by others, until the exercises appointed for the evening were announced.

A reception committee of ladies and gentlemen awaited the guests in the ladies' parlor, and presented them to Dr. and Mrs. Cooper and Mrs. Goodell, in the parlor of the parish chapel. Eight of the nine original members of the church still with us, were gathered in the inner parlor of the parish chapel and received the congratulations of many friends. The entertainment committee had prepared a bountiful collation in the refreshment room below, and served supper from five until eight o'clock.

The society rooms had been tastefully fitted up by the decoration committee, to receive portraits and photographs of former members of the church, and interesting relics of the olden days. These rooms were a center of attraction during the whole evening. This collection of portraits was especially interesting, including those of James North, the father of the three North brothers, who were so largely instrumental in the formation of the church, Mr. and Mrs. Seth J. North, Mr. and Mrs. Henry North, Deacon and Mrs. Chauncey Cornwell, Dr. and Mrs. Samuel Hart, Horace Butler, Dr. and Mrs. Lucius Woodruff, Mrs. F. H. North, William H. Smith, Henry Stanley, George Hart, Mr. and Mrs. C. B. Erwin, Mr. and Mrs. Oliver Stanley, O. B. Bassett, Elnathan Peck, F. T. Stanley, C. M. Lewis, Deacon House, Rev. and Mrs. Charles Nichols.

Deacon and Mrs. Seymour, Gad Stanley, W. S. Booth, Chauncey Arnold, W. B. Stanley, Mrs. Chester Hart.

On the old hair-cloth sofa, which stood in the old church behind the communion table, was the marble corner-stone of the old church itself, bearing the date 1841, the building having been begun and the corner-stone laid a year before the church organization was made. On the wall was a drawing of the old church, and beneath it a plan of the pews, with the names of the pew-holders of those days written in. Here also were the contribution boxes, the Sunday-school bell, the "double bass," the minister's prayer meeting chair, and last but not least, the old pulpit Bible and hymn book.

At eight o'clock, Dr. Cooper bade the people welcome to this social entertainment and Rev. Dr. F. G. Woodworth offered prayer.

The musical selections of the evening were interspersed through the two hours of speech-making and letter-reading that followed, and were rendered by Miss Jessie Leigh, Miss Mack and Messrs. Charles E. Wetmore, Robert H. Stanley, Frank S. Pierce, Mortimer H. Stanley, and Walter P. Stanley.

The first literary exercise of the evening was the reading of a

THANKSGIVING ODE

by the Rev. Levi Wells Hart, of Brooklyn, N. Y., the son of an original member of this Church. Mr. Hart depicted three phases of our city, the present, past, and future. The following selections are given from a very interesting poem:

THE PRESENT.

"Better fifty years of Europe
Than a cycle of Cathay."
Thus sang the English poet
So lately laid to rest
In grand Westminster Abbey,
Where England's noblest pressed.
Yet the "fifty years of Europe"
Show less of triumphs won,
Than a decade of our nation, —
Bride of the Western sun !

It numbers seventy millions;
Its wealth, though new, is vast;
While on and upward ever
Its tides are rising fast;
The tide of immigration,
And of nature's swift increase,
Fresh wealth from seas, mines, prairies,
New arts of skill and peace!

THE PAST.

Count back five thrilling decades:
See! Changes manifold
Within our city's limits
Have swiftly been unrolled.
To tell them fills the volumes
Of Andrews and of Camp.
Schools, mansions, churches, factories;
For hills and farm and swamp,
One road, a few spare houses,
The stage-coach, sheep in flocks,
The loom, dye-tub, and tailoress,
Plain homes, few bars or locks!
Our people all were kinsmen;
A homogeneous clan;
Whereas, we now are specimens
Of heterogeneous man.
The soul was then New England's,
Devout, hard-working, staunch;
But now is cosmopolitan,
From many a foreign branch.

. . . . .

The Puritans! brave settlers!
And their sons who kept the faith!
Embodying Christian virtues
That conquer sin and death;
May we emulate their manhood,
And love the path they trod,
Devoting their best talents
To an humble walk with God;
Till at last we join our loved ones,
When Jesus speaks the word,
And in bliss with them inherit
The fullness of the Lord!

. . . .

THE FUTURE.

God grant this golden wedding
Of Christians to their Lord
May prove a holier baptism
To the Lamb whose blood was poured;
A full re-consecration
To the Mighty Son of God,
Whose death brought our salvation,
And whose love is shed abroad !
God make this church the symbol,
With its flowers and greens and psalms,
Of the Saviour's " many mansions "
And His host with victor-palms !
God make us faithful stewards
Of all Thy boundless grace;
And sanctify us wholly
That we may see Thy face !
Grant us, as Christ's own members,
To bear his image here;
And with Him at His advent
In glory to appear !
Thus shall we keep Thanksgiving,
Where many nations be,
And sing our Hallelujah
Upon the crystal sea.

LETTERS.

A large number of delightful letters have been received by the committee on correspondence, from friends and former members who could not be present at the exercises. Selections from many of these letters were read by the committee, some extracts from which are here given.

The first letter read was from Mr. Frederick H. North of Chicago, the son of Major Seth J. North, so often referred to in this volume.

" This invitation carries me back to the early beginnings of the South Church.

" When in my 'teens' it was my good fortune to be present on an occasion which marked the inception of the undertaking. Among other reasons there had been some talk in a general way of the desirability of organizing a church which should better accommodate the residents of the south end, the old church on the site of the present Burritt school, being at that time located at almost the extreme northern limits of the village.

"The occasion above referred to was an entirely informal one, there being but two others present besides myself (Mr. North's father and uncle), but the subject had engrossed their minds for some time, and they believed the time was ripe for its initiation. With them to decide was to act, and, as the edifice could not be expected to rise without material aid, they together pledged themselves for one-half the amount which they considered would be necessary to complete the structure. There were those in the village who doubted if the place was large enough to support two churches of the same denomination, and they were not sure that the call to build was from God, but courage was not wanting and faith was strong, and we have reason now to believe that they 'builded better than they knew.'

"In those early days the church prayer-meeting was always held in the afternoon, and there are those who will recall the announcement every Sunday from the pulpit — Church prayer-meeting Friday afternoon. There was good reason why the afternoon and not the evening should be selected, for good old Horace Butler, Josiah Dewey, Deacon Cornwall, Alvin North, and Professor Andrews, were not greatly in the habit of venturing out evenings, and upon these the pastor mainly relied for remarks and prayer. The remarks were generally short and sometimes far between, but the prayers made up for what was lacking, and in their generous proportions took up whole countries and the islands of the sea, together with all the ends of the earth and the inhabitants thereof.

"Those were not the days of Young People's Societies of Christian Endeavor, and I am not now able to recall an instance of any young person taking part in the exercises. Indeed, it was not always the case that enough young people of both sexes were present to aid appreciably in the songs of worship, but the older people who managed the singing were quite familiar with many of the good old tunes, and 'Old Hundred' and the tune that was always set to the hymn, 'Hark, from the tombs a doleful sound,' could always be relied on.

"Those early days recall to mind the grand old company of ministers who were set upon the watchtowers in the surrounding towns, and whose labors aided and encouraged the upbuilding of the new association — Doctors Horace Bushnell, Joel Hawes, Noah Porter, Rev. Mr. Jones of Southington, Rev. Mr. Robbins of Kensington, and last but not least, Rev. Joab Brace. The sermons of the latter did not always impress the young people with a due sense of the folly of trangressors and the terrors of the law, but an encounter with the steady gaze of the black piercing eyes that looked down at them from the pulpit and right through them, was sure to convict.

"It was under such influences, and encouraged by the noble host of ministers and divines, some of them of world-wide influence, that the fathers and mothers of fifty years ago, in faith and prayer, undertook the work of organization of the South Church, and, like the founders of the republic, their descendants approve the wisdom of their action."

The reminiscences in the letter of Mrs. Mary E. (Bassett) Mumford of Philadelphia, are as delightfully entertaining as they are realistic.

"Though not there in the body I shall certainly be present in the spirit, and celebrate with you; but with this difference, that while your memory dwells mainly within the new South Church in its elegant dress and gracious plenty for its children, the "South" I go back to, tenderly, is the old white wooden structure, bare and unpicturesque, which, thirty years ago, meekly reared its Grecian front upon the village street.

"How ugly, how forbidding it was! And yet to childish eyes it had some elements of grandeur. What an exceedingly high flight of steps was that which led up to the front church door, and how imposing the Grecian pillars which held up the pediment, the clock, and the square tower atop of all! Stiff and uncompromising in its exterior, the inside was equally cold and white and bare. We didn't care to go in. We would rather have lingered in the porch, and looked at the worshipers as they came slowly thronging up the steps in their best Sunday clothes, or watched the carriages of the country members arriving one by one, delivering their burdens at the foot of the steps, and then defiling soberly around to the sheds in the rear. But if we must go in, and decorum whispered that there was no alternative, then we sought to linger a little by the stove which stood just inside the door, and sent its long black pipe across the church to now and then weep dark sooty tears down upon an innocent Sunday gown.

"What pleasure on a cold or stormy day to listen to the group of older people who exchanged civilities or bits of gossip as feet were warmed or dried before proceeding to the distant pews. How we wished we dared to ask to sit by the stove all day rather than go on to the cold family "slip," and how reluctantly at last we followed our elders up the long aisle and found our places in one of the "Amen pews." Oh, the cold white pulpit! Oh, the cold black horsehair sofa and chairs! Oh, the long words we couldn't understand! What a boon when the monotony was broken by the announcement, 'Such a man and such a woman intend matrimony.' Ah! there was something human at last. We understood what that meant, and it woke us up for the rest of the day. The Fast-Day proclamation, sent by the Governor was always another joyous break, and as for the Thanksgiving announcement, nothing would have kept us home on the day we knew that was coming. Don't I remember that grand peroration to this day! What a roll it had under the tongue: 'Given under my hand and the seal of the State, this 20th day of November,' and signed by his mysterious highness, the Secretary of State.

"We worried through the sermon at last, diverted now and then by the palsied old lady in the front pew, who looked up at the preacher and shook her head as if denying every word he said; or, again watching the nodding gray heads adown the middle aisle, or counting the rosette-like ornaments which ran around the front of the long white gallery. Then came Sunday-school, when we crept down the narrow little staircase which led to the basement, and sat on bare settees, with our feet dangling in the air. To this basement we sometimes came on Saturday afternoons for a singing school, and later on to evening meetings, where in the dim lamplight we heard prayers and exhortations, or sat in long silences, broken at last by the good deacon with the unvarying resource, 'Sing Balerma.' The church you celebrate, my dear friend, is rich and warm, and full of color and comfort. Mine is the old white edifice, cold and square and barn-like. This is the picture stamped indelibly upon my childhood. In the new church I have only been a visitor.

"But though I see it now, I did not think it cold or empty then. The young people of those days were full of their own pleasures, while the older heads ran over with wisdom and kindly counsel.

"The men and women who made New Britain sat in those straight-backed pews. The Norths, and Stanleys, the Browns, the Smiths, the Pecks, the Corbins, and their heirs to-day enjoy the heritage they won. Of the women of the old South Church, let me mention but two out of many, and these because they left an impress upon my own life. These were Miss Clara North and Miss Harriet Stanley. Both were Sunday-school teachers of mine, the earliest I remember, and happily I was for quite a series of years under their instruction; and the best I know of Bible lore and religious doctrine, I owe to them. Though very different types of character, each had gracious, charming manners with little folks, and inspired personal admiration in their young pupils. May I also mention by name one man, who was the heró of my childish soul, and chiefly, as I suppose, because he always bowed to me on the steps of the old church on Sunday mornings, and lifted his hat with the same deference he would have shown to an older person. This hero, to my childish mind, was Hubert North, who, with his gentle, high-born courtesy, which never forgot even a child, won a love and remembrance as fresh to-day as it was forty years ago.

"There is a parable in these things, though I may not dwell upon it here. About the time my connection with the 'old South' ceased, the new day began to dawn — the child's day, I may call it — and Sunday-school reform came in; songs and lessons adapted to infant needs, books that would attract the immature mind. We were no longer expected to enjoy Alleine's Alarm or d'Aubigne's History of the Reformation, or memoirs of suffering missionaries. The forcing of old ideas upon young minds was seen to be valueless, if not pernicious. The child's nature was consulted in his education; a new era had begun. But I must not reminisce further or you will find out that I have passed my own half-century mile-stone, and become garrulous and prosy.

"I wish the good old church (born the same year as myself) God speed, and may the richest blessings, spiritual and temporal, rest ever upon her."

In somewhat the same strain Mrs. Abbie Peck Lee, now of Denver, Colorado, writes:

"The early, and some of the sweetest recollections of my life, are associated with this church in the first period of its history, when the days and years were much longer to me than now. I was for a time a member of the choir and took great delight in the service. I well remember my place in the Sabbath-school, when it was held in the damp and cheerless basement of the old frame building where worship was conducted; also the kind teachers, who strove so patiently to guide my wandering thoughts to what seemed the mysterious teachings of the Bible.

"I can think of so many who were then active members of the church, for whom I had a reverent regard, who have been long on the other side. One, the dear pastor (Rev. Samuel Rockwell), under whose teachings I was led with many others to take upon myself the vows of church membership, having perhaps feeble ideas of what I was doing, though I am convinced that it was the threshold of an experience which has been growing ever since. I love to think of those days, and the dear faces I was accustomed to see every Sabbath, when it seemed as if everything was always to be the same.

"How I should love to be with you. But a distance of two thousand miles is too great an obstacle to be overcome."

Mr. Mortimer A. Warren, of Greenwich, Conn., writes feelingly on the subject of growing old:

"I remember very well, how, as a child, I went one evening with mother to see the foundation walls of brick of the new old South Church building. That must have been in the summer, they say, of 1841, but I think there must be some mistake about the date. It was only a little while ago.

"Can it be that we are growing old? I saw a sunset last evening. It was just like the sunsets of my boyhood. I didn't see any improvement. It didn't show any marks of age. When I go to New Britain I am a boy again. I go about the streets or climb Walnut Hill; and I am a boy again, — but not quite a boy. There is something the matter. Things are different, yet the same. The old Normal School building is not half so tall, nor half so grand as it used to be. The new South Church is no longer painted white with green blinds. Walnut Hill is not such a very big hill. The boys and girls look like middle aged men and women. And some of them are crazy.

"Let me give you an instance. A little while ago I was passing through the village — New Britain, I mean — when an old schoolmate came into the train. I greeted her cordially, as why shouldn't I? It was only a few years ago that we were at school together. She had a a little girl with her. Speaking of the child, I said: 'Your daughter, I presume?' 'Yes,' was the reply, 'my grand-daughter!' Yet this old school-mate of mine seemed sane enough on all other subjects. Beware of one temptation. Beware of thinking, or feeling, or fearing, that you are growing old! You are just a boy, with a little more of experience than you had once."

The Rev. William M. Brown, president of Tillotson Institute, Austin, Texas, writes appreciatively of old friends and former days:

"The longing to go to Connecticut comes over me very strongly, but the hindrances in the way seem quite insurmountable. I am sure the anniversary will be a pleasant one. Not many will be present who remember Mr. Rockwell and the old 'meeting-house'; nor the melodeon at which Mrs. George Rockwell presided, and the bass viol from which Mr. Booth drew most lugubrious tones. It certainly will not be a repetition of the time when grey-haired men wept at the recollection of the former house and its glory.

"For myself, I can say that I have never known happier days than when I used to scramble for a front seat in the infant schoolroom, so as to be as near as possible to Mrs. North, whom I adored. And now it is almost a quarter of a century since I united with the South Church."

Col. Homer B. Sprague, once principal of our State Normal School, sends kindly greetings from across the continent, dated from the University of California:

"On behalf of Mrs. Sprague and myself, I heartily thank you for the invitation we have received and we greatly regret that the breadth of a continent intervening will necessarily prevent our being present on this most interesting occasion. . . . . Heartfelt wishes for the continued prosperity of this efficient branch of the great Church of Christ, with which are connected in my mind many hallowed and tender memories."

Prof. Henry B. Buckham writes a genial note from Fayetteville, North Carolina:

"I am sure I should meet many old friends, and it would do me good to see their faces and to hear their voices. But I cannot come, and can only send greeting and hearty good will to all, with the prayer that grace, mercy, and peace may be with all. Mrs. Buckham joins me in this."

The Rev. Henry E. Hart, of Franklin, Conn., speaks heartily of his former relations with Dr. Goodell:

"Your anniversary suggests to me so much. It covers some of my tenderest and most delightful experiences. Dr. Goodell married us. A package of letters, written by him during the perplexities of my first revival season, is somewhere among my treasures. His encouragement got me on my feet before the first State conference. His patience and self-control have been to me a wonder and a thing deserving imitation. . . . . A church anniversary covers so much. Fifty years of ministerial and church work! . . . . May the Divine blessing be on the dear South Church and all its people."

The Rev. William A. Lamb, of Newton, Mass., who went out from his work here to enter the Christian ministry, says:

"The South Church has been my Alma Mater in spiritual life. Gladly would I add many leaves to her wreath of glory. Should I not be permitted to be with you, I certainly shall be in spirit and in warm love."

Mrs. I. N. Carleton, of Bradford, Mass., gives a mother's testimony, which is dear to us:

"I am thankful that we ever had the privilege of belonging to the South Church, and especially for the strength and support which I derived while my children were young, from the meetings of the Maternal Association. The South Church, New Britain, comes nearer, in my mind, and I say it sincerely, to the modern and Christian conception of an organization for doing a given work in the world, than any other that I have been familiar with."

Mrs. L. L. Camp, of New Haven, the daughter of our early deacon, Chauncey Cornwell, expresses her regret at being unable to be present:

"The dear old Church was very near the hearts of my parents and also to my own, and, although many years have passed since I left New Britain, I do not forget that under its roof I was welcomed to its fellowship when a child and that there my marriage vows were spoken."

It was a real pleasure to us to receive a number of excellent letters from the younger members of our church, who are temporarily away at school or in business, or who have recently removed from us. Mr. Watson Davis, of Lynn, Mass., says:

"Not one of its members would enjoy being present more than myself, for it was there I first felt real love for the Master's service, from which time He has blessed me richly."

And Mr. Buell B. Bassett, from the U. S. Military Academy at West Point, regrets the military law which compels him to be absent:

"I have a very great love for the church in which I was raised, and am often led to wish for the advantages which I there enjoyed for the worship of God and the study of His Word. I know that this anniversary will be a happy event, and, as it should, add to the glory of His name."

The last letter to be read was from Mr. William E. Peck, of New York city — a thoroughly lively letter of personal reminiscences of the small boy of thirty years ago. Only a small portion is given here :

"It seems but yesterday that I was trotting to the old South Church, trying to keep up with my father, and bearing in my hand a hot soapstone to keep my feet warm during Mr. Goodell's long discourse. I believe that the first children baptized by Mr. Goodell were my sister Minnie and myself. During this period, 1862-1866, my father was one of the heavy-weights in the choir, and Mr. Eli Porter assisted on the 'double bass.' This old instrument I afterwards borrowed and learned to operate as a member of the Williston Seminary and Yale orchestras. . . . .

"Many a time did I climb to the top of the old square belfry, and it was fun to be there when the bell was ringing and feel the jarring sensation. . . . . You doubtless remember Rev. Mr. Rockwell's remark as the old church burned down. It was then the 'Union Hall,' and the saintly edifice had been disgraced with low entertainments. The white-haired old gentleman watched it burn for some time, and after choking with the thought of its later uses, spoke these words: 'At last it is purged by fire.'

Letters were also received from Mrs. Sarah D. Acker, Mrs. Samuel Brace, Frederick A. Bassett, Mrs. J. C. Breckenridge, Mrs. Charles H. Cornwell, Mrs. Charles O. Collins, Mrs. Emma Conklin Clark, Mrs. John B. Cowles, Mr. and Mrs. E. W. Dowd, Mrs. Annie Conklin Fair, Mr. H. J. Gillette, Dr. and Mrs. Fred. M. Hemingway, Dr. and Mrs. E. B. Hooker, F. L. Hungerford, Esq., Mr. and Mrs. William Killam, Mrs. Jennie Hart Lewis, Mr. and Mrs. Isaac S. Lee, Mr. Joseph E. Marvin, Mr. Charles F. North, Miss Frederica North, Mr. and Mrs. J. N. Oviatt, Mr. and Mrs. Edward F. Peck, Mr. and Mrs. J. A. Pickett, Mrs. Carrie Copley Rundlett, Mrs. Martha J. Rand, Mr. and Mrs William N. Shepard, Mrs. J. A. Stillman, Mrs. Jennie M. Shepard, Miss Harriet A. Stanley, Mrs. Martha F. Stanley, Mrs. Julia Smith Townsend, Mrs. Elihu Thomson, Mr. Meigs H. Whaples, and others.

Among those who attended the services from out of town, besides a few mentioned in the list above, were Hon. Henry F. Peck, Mrs. Peck, the Misses Peck, Mr. and Mrs. John H. Peck. Morton S. Judd, Hubert L. Judd, Mr. and Mrs. Theron Upson. Timothy W. Stanley, L. P. Buell, Mr. and Mrs. W. C. Williams.

Mrs. Thomas S. Hall, one of the charter members of the church, the youngest of that original one hundred and twenty, read a commemorative poem, from which the following verses are selected.

COMMEMORATIVE POEM.

O Lord, on this memorial day
    We lift our hearts in praise,
For all the blessings of our way
    Accept the song we raise.

We thank Thee that Thou didst impart
    To our beloved sires
Unwavering faith, a steadfast heart,
    High hopes, and pure desires;

That Thou didst lead Thy servants here
    Thy holy work to share,
A temple in Thy name to rear,
    And here Thy truth declare.

Full fifty years have sped their round
    Since that bright, happy day
When on this consecrated ground
    We met to praise and pray.

We made a covenant with our God,
    And though in numbers few,
This little Church, fed with God's word,
    In strength and members grew.

And often in this sacred place,
    We felt the Spirit's power;
We witnessed burdened souls embrace
    Their Saviour in that hour.

And many who once worshiped here
    Now see the Lord they love;
May not their spirits hover near
    And beckon us above?

Yet now, dear Lord, we would implore
    Thy help to conquer sin,
We pray that we may love Thee more;
    That we more souls may win.

> We need the Pentecostal fire
> To purge away our dross,
> To quicken every pure desire,
> And keep us near the cross.
>
> Soon shall the precious word divine
> Be preached the wide world o'er ;
> Through all the earth Christ's light shall shine,
> And darkness be no more.
>
> Now may the Church of God arise,
> And to her Lord draw near,
> Ere trumpet sounds ring through the skies,—
> Jesus, our King, appear!

ADDRESSES.

A striking feature in the evening's entertainment was the bright and felicitous speeches of the Hon. Valentine B. Chamberlain, of the First Church, and Noah Cornwell Rogers, Esq., of New York city.

Judge Chamberlain spoke for the "Daughters of the Church." He pleaded guilty to the charge preferred against him, viz. : that he had stolen his wife from the South Church. He admitted the facts which had been recited by Dr. Cooper. "But," said he, "it was not under the cover of the darkness. I well remember the time. It was a beautiful afternoon in May, twenty-one years ago. The bright sun was shining, the birds were singing, and all nature was awake with joy, when I led my young bride from this church where we had received the benediction of the Rev. Mr. Goodell. She was good and lovely then, and she looks no less lovely to me to-day." He thought, therefore, that he ought to be pardoned for the theft, and so, in his opinion, ought every young man who looks covetuously upon the fair daughters of the South Church.

The Judge then recalled his own intimate relations with this church during the past thirty-five years. His three cherished friends, Oliver Stanley, Theodore Stanley, and William Corbin, were all members of the South Church. Mr. Corbin died in 1860. Lieutenant Stanley died during the Civil War at Washington from wounds received at Fredericksburg, and Oliver

Stanley has but recently passed away. The members of the South and First churches mingle so freely in social life that it is difficult to know who belongs to the one or the other. He did not care for the distinctions made by the names of different churches. We are all one. When a child is brought to the font and is baptized, that child belongs to the family of God. He belongs to the great, broad church of Jesus Christ. He has a claim on Christian people everywhere. It is this strong and tender bond of Christian love that we are to feel drawing us to each other and to God.

Mr. Rogers spoke for the "Sons of the Church." Referring to Dr. Cooper's remark about the offense of a man outside of the church coming into the fold and carrying off one of the daughters of the church, he said that he, in one respect at least, ought to be a man after Dr. Cooper's own heart, for he, a son of the church, had married a daughter of the church and was also very much interested at present in a little granddaughter of the church, both of whose parents, all four of whose grandparents, and at least two of whose great-grandparents had been members of the South Congregational Church.

Referring to the story of the Prodigal Son, he said it was the good son who stayed at home and the other that journeyed into a far country. In the present case the good sons had almost all stayed at home. In professional life, in the banks, in the offices and places of business and manufacturing, they hold important positions of trust and are an honor to the community; they had already begun to be called to responsible positions in the church, and as those who were older passed away to their reward, they would be found able and willing to assume the heavier responsibilities that might devolve upon them with credit both to themselves and the church. Some of the other sons of the church, like William Peck and himself, had wandered off to the far countries. William Peck, after traveling over all the civilized countries of the world, and several of the uncivilized, had finally ended up in New Jersey, while he had settled down in New York; and they both, like genuine prodigal sons, enjoy coming back to the father's house and receiving a welcome, as they partake of the feast that had been prepared.

He then referred to the fact that he had had the good fortune to know all four pastors of the church. He remembered good old Mr. Rockwell, who used silently to come in and go out before them; had an intimate acquaintance with Dr. Goodell, whom they all remembered with love. The year 1872 was quite a memorable year, for it was in that year that a great number of the then boys and girls, now young men and women, joined the church. It was the last year of Dr. Goodell's pastorate, and was twenty years ago, so that this is really an anniversary of that occasion. They all remembered Mr. Griffin, although he stayed so short a time, his genial ways and his scholarly talks and sermons; and they have often had the pleasure of meeting the present pastor of the church as they have come back from time to time. They are gratified to hear, in their far-off fields of work, of the prominence and influence in religious and educational councils which Dr. Cooper has gained; and are likewise rejoiced to note the prosperity, in all temporal and spiritual things, of the church itself under his leadership. He closed by referring to the glorious past of the church and hoped for an even more useful and glorious future.

The time had now arrived when the exercises of the evening, and with them the services of two days, should be brought to a close. Other friends were with us from whom it would have been a joy to hear, friends who had come up to spend this happy anniversary with the church which they had learned in former years to love, and whose presence with us has added a peculiar charm to the interest of the occasion; but the late hour admonished. We had taken such review of the past as inspired both gratitude and hope. Our faces must now be set toward the future.

The Pastor announced as the only fitting and most expressive closing song, the ancient "Doxology," in long meter, "Praise God from Whom all blessings flow." The benediction was pronounced, and the formal celebration of our semi-centennial passed into history.

www.ingramcontent.com/pod-product-compliance
Lightning Source LLC
Chambersburg PA
CBHW032135160426
43197CB00008B/658